Poker books f~~rom D&B~~

Think Like a Poker Pro
by Byron Jacobs
978-1-904468-55-4, 304pp, $34.95 / £21.99

Advanced Limit-Hold'em Strategy
by Barry Tanenbaum
978-1-904468-36-3, 256pp, $24.95 / £14.99

Secrets of Sit'n'gos
by Phil Shaw
978-1-904468-43-1, 224pp, $24.95 / £14.99

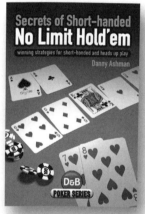

Secrets of Short-handed No Limit Hold'em
by Danny Ashman
978-1-904468-41-7, 208pp, $24.95 / £14.99

Secrets of Pro Tournament Poker, Vol. 1
by Jonathan Little
978-1-904468-56-1, 272pp, $27.95 / £16.99

Secrets of Short-handed Pot-Limit Omaha
by Rolf Slotboom and Rob Hollink
978-1-904468-44-8, 336pp, $27.50 / £15.99

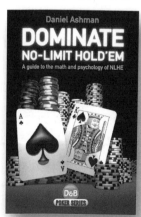

Dominate No-Limit Hold'em
by Daniel Ashman
978-1-904468-57-8, 272pp, $24.95 / £16.99

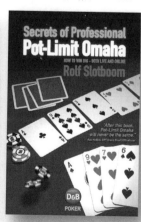

Secrets of Professional Pot-Limit Omaha
by Rolf Slotboom
978-1-904468-30-6, 240pp, $25.95 / £15.99

Limit Hold'em: Winning short-handed strategies
by Terry Borer and Lawrence Mak with Barry Tannenbaum
978-1-904468-37-0, 352pp, $25.95 / £15.99

Reviews of *Secrets of Professional Tournament Poker, Volume 1*

Little does an exemplary job of analyzing situations and giving sound advice in an easy-to-read writing style that keeps you turning the pages.
Gamingtoday.com

Jonathan Little's book may well be the best tournament poker book written since Harrington's.
PokerQ4.com

Here is the penultimate sentence in Secrets of Professional Tournament Poker: "If you become lazy, you will be left in the dust." Memorize, grasp, understand, use the information Little offers, you'll be the one kicking up that dust.
Jack Welch, Pokerheadrush.com

This book is a blend of analytical and common sense. For people who want to be competitive in MTTs as they are currently played, I think that this book is essential.
Thegoodgamblingguide.co.uk

This book may not be a break through book in the history of poker writing, but it has all the masala to get you going and reach heights. After all this book comes to you by someone who has already been there, seen it and done it all! Go Grab it!
Pokerstarus.com

If you're looking to improve your game and pick up a book that can help you do that, then give SOPTP a try.
Chad Holloway, PokerNews.com

Jonathan Little is one of the premier tournament poker players in the world today. I personally have learned so much from him and you can too.
Shannon Shorr

Jonathan Little

Secrets of Professional Tournament Poker

Volume 2: Stages of the tournament

www.dandbpoker.com

First published in 2012 by D & B Publishing

British Library Cataloguing-in-Publication Data

A catalogue record for this book is available from the British Library.

ISBN: 978 1 90446 858 5

All sales enquiries should be directed to D&B Publishing:

e-mail: info@dandbpoker.com; website: www.dandbpoker.com

To my parents, Larry and Rita Little

Cover design by Horatio Monteverde.

Printed and bound by Versa Press in the US.

Contents

Acknowledgements

In *Secrets of Professional Tournament Poker: Volume 1*, I gave thanks to everyone that helped me become a technically sound poker player. In this volume I would like to thank everyone that helped me learn to be successful at life. First, I would like to thank my parents for always helping me in every way they knew how. I owe them a great debt for supporting me in everything I tried. I would also like to thank the rest of my family, including my brother Garrett for always being there for me.

I would like to thank Daniel Stanley for helping me with my numerous poker training businesses. If I didn't randomly meet Dan a few years ago, I could have easily given up on helping people learn to play poker. He has made my life much easier and better in so many ways. I would like to thank Shannon Shorr and Dave Benefield for helping me to meet everyone I know in the poker world. If I didn't meet these two guys, I could easily have very few friends in poker. Instead, I have too many to count. I would like to thank Steve Begleiter for teaching me so much about life. I had the opportunity to coach Steve for his WSOP main event final table. Even though I was officially the coach, I was really the student. I have learned a ton from Steve about numerous aspects of life.

I would like to thank Hoyt Corkins for introducing me to the wonderful world that is outside my house and away from the poker table. Hoyt has shown me all around the mountains and deserts of Nevada and California. If I had never met him, I would be much more tilted and unhappy in my day-to-day life. I would like to thank Amie Broder for offering numerous great ideas that helped me make this book more complete. She constantly looks out for me and helps me become a better, more complete person. I would be lost without her. I would like to thank Byron and Dan at D&B Publishing for having the faith to trust a previously unpublished author to write what we all hope to be the definitive series on tournament poker.

Finally, I would like to thank all my students. If I did not have such a dedicated group of learners, I would not have been motivated to write this book. It excites me every time I open my email box and read another success story about how someone watched my training videos, either from www.JonathanLittleSecrets.com or www.FloatTheTurn.com, and transformed from a breakeven or losing player to a big winner. It goes to show that if you work hard and study a lot, pretty much anyone can learn to beat poker. If this book helps you improve your game, email me and let me know.

Introduction

I outlined a strategy in *Volume 1* to make you a winner at tournament play. In this book I will explain how to alter your game at each level of a tournament and squeak the most equity out of every situation. You do this by constantly adjusting to your opponents, learning their tells and staying in shape, both mentally and physically. I will teach you how to think, which will help you win at the game of life, which should be everyone's ultimate goal. After all, if you sit at a poker table all your life, you really haven't accomplished anything. I will also answer some of the questions that come up most often in my private coaching sessions. I hope you are ready to learn everything it takes to be a pro, both on and off the felt.

Chapter 1

Stages of a Tournament

You must significantly alter your game as a tournament progresses. This is because the person that takes first place does not win the entire prize pool. In a standard tournament, first place will be between 20 percent and 50 percent of the total prize pool, depending on the number of entrants. In general, the more money that is awarded to the top finishers, the more likely you should play to win. Sometimes though, you will find spots where you gain a lot of money by folding.

For example, you are down to three players in a World Poker Tour (WPT) event. You have 1 million chips, one player has 3 million chips and the other has 10 million chips. Suppose the player with 3 million chips goes all-in and the player with 10 million chips calls. If the payouts are $1 million for first, $500,000 for second and $250,000 for third, you should fold almost every hand. By folding, you give yourself a great chance to go from almost certainly getting $250,000 to perhaps getting $500,000. In this spot, depending on the blind structure, you can easily justify folding hands as strong as A-K or J-J.

When you play a tournament, you need to know the prize structure. If an unusually large share of the prize pool goes to first place, you should play the tournament as if winning is the only thing that matters. If a large percentage of the field gets in the money, you should play fairly tight until you get in the money, and then play to win. In a standard online sitngo, 30 percent of the field, three out of 10 players, gets paid. This causes some pretty wild situations because it is not too tough to get in the money. In these tournaments, your main concern is to get in the money unless you know everyone else cares about the money more than you do. This usually occurs on the bubble, which will be addressed later in this section.

The early stages of a deep-stacked tournament are played much like a cash game because you are usually a long way from the money. Your chips are worth about what you paid for them, whereas in the later stages their value is significantly diminished because money will soon be taken out of the prize pool to pay players. You can play the strategy outlined in the "Playing Poker" section of *Volume 1* of this set with little or no modification.

As stacks get shorter, you will have to adjust. Some tables will let you run them over, winning every blind and ante, while some will never let you see a flop for less than 10 big blinds (BBs). You will have to adjust to each table, as well as the structure. Poker is a constant balancing act. Whoever can juggle all the variables the best will come out on top in the long run. This section will help you do just that.

Early Levels

In the early levels of a tournament, some players show up running on all cylinders while others play very tight. You must quickly determine who is scared to bust and who is going out of his way to get chips or go home early.

I never show up to a tournament with a specific game plan. As in all forms of poker, you should take what the table gives you. If you are constantly being re-raised, you need to be tight, and if you pick up every pot before the flop with a small raise, you should attack the blinds relentlessly.

The penalty for being tight is fairly small when there are no antes in play, as is the case in the early levels of most tournaments. You can blind off for a while before your stack starts to diminish significantly. Most tournaments start you off with a very deep stack, which is another reason why you can play tight for a while. I played a charity tournament where we started with 1,000 chips playing 5/10 blinds with 20-minute levels. I was totally card dead for the first hour but only blinded off 15 percent of my chips. I finally got a good hand and doubled up. Waiting an hour for a hand cost me very little, so it was the best play, especially since the players at the table didn't care about my image.

I used to get upset when I lost chips in the first few levels of a major tournament. I eventually realized that it wasn't the end of the world if I started a tournament with 30,000 chips and went into the middle levels with 28,000. Do not become result-oriented about your stack because in reality, it doesn't matter much. If you can make it out of the early levels while giving yourself a few opportunities to gather chips, you have done your job well regardless of whether you actually get them.

When you first show up to a tournament, your goal should be to figure out who is going to give you free chips. This requires you to pay attention. Don't be eating breakfast or watching sports on TV. Pay attention to the poker game. I play a bit tighter than normal at the start of most tournaments. This keeps me out of trouble while I am getting a good handle on everyone at the table.

I tend to get my chips from two types of players. The first is the tight player that vastly overplays top pair or any big hand. These guys will raise and re-raise their big hands post-flop regardless of what comes on the board, which is obviously a huge mistake. They are usually older players with some experience, but not a lot. You can usually pinpoint them by their tightness, and also by their aggressiveness after the flop with hands like an overpair that don't warrant such action. If you don't know the correct way to play hands like over-pairs, please reread *Volume 1*.

The way to beat these players is to play as many pots as possible in position against them. Ideally, you will all be fairly deep-stacked and you can see a flop for 3 BBs or less. Some of these players raise larger pre-flop, to around 5 BBs, but even then you should rarely fold hands like 9♠-7♠ or 2-2. Call with these hands because these players are going to flop a hand like top pair and be unable to fold to your aggression when you flop a monster. Also, they think they are supposed to raise and reraise the flop with top pair, which we already know is a huge mistake. So, see lots of flops in position with hands that have high implied odds, like A♠-4♠, 9♦-8♦ and 3-3. Don't call their raises with hands like A-9 or K-10. These will make you the second-best hand quite often against their raising range, so avoid them like the plague.

You will get a lot of chips from the loose players. They come in two types: good and bad. You can spot them by the fact that they are involved in a decent number of pots. The good ones will randomly spew chips into the pot, usually when they think you are weak. The bad, loose players tend to overplay every hand they make, and they usually can't fold a hand better than middle pair.

Against the loose-aggressive players, tend to act weak when you are strong and go into pot-control mode. Be happy calling three barrels with hands like top pair. Act as if you are debating every decision, which will induce most bad players, who think they are great at reading tells, to bluff like crazy. Once they see how you tricked them, you should play a fairly normal game without much hollywooding. If the loose players are calling stations, feel free to value-bet with a wide range of good, but not great hands if you think they can call with worse. Some of these players will constantly find ways to call down with ace-high. Against these players, hands that normally have high reverse implied odds, like K-J, become very playable because you are looking to induce bluffs when you make a hand like top pair, bad kicker. You obviously should play all hands with high implied odds because when these players decide to get super-aggressive, you will prefer to have a strong hand.

Once you have found the player that is going to give you his chips, try to enter pots with him anytime you have a hand that plays well against his range. You can still play pots with everyone else, but be mindful of the weak players. Also, there may be more than one weak player at the table. Sometimes everyone at the table is weak. In this case, try to pinpoint the worst players and go after them.

There are times when you should deviate from your standard game to play a pot with a weak player. Suppose everyone has 200 BBs and a good, loose-aggressive player raises from middle position, a player that is overly aggressive with any top pair calls in the cutoff and you pick up A-Q on the button. This is a good spot to just call instead of re-raise because if you get an A-x-x flop, you can be happy playing the pot against either player, whereas re-raising may force the weak player off a hand like A-4 that would have paid you off on favorable flops.

I am all for going after the bad players, but don't get carried away. Some professionals play so many hands against the weak players that their edge vanishes. No matter how bad a player is, you shouldn't be calling his raises with hands like Q-4. Be smart and go after the dead money when you are the favorite.

While you do have to survive to make it deep in a tournament, if you are not constantly giving yourself opportunities to gather chips, trying to survive will lead to death. You see some players at the top of the tournament leader board every so often. While it doesn't mean much if a person is at the top of any individual tournament, the people that consistently have the most chips tend to bring home the titles.

Tournament poker is often compared to a marathon, at least by the tight players. I view tournaments as a marathon where the winners are required to sprint from time to time. You can and should have many gears in your game. Your early-level play should depend entirely on your table. Most tables will let you get away with a few plays and will often give you some great chances to pick up chips with little risk.

Suppose someone raises from early position to 3 BBs out of a 200-BB stack and you are in middle position with 8♠-6♠. Most tight players will fold here, saying they want to conserve chips and not gamble, but this is an excellent spot to see a cheap flop. Some players refer to a cheap pot as one you can limp into. This is silly, as the difference between one and three big blinds isn't too much when you are deep-stacked. Also, you would sometimes prefer the pot to be larger pre-flop because pots grow exponentially in holdem. You need some sort of pot early in the hand if you want it to grow large by the end.

So, you call with your 8♠-6♠ and the big blind calls as well. The flop comes A♣-7♠-4♦. Everyone checks to the initial raiser, who bets 6 BBs.

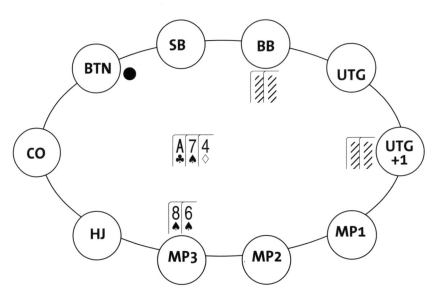

This is another great spot to call, even though you only have a gut-shot. Notice that you also have a backdoor flush draw. The important concept is that you are getting huge implied odds. Your opponent probably has an ace, which means you can easily get two big bets in on the turn and river if you peel your 5. You can also see a river if you turn a flush draw. Finally, if your opponent checks the turn, you can usually take a stab at the pot because he may not have an ace. So, one of two good things can happen. You can hit your 5 and win a large pot or bet the turn when your opponent checks and win a small pot. When you bet the turn after he checks, you will still see the river if he calls, and will almost certainly get paid off if you hit your 5. When you miss and your opponent bets the turn, you can just fold, losing 8 BBs out of your 200-BB stack. You can either pick up a nice pot or lose a tiny one. You should be willing to risk a little to gain a lot.

Many spots look great but should be avoided. Suppose a player raises from middle position to 3 BBs and you are on his left with 3♠-2♠. I would just fold pre-flop because 3♠-2♠ flops poorly. But pretend you call and the small blind calls as well. The flop comes J♠-8♠-4♣. The initial raiser bets 6 BBs and you call, which is fine. The small blind raises to 24 BBs and the initial raiser calls. It's best to fold, even though you have a flush draw. Your hand may be good if you hit, but it is tough to know with any certainty. Even if you do peel the flush, you will be stuck playing pot control and could lose a large pot to a bigger flush, which is certainly in both your opponents' ranges. You will rarely be able to bluff and pick up this pot later. Save yourself the trouble and get out of the way.

It is interesting that sometimes you should easily call with a gutshot and other times you have an easy fold with a flush draw. You should take small risks to gain a lot of chips at times, while other times you should fold without a second thought. You should have very few problems if you play intelligently and think ahead about what could happen later in a hand.

You may remember how I suggested using pot control often in tournaments. This is another way to avoid getting a lot of money in when you are in bad shape. You will occasionally give up thin value on the river in exchange for keeping some chips when you are wrong.

I played a hand where everyone started with 6,000 chips. I raised with 9♠-7♠ from middle position to 150 and the big blind called. The flop came Q♥-7♣-2♠. My opponent checked and I bet 200. He check-raised to 525 and I called because I thought he was fairly weak. Plus, I had draws for two pair or trips and a backdoor flush draw. The turn was the 3♠. My opponent bet 1,200. I was pretty sure he had a big hand at this point, but I would be happy getting more money in if I hit. The river was the Q♠. My opponent bet 2,500 and I just called. I didn't push with my last 1,600 chips because of the hands he would call with, I only beat a queen that didn't make a full house.

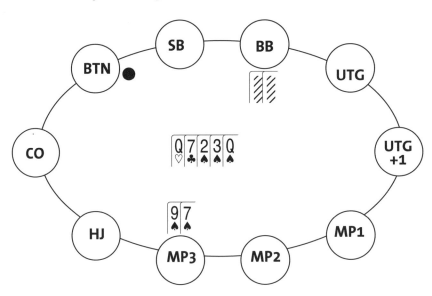

My opponent showed A-Q and the table went nuts wondering why I hadn't raised. The answer is that winning an extra 1,600 chips when my opponent didn't have a full house was not worth going broke when he did. Even if he had a full house only 40 percent of the time, meaning I would win 1,600 more chips 60 percent of the time and go broke 40 percent of the time, I would still just call. Having 1,600 chips at 25/50 is worth a lot, whereas the difference between 10,400 and 12,000 is miniscule. This is another example of how chips change value in a tournament. As your stack gets shorter, your chips become much more valuable and should be conserved when possible.

As you can see, some risk is good and some is bad. Think about what you want to accomplish on each hand and whether it is worth the risk. In general, if a lot of good things can come from an investment, go for it. If only bad things can happen, fold and wait for a better spot. Constantly think about these things and you will find yourself in great spots and avoiding bad ones.

Some players have a style that ensures they either go broke or double up fairly early in a tournament. This is a terrible idea if playing that specific tournament is the most important thing in the world to you. If you would rather be doing something else besides playing a tournament, skip it. That being said, some people do not care about any individual tournament, so they either want to double up early or bust. Some players believe their edge over their opponents greatly increases as their stack size grows larger than everyone else's. I believe this is mostly a mental problem, although I am sure some of them play better with a big stack. That being said, if you play tournaments for a living and winning each one is important to you, you shouldn't be too willing to throw your chips in the pot early in a tournament without a great reason.

Here's an example. I played a $10,000 WPT event at which someone raised from first position. Another player called and a player that tries to double up or bust re-raised to 15 BBs out of his 300-BB stack from the button. The original raiser four-bet to 50 BBs. Everyone folded back to the button, who went all-in. The initial raiser called with A-A and beat the button's 9♠-7♠. While this might appear crazy, it actually has some merit because 9♠-7♠ will do decently well against his opponent's calling range, which is something like A-A, K-K, Q-Q and A-K. Some opponents will even fold K-K, Q-Q and A-K to an all-in in the early levels of a tournament. Nevertheless, you will never see me making these plays.

These huge bluffs are rarely worth it unless you have something more important to do. You are much better off biding your time and waiting for someone to give his stack to you. I am pretty certain I have never given my stack away in the early levels without good reason, such as a read that turned out to be incorrect. If you are patient and play as I suggested in the "Playing Poker" section of *Volume 1*, you will have no problem finding great spots to get your money in during the early levels without getting it in bad too often.

Middle Levels

Antes come into play after a few hours in most tournaments. This forces everyone to loosen up or be blinded off at a much faster rate than before. Most tournaments slowly introduce the antes, and amateurs tend to ignore them. For example, in most large tournaments, the blinds will go 25/50, 50/100, 75/150, 100/200, 100/200-25 (i.e., 100/200 with 25 ante). Many players say 100/200 and 100/200-25 are the same, but they are not. One orbit of blinds at 100/200 costs you 300. You pay 550 in blinds and antes at 100/200-25, almost twice as much because of that tiny 25 ante. That also means that a steal brings in 550 chips instead of 300.

Most players fail to adjust their pre-flop raises to account for the pot being almost two times larger with that small ante. While good players can get away with raising to 2.5 BBs, most amateurs continue to raise to 2.5 BBs or 3 BBs. This is generally a mistake because they are giving the rest of the table great odds to call, and they likely don't play as well as they believe. They should instead raise to 3.5 BBs or 4 BBs. Good players can continue to raise to around 2.5 BBs before the flop when antes are introduced. Notice that if you raise to 500 pre-flop at 100/200-25 and pick up the blinds and antes half the time, you will show a profit even if you check-fold every hand when called. You should also profit when called, which makes stealing with a wide range very profitable.

You should instantly notice that if you only steal the blinds and antes every 1.5 orbits, you will lose money over time. This is what happens to tight players. They wait for premium hands that sometimes never come around, and end up blinding off. In fact, most weak-tight players stand little to no chance in high-buy-in tournaments because they fail to adjust to the antes. This is one of the main reasons why cash-game players fail at tournaments. They simply play too tight.

They also fail to adjust to the fact that everyone's stack slowly diminishes. Depending on the tournament, you may have 200 BBs once the ante comes into play or you may be starting to get short-stacked. Despite your chip stack, the general strategy outlined in the "Playing Poker" section of *Volume 1* will work well. You will stay well ahead of the field as long as you constantly raise and steal pots. In fact, most professionals' stacks start growing once the antes enter play.

You should actively attack the blinds of tight players who wait for premium hands. As long as an opponent isn't super-aggressive, you should raise his blinds with any mediocre hand, especially when you are in position. If a tight player re-raises, you can simply fold unless you are deep-stacked and have a hand with huge implied odds. Remember that you profit if you pick up the blinds just half the time. This means you can afford to wait for better spots than before, as long as you are deep-stacked and don't have to worry about going broke or risking too much of your stack on a steal.

Sometimes you will find yourself in the middle levels of a tournament with only 25 BBs or so, especially when you start with a modest stack of chips or the tournament has a poor structure. When this happens, just push over top of the raise of an overly aggressive player. If you can find a few tight players, attack their blinds relentlessly by raising to 2.25 BBs or so, assuming they will fold to such a small raise. Some players will always call 2.25-BB raises before the flop. Against these players, don't be scared to raise to 2.5 BBs or even 2.75 BBs. Remember, much of your profit will come from making your opponent fold when he is getting proper odds to call. Attack the blinds and play in position as much as possible and the chips will come your way.

The Bubble

Besides the final table, the bubble is my favorite situation in tournament poker. This occurs when the next person out gets nothing and everyone else gets paid. For example, if 36 people get paid, the person eliminated in 37th place is said to have busted on the bubble.

No one wants to play for a long time in a tournament and go home with nothing. You can exploit the players that care about cashing for the minimum. Don't worry about bubbling in a multi-table tournament. If you do, you are forgetting that most of the money goes to the top few finishers, or you are playing well out of your bankroll.

Some players finish in the top 10 percent of the field over 30 percent of the time and lose money in the long run, whereas some make the money only 8 percent of the time and are huge winners. The former drastically hurt their chances of winning the tournament by blinding off while on the bubble.

If you ever want to win at tournament poker, you must accept that you will bubble sometimes. Exploit the weak players that are concerned about winning the minimum. In fact, you should be happy when your weak opponents are rewarded in this way, as they will continue to play tight in future tournaments. Just remember that you will be going for the 100 buy-in first prize far more often than they will. As stacks get deeper you should play a more standard strategy and almost ignore bubble concepts in small pots. As each pot starts to take up a larger proportion of your chips, which will be the case in most tournaments, you must drastically alter your play.

There is a tool called the Individual Chip Model (ICM) which uses fairly intense math to determine each player's dollar equity, which is how much of the prize pool each chip stack is worth. The math is too difficult to perform at the poker table, so I will sum it up for you. ICM is normally used in sitngos, where fourth place usually gets nothing and third place gets paid, but you can also apply it to multi-table tournaments. The general concept is that when there is a large pay jump looming, you need a much stronger hand to call a shove than to shove yourself. This remains the pattern throughout the rest of the tournament, as you will win more money whenever a player busts. Even though a play may win you chips on average, it can still have negative expectation in terms of dollars, which is what matters in the long run. Keep this concept in mind as you move forward.

I start to adjust my play, sometimes drastically, when I get around 15 percent of the field away from the bubble. So, if 36 people get money, bubble play starts in my mind when we get down to around 42 people. If 1,000 people get money, bubble play starts when we are down to around 1,150 players. Some players start thinking about getting in the money way before I do. These players are usually super tight. Some of them will even tell you they are going to wait for a strong hand or just fold until they get in the money. Try to steal these tight players' blinds every time from basically any position, especially if your table tends to let people steal. If they play back at you, be willing to fold some huge hands. Sometimes, if you act like you are strongly considering a call, they will even tell you what they have.

In a $1,500 World Series of Poker (WSOP) event, which is known for having extremely tight bubbles because the $3,000 cash for breaking the bubble is worth a lot to most entrants, I raised A-Q from middle position to 2.25 BBs out of my 30-BB stack and the big blind went all in for 12 BBs. As I counted out my chips to call, he said in broken English, as he was from another country, "I have aces." I asked him to repeat himself and he again said he had aces. I asked why he said that and he said he wanted to get in the money and didn't want to risk going broke. I decided he was telling the truth, which most amateurs do under pressure, and folded. He flipped up the aces. I am glad he saved me 10 BBs. I am also glad he got in the money because he will probably continue to play that way for the rest of his life.

I also had the pleasure of playing in a $1,500 WSOP event with another person that stated he was only going to play A-A and K-K and was going to guarantee he got in the money. He claimed he only had $20 to his name, and cashing for $3,000 would get him back on track. He proceeded to blind off from 10 BBs all the way down to 1 BB. In fact, I raised his blind with 9♠-3♣ when he had 3 BBs left because I knew he would fold. You normally have no fold equity before the flop when the big blind has 3 BBs, but situations like this occur occasionally. Pay attention and don't pass them by.

You can get away with some really weak re-raises on the bubble against aggressive but not great players. Most decent players know they are supposed to go out of their way to steal as many blinds as possible on the bubble. You can re-raise them with basically any two cards if you know they will fold a huge percentage of their range. If your stack is between 15 and 30 BBs, you can re-raise them all-in with a wide range as well. You can't fear going broke on the bubble. You must know your opponent well before re-raising him all-in with nothing, but if you are confident in your reads, you can pick up a lot of chips on the bubble, even with a short stack.

I was playing a $10,000 WPT event when an overly aggressive online player raised to 2.25 BBs, I pushed from the small blind with Q-9 for 16 BBs and he folded. The very next hand, he raised again and I pushed with 8♠-7♠, this time for 21 BBs. He folded again. He raised a third time and I was holding A♠-A♣. If I hadn't pushed the previous two hands, I probably would have made a small re-raise to induce action, but since I had already pushed on him the last two hands, I decided to go all-in. As soon as the action got back to him he instantly called and proudly flipped up his A♥-7♦. I doubled up and he bubbled shortly thereafter.

This goes to show that you really need to know your opponent. If he had a great read on me, he probably wouldn't have called. You can be pretty certain that you have an easy fold with A-7 in his spot, because few people will go all-in three times in a row with weak hands. Also, I had to assume he had at least something in order to raise a third time. This is just another pitfall you must avoid on the bubble.

This also shows that you should tighten up if people are not letting you steal on the bubble. There is no set rule that says you must try to steal every pot on the bubble. One of the biggest mistakes great online players make is assuming that everyone is trying to outplay them. They find themselves in large pots on the bubble against players that are just trying to sneak into the money. They run into a few monsters and can't understand why they constantly lose on the bubble. They are playing too loose against opponents that never bluff. If the table isn't letting you steal, then don't steal. That being said, becoming a total nit and folding every hand is usually wrong. Maintain some aggression but stop raising every hand.

Occasionally you will encounter a player who goes out of his way to put you in a tough spot on the bubble. To deal with this, you must have a great read on your opponent and determine if he is trying to put a move on you or if he actually has a hand. One incorrect read can turn a great opportunity into a huge spew.

I have run into some pretty interesting leveling wars with great players on the bubble in major tournaments. On the bubble in the WPT event in San Jose, the reigning online player of the year raised 2.5 BBs into a tight player's blind from middle position. I was on the button with 8♠-7♦ and decided to re-raise to 7.5 BBs. I knew the player of the year would be attacking these blinds, as they were both tight, so I was pretty comfortable re-raising him. The action folded to him and he four-bet me to 18 BBs or so out of his 60-BB stack. I assumed he knew I was attacking his raise and was good enough to do something about it. I had more chips than him, so I wouldn't bubble even if I lost. I also noticed that he had stopped breathing, which usually indicates that a player is scared to get any more action. All of this convinced me that the best play was to go all-in, so I pushed. He thought for a while and folded. While stealing the blinds on the bubble is supposed to be easy, sometimes players will try to make your life difficult.

I was on the bubble of a $1,500 WSOP event when I played a hand against a young player I had never seen. I watched him play for a few orbits and thought he was playing just well enough to get by. He raised to 2.5 BBs out of his 100-BB stack and I re-raised with A-Q to 7 BBs out of my 80-BB stack. He four-bet me to 25 BBs. I decided he was trying to put a play on me since he was young. I went all-in and lost to his A-A. I picked up his name through the table talk and looked him up online when I got home. He regularly played $200 tournaments in his home town, which meant he probably wasn't capable of pushing there with a wide range. I made a bad read because he was young and had a lot of chips. He probably only re-raised in that spot with the nuts, which made A-Q an easy fold.

While I do suggest aggressive play as your default on the bubble, you should not go out of your way to bust the bubble and allow everyone else to get in the money. Sometimes, you actually want to stay on the bubble, especially if your table lets you pick up the blinds every hand. This may seem counterintuitive, but if you can gather more chips on the bubble than in the money, there is no reason to end the bubble. Suppose you are playing a $10,000 tournament where 18 people get money, with 18th place getting $20,000 and first place taking $700,000. You are the chip leader among 19 players, with 50,000 chips. Everyone else has between 7,000 and 15,000 chips. The blinds are 500/1000-100. If you are playing six- or seven-handed at three tables, you should go all-in with any two cards if you are first to enter the pot. Everyone else will be waiting around for the bubble to bust. Someone who calls your all-in must win more than half the time to break even. He gets nothing if he loses, and if he wins, he still might not finish in the money, as he will have between 15,000 and 30,000 chips and could still go broke. Also, it doesn't guarantee that he moves up beyond 18th place.

They actually need around 65-percent equity to justify a call, which is surprisingly difficult even if they know you are pushing with any hand. They should only call with A-K and 8-8+. This means that when you have a large stack on or very near the bubble, you should be using it to get a giant stack. If the bubble doesn't break anytime soon in the example above, you can easily go from 50,000 chips to 75,000 with no showdown. You will eventually be called and you will be way behind, but you will still be free-rolling because of all the dead money you will have picked up.

I will go out of my way to prolong the bubble at a cooperative table that lets me steal the blinds every single hand. Suppose everyone folds to the small blind, who goes all-in for 7 BBs, and you have A-7 in the big blind. While this would normally be a snap call, you should consider folding if everyone is giving you their blinds. You will win around three sets of blinds per orbit if you fold this hand because you can continue pushing. If you call and lose, you have fewer chips, which means one failed steal will put your stack on a par with everyone else's, and if you win, you have another 7 BBs but can no longer steal the blinds constantly. Either way, you are unhappy. Fold in this spot and continue picking up the blinds.

Notice also that when you are close to or on the bubble, you need a much stronger hand to call an all-in than you do earlier or later in the tournament. This is because your tournament equity doesn't double when your stack does. In the example above, if a 10-BB stack doubles to 20 BBs, the player's equity might increase from about $40,000 to $60,000. I made up these numbers, but they are similar to what happens in the real world. To call, you need a hand that is a heavy favorite against the pusher's range or you need great odds, which is rarely the case. Hence, you should push often and rarely call. You can profitably push a wide range on the bubble. Your opponents can't call without throwing away money.

Suppose everyone folds to the small blind, who pushes for 10 BBs. You are in the big blind with 10 BBs as well. What range should you call with? You need around 60-percent equity against his range to break even due to the prize payouts. Suppose you know he is pushing every hand from the small blind. You can call with something like 6-6+, A-8+ and K-Q. If his range is tighter, you should call even tighter. This allows you to push a very wide range on the bubble as long as most people are short-stacked and unwilling to call without a very premium hand.

You may also be in situations where you want the bubble to end, such as when the table is not cooperating at all. Suppose a short stack goes all-in for 5 BBs and two players call. You are in the small blind with 7♠-6♠ and 20 BBs. I would call here every time if the big blind is not prone to pushing in these spots to get the pot heads-up, which would probably be a good play. By calling with a hand such as 7♠-6♠, which tends to have equity against every hand, you are locking up at least 25-percent equity in a four-way pot, which is almost always a good thing. Fold if you have a hand like K♠-2♣, which will often be dominated.

Notice that if you are abusing the bubble with a big stack, someone pushes for 5 BBs and three people call, you should go all-in with any two cards. You can usually get heads-up with 15 BBs dead, as the three callers will almost always assume you have a strong hand and fold. Don't be surprised if they cuss you out after you flip up your 9♠-4♣.

There is one situation where I would suggest blinding off for a while to ensure you get in the money. If you have around 10 BBs and a player with one or two big blinds will be taking the blinds soon, you should go out of your way to not go broke. Your 10-BB stack usually won't be worth much, but it will be worth a lot more than a 1-BB stack. If yours is one of several short stacks with 10 BBs or so, do not wait for one of them to bust out. These other short stacks will often blind off to their very last chip, costing you equity if you blind off as well. Waiting for them to bust is a huge mistake because you will lose any chance of winning the tournament.

Some players justify playing tight by saying they got in through a satellite and the money means a lot to them. In order to be a great poker player, money cannot mean anything to you. If I were on the bubble of a $1 million buy-in tournament and bubbling would cost me $2 million in real money, I would play my normal game because I know the proper strategy is to play for first place. Winning the minimum should not be a good result in your mind. In fact, it should be somewhere between neutral and bad. Even if you have $50 to your name and cashing in a tournament will give you 1,000 times your net worth, you should still play good poker. If the money means that much to you, you shouldn't have played the tournament. Be smart and only play tournaments you can afford to play optimally.

The bubble is a fascinating and troubling stage to play. I can't stress enough that you should not play to win the minimum. If you play great poker, you will make money in the long run regardless of whether you cash in any specific tournament. Pinpoint the players that are too tight and raise their blinds whenever you have a chance. Gun for the players that try to steal the blinds too often. Make sure you have a good read on your opponent and think about his range of hands. Ranges on the bubble are either very tight or very loose. Figure out who you are playing against and it becomes an easy game.

In The Money

In most tournaments, everyone breathes a sigh of relief when they get in the money. Sometimes people even clap and cheer. Getting in the money is nothing to be proud of. Most tournaments will last at least a few more hours, so being content with what little cash you have won makes no sense. Your eye should be on first prize.

As soon as you get in the money, an unusual number of short stacks will be ready and willing to go all-in. At this point you should tighten up your pre-flop raising ranges a little because it's likely that a short stack will shove on you. For example, say you just got in the money and you pick up 9♠-8♠ in middle position. You have 50 BBs and everyone behind you has between 15 and 25 BBs. This is an easy fold because everyone behind you has a great stack for shoving. With A-J instead, you should be more than happy to raise and call a push from one of the short stacks because their ranges are usually going to be abnormally large, making A-J a decent favorite.

Some players who have large stacks from pushing people around on the bubble may keep up the aggression, not adjusting their game at all. Be very willing to re-raise them, especially if you have a great stack for a three-bet push. Suppose one of these overly aggressive big stacks raises from the cutoff and the action is folded to you in the big blind. If you have between 20 and 25 BBs, consider going all-in with any two cards. I would usually push a touch tighter, with something like the top 50 percent of hands. Be careful to accurately estimate the aggressive player's range. If you think he is still raising wide when he has actually tightened up, you could be making a huge blunder.

Most of the short stacks will either bust out or double up after a little while. Despite this, most players' stacks in some events will be only 20 BBs. If most people have a stack between 15 and 30 BBs, which is optimal for re-raising all-in, you should raise fairly tight if they know you will go all-in fairly wide. If they are all rather tight and don't know they should be pushing over your raises, feel free to continue raising with a wide range. You can widen your range and attack the blinds often if most stacks are deeper than 30 BBs.

As you get deeper in the tournament, some people will tighten up as you approach a pay jump. In most tournaments, the payouts increase as groups of nine players are eliminated. For example, if 45 people get money, 45th to 37th will get the same amount, and 36th to 28th will get the same, greater amount. When you get down to around 38 players, you can loosen up even more against those that are concerned with moving up to the next pay level. Remember that your goal should be to win, not to move up a few more dollars.

You will sometimes play short-handed as players are eliminated. Normally you will play nine-handed, but you may play as low as six-handed. My advice for playing six-handed is to play your standard nine-handed game and pretend the first three players have folded. So, first position at a six-handed table should use my opening ranges from the "Playing Poker" section in *Volume 1* for middle position. Most players go overboard, raising and re-raising really wide once they get short-handed. Do not fall prey to this temptation. You should be fine if you can steal the blinds more than once per orbit.

Revert to your normal game after you get in the money and the short stacks bust, constantly attacking the blinds and weak pre-flop raisers while trying to put a lot of money in the pot only with a strong hand. If you can keep this up, you will soon be on the final-table bubble.

The Final-Table Bubble

The final-table bubble is similar to the money bubble except you are always short-handed, as there will be 11 people left playing either five- or six-handed. This is similar to the money bubble when you are down to 19 people and only 18 get paid, but the big stack will have an even greater edge. However, there is a huge difference between untelevised and televised final table bubbles.

Play your normal aggressive bubble game if you're not on television; the only incentive to make the final table is to say you made the final table, which really doesn't matter. This is because the payout jumps from 11th to 10th place usually are not that big compared to those later in the tournament. Remember that you are playing to win, not to take 10th place. This, however, doesn't mean everyone else is playing to win. Some players take great pride in making final tables. Steal their blinds as often as possible. Try to stay out of the way of players who are there to win, as long as they aren't getting too far out of line.

Televised final tables are entirely different. Most players dream of being on TV. Most of them, including top professionals, go out of their way to do so. I mean, who doesn't want to be on TV? Because of this TV craze, you should go out of your way to steal each and every pot on bubbles for televised final tables. The number of players who get to be on TV varies significantly by tournament, but whatever it is, be aggressive right before you reach that number. For example, the WPT puts six people on TV. When you are down to seven or eight players, go nuts and steal as many pots as possible. The WSOP puts nine people on TV. When you are down to 10, steal to your heart's content.

When you are on the TV bubble, if someone, especially someone who wants to make the final table badly, plays back at you, get out of the way quickly. He almost certainly has a huge hand. You can watch basically every WSOP Main Event final-table bubble for the last few years and the player that busted in 10th place got fairly unlucky. You can fold big hands when things don't feel right, especially if players are letting you steal most of the blinds.

On these televised final-table bubbles, I generally raise to around 2.25 BBs before the flop if most people aren't short-stacked; I want to steal the blinds often pre-flop and I don't mind if the blinds call, because I will be in position. Most people play straightforwardly on the final-table bubble. If your opponent is willing to put a lot of money in post-flop, you usually need two pair or better to continue unless he's a maniac.

If you have a large stack on the final table bubble, you should be stealing from everyone. If another aggressive, large stack raises, go ahead and re-raise with a wide range as long as you are not committing yourself to the pot. Also, go out of your way to raise the medium stacks. These players usually assume they will make the final table if they are tight and wait out the short stacks. If they have this attitude, steal as much as possible from them. You do need to be a bit careful when stealing against short stacks, especially if they have no fear of bubbling. If they are tight though, attack them often.

If you are a medium stack on the final-table bubble, you are almost forced to sit back and wait. If you have around 25 BBs, feel free to push over an aggressive big stack's raise with a wide range. Attack the short stacks as much as possible if they are not fighting back.

If you are a short stack, you need to get to work. When everyone folds to you, you should be going all-in with a fairly wide range if you have 10 BBs or less. Even picking up the blinds and antes is a huge boost to your stack. Don't be scared to go broke against an aggressive, big stack. Some players fear the big stack because he can bust you. Remember that you are playing to win, and you have to get some chips if you're to have chance.

Keep your eyes and ears open to figure out how much each player wants to make the final table. At the WPT event at Mirage that I won, a friend that was watching me overheard the player on my direct right talking to a family member about how his first and main goal was to make it on TV. Once my friend relayed this information to me, I re-raised that player most of the time when he raised before the flop. He folded every time. Without this information, I would have missed a lot of opportunities to steal chips.

At the same time, I had Phil Ivey two seats on my left and he must have thought I wanted to make the TV final table, because every time I raised, he would re-raise me. After the second time, I decided he was using my loose raising range as a great reason to re-raise me with any two cards. I kept raising my wide range but every time he re-raised me, instead of folding, I went all-in. He folded every time. This happened a few times before the final table bubble broke, and was the main reason I made it to the final table with a big stack.

If you are constantly in each opponent's head, you should be able to determine what to do in every situation. Poker is not about playing your cards. It is about playing your opponents. Once you realize most players just want to be on TV, you can go out of your way to abuse them until everyone is rewarded with a spot on a TV show. Most of the time, you will be the one sitting there as the chip leader.

The Final Table

Making the final table of a major tournament is a dream come true for most amateur poker players. For a professional, the only dream should be to win a major tournament. Your goal at any final table should be to gather as many chips as possible before the blinds get too large to play a super loose game. Once this happens, you simply need to tighten up, play a solid short-stacked game and hope for the best.

The players usually get some sort of break once they make it to the final table. Use this time to gather as much information as you can before play resumes. Before every WPT final table I have ever played, I have watched at least four hours of video on the big-name players I'll face. I am sure that this greatly increased my chances to win. I google every player to see how much the money will effect them. Some players are billionaires and some are near broke. Clearly, a billionaire isn't worried about the money. His only concern is to win. If a player owes $150,000 on his house, moving up the payouts enough to pay off his house will be his main concern. If you spend enough time collecting information about each player, you will be much better equipped to play with them at the final table.

I have had two pretty huge victories in the information war when studying opponents. The first came when I learned that a player was $200,000 in debt and desperately wanted to get out. It happened that fourth place was right around $200,000. Sure enough, he started playing the final table tight. I stole his blinds relentlessly and he never played back at me. Once we got down to four players, getting the player out of debt, he became a maniac, raising and re-raising every hand. I eventually made a fairly big call to bust him. Had I not known about the debt, I may have missed the big call to bust him as well as a few blind steals early at the final table.

A more recent success occurred during the $10,000 heads-up tournament in the 2010 WSOP. I won my first round and knew I was going to play Daniel Negreanu in a few hours. I didn't have time to go home, so I was just going to chill at the Rio until our match. I then remembered I had a book in my bag that used examples from the NBC heads-up tournament. Negreanu was involved in around five hands in the book. I read over all of them and headed off to my match. I had a lot of good hands but on one, I made a very uncharacteristic fold with top pair, bad kicker because he took the exact line he had taken with the nuts in the book. I won the match in 20 minutes thanks to his making strong, second-best hands, but had I not read that book, I may have lost a lot of chips with top pair, bad kicker earlier in the match.

Once you get to the final table, assuming the big stack played the bubble well, there will be one or two large stacks and a bunch of shorter stacks. If you have a large or medium stack compared to the rest of the field, you should generally tighten up once you make the final table. Attack the blinds if you have a small stack and everyone folds to you. You simply must get some chips to give yourself a chance to win the tournament. The difference in payouts between 10th and fifth place is usually only a few buy-ins, but the difference between fifth and first is huge.

As when the first bubble broke, most of the short stacks will go a little crazy. From time to time, one of the big stacks will go nuts and give away his chips as well. If you see someone getting out of line, buckle up and get ready to get all-in against him as soon as you pick up a good hand.

For example, suppose everyone has between 10 and 30 BBs. Everyone folds to the button, who has reduced a 50-BB stack to 10 BBs by raising and re-raising weak hands. He goes all-in. The small blind folds and it is up to you, with a 15-BB stack. What hands should you call him with? Most likely, if he went from chip leader to being nearly out of the tournament, his range is going to be wide open. I would assume he is pushing around 90 percent of hands. There are around 3 BBs of dead money in the pot, so you have to call 9 BBs to win 13 BBs, meaning you would normally need around 40-percent equity to call. However, you still need a much better than breakeven hand because doubling your chip stack will not double your equity in the tournament. I would estimate you need about 50-percent equity to break even here, assuming there are no abnormally large or small stacks. Remember, we need to do a little better than break even, so we need something like 54 percent to profit here. I would call with 4-4+, A-2+, K-7+, Q-9+, and J-10. Notice that even though he is pushing wide, I must call with a tight range. As you get deeper and deeper into the final table, pushing goes way up in value and calling goes way down.

If he is a super nit instead of a maniac, he will only push from the button around 20 percent of the time, and I will only call with 8-8+ and A-J+. Keeping a decent stack and utilizing fold equity is the way to grow a short stack into a medium stack quickly.

Once everyone settles down and the short stacks bust, you need to revert to your normal game. You should constantly pick on the players that are trying to move up and avoid the better players. If everyone has a short stack, play good push-fold poker and look for as many spots as you can to go all-in from late position where you expect to have a lot of fold equity. Eventually, you will be sitting at a final table with only six players competing for the grand prize.

Chapter 2

Short-Handed Play

A great deal of tournament play is contested at tables with 9 or 10 players. In this chapter we are going to consider situations where there are fewer players at the table, from six right down to heads up play. Some online tournaments are actually played out on six-max tables and, obviously, even tournaments with the more normal nine- or ten-player tables will drop to smaller numbers if you make it to the late stages.

Six- to Four-Handed Play

In this book I consider play to be short-handed when there are between four and six players at the table. Your goal when playing short-handed is to pick up as many blinds as possible and to re-raise from time to time to steal an aggressive player's pre-flop raise. Don't put a lot of money in the pot against a tight player without a fairly strong hand. Be prepared to put a lot of money in with a fairly weak hand against an aggressive player if the situation calls for it. Determine each player's range and act accordingly.

Short-handed poker gives many players headaches because they fail to adjust to individual players. As you play more hands with the same players, you must constantly adjust to their adjustments so you can stay one step ahead of the game. Some players think short-handed poker is about being more macho than other players. If you can spot these players before they make a ridiculous bluff, you can win a lot of chips. Short-handed poker is about remaining calm while everyone else goes on tilt.

Tight players are sometimes referred to as "dead money" in a tournament because they fail to adjust to the losing players. They sit around and wait for a premium hand until they blind off. When the blinds and antes come around much faster, as they do when short-handed, you have to raise a little more often from late position. Failure to keep up with the blinds is the reason why these players have little chance to win a tournament.

Loose-aggressive players become extra loose once the table gets short-handed, which tends to get them in trouble. Despite their usually –EV play, poor loose-aggressive players always have a chance to win the tournament because they are aggressive, which is never a bad thing.

I play short-handed a bit tighter than most players out of position and a bit looser in position, because you win more hands in position than out of position. If you constantly raise weak hands out of position, you will land in many tricky spots after the flop. For example, you can usually get away with raising J♠-8♣ from first position at a six-handed table, but occasionally you will flop top pair and run into a better top pair, which will usually cost a decent number of chips. I would much rather raise 7-4 late than J-8 early because you gain a lot of fold equity in late position. When you raise with hands like 7-4 from the button, you have to be aware that you are merely trying to steal the blinds. If the flop comes J-4-3 and your opponent check-raises your continuation bet, you generally will need to fold. Basically, you should loosen up in position but don't go crazy with huge post-flop bluffs.

You'll do well in all forms of short-handed poker if you remember to play as if the table is full and everyone has folded to you. In the "Playing Poker" section in *Volume 1*, I suggested raising 2-2+, A-2+, K-7+, Q-9+, any suited hand where both cards are 9 or higher, offsuit connectors and one-gapped hands down to 7-5 from the cutoff. This is a pretty wide range, and I suggest you raise with this range from the cutoff whether the table is four- or 10-handed. From the button you can raise with basically any two cards if the blinds are tight, although you should usually fold hands like Q-3, 10-4 and 7-2. This means that you should raise a wide range from the button even when there are four players.

I also advised not to raise every hand from late position every time the action is folded around to you. You can fold from time to time. You can still fold when short-handed, but not as often as when 10-handed. You have to raise every few hands just to keep up with the blinds. You'll quickly fall behind if you fold the button often.

Some players call too loosely from the blinds. Even short-handed, I only defend my blinds by calling with hands that flop well, such as 5♠-5♣ and 8♠-7♠. I rarely call raises while out of position with hands like A♣-4♣. You are usually better off re-raising these hands before the flop. Throughout this book I have preached tight play out of position, and short-handed play is no different. Play your normal, aggressive late-position game when short-handed and you will have no problem.

Three-Handed Play

You will always have the option of raising from the button when you play three-handed, as you will be first to act before the flop. This huge advantage of always being able to play the button every round means you can actually get away with playing a bit tighter than most people think.

On the button in a three-handed game, if the blinds play fairly tight, which they should, you should be raising around 80 percent of your hands. If the blinds play back at you often, you can cut it down to about 50 percent. Raising any less than this at a three-handed table is usually a mistake because you will basically be blinding off. As long as you keep raising and firing out continuation bets, you will win more than your fair share of pots from the button.

From the small blind, you should re-raise or fold most every hand you intend to play. The big blind has a great squeeze opportunity if you just call. If you know the big blind will rarely squeeze, you can call with a slightly wider range of hands that flop well. If you are dealt a hand like A♣-4♠ in the small blind and the button raises, you should always either re-raise or fold, depending on how wide the button is raising. If the button folds, consider folding a decent number of hands from the small blind. I would raise something like 2-2+, A-2+, K-7+, Q-8+, J-9+ and connectors against a generic opponent, which you will rarely face. I will raise every hand in the small blind against a tight big blind. If he is loose and aggressive, constantly re-raising you, feel free to limp and call his raises. This will let you see cheap flops with almost a guarantee of decent implied odds. For example, I would raise a tight big blind every time with J♠-9♠, but I would consider limping with that hand against a loose, aggressive big blind. Another option is to raise and four-bet if he re-raises. Again, you must know your opponent well, but if you have been paying attention at the final table, you should have some kind of read on each player.

You can call a button raise in the big blind with most hands that flop decently well. Re-raising is also an option. You can fold fairly often if the button is not getting too far out of line. Fold hands like A-3 if the button is tight, but re-raise every time if he is loose. You can often call the small blind's raises in position if the stacks are over 40 BBs or so. Basically, you are looking to either hit a flop or get a flop that enables you to represent a hand. For example, if the small blind raises and you call in the big blind with 7♠-4♠, you should be very willing to either float or raise if the flop comes 9♥-8♥-5♦. Pile on the aggression in spots like this because most players can't take the heat.

The effect of position becomes magnified as the game becomes more and more short-handed. It will be tough to make too many mistakes if you play loose and aggressively in position and tight out of position. I suggest you play some six-handed sitngos online to get practice playing short-handed with shallow stacks. The game will eventually turn into a push-or-fold situation where the first person to go all-in usually wins the pot. If a tournament becomes three-handed and everyone has a shallow stack, you need more than normal equity to make a profitable call because of the prize payouts. The difference between the second and third place payouts is usually significant, so you do not want to bust in third when you could have easily snuck into second place.

For example, say you're playing 200/400, the big stack has 10,000 chips, you are the middle stack with 5,000 and the short stack has 1,000. The short stack folds on the button and the action is on the big stack in the small blind, who goes all-in. You need a very strong hand to call here. Calling with Q-Q may even be incorrect, depending on how the table is playing.

This situation is basically another bubble. In fact, at the final table, every prize jump will cause some people to play as if they are on the bubble. I tend to care about the prize jumps only after I get to fourth place or so, as the previous jumps usually aren't too large. Notice that if you are a big stack playing a short and medium stack, as in the example above, you can push players around on this three-handed bubble easily because the middle-stacked player will be looking to outlast the short stack.

As the big stack, you may even want to keep the short stack alive so you can blind off the middle stack. Suppose there is a medium stack of 5,000 chips on the button, a big stack of 10,000 chips in the small blind and a short stack of 1,000 chips in the big blind playing 200/400. As long as the 5,000-chip stack is passive, the big stack should fold basically every hand from the small blind if the short stack is not doing anything too wild. If the big stack folds, he can go all-in on the next hand, winning the blinds if the small stack folds or getting all-in with decent equity if he calls. If the short stack shoves on the next hand, the big stack, which is now in the big blind, can fold. On the next hand, he can steal from the short stack, then again from the middle stack on the next hand. Basically, the big stack should steal twice per orbit and give up his blind or get a walk when he is in the big blind. Always look for spots like this to exploit because when they come up, they are among the most profitable situations in poker because you stand to win a lot of chips with very little risk.

Heads-Up Play

If you are fortunate enough to make it to heads-up play in a major tournament, you will probably be worn out. You will have been playing for five days straight, and will now play heads-up for a huge amount of money. If you face a competent heads-up player and you have no clue how to play heads-up poker, you will quickly lose chips. Heads-up poker is full of variance. If the best player in the world played heads-up against an average player and both had fairly short stacks, he would be lucky to win more than 57 percent of the time in the long run.

You would be wrong to take this to mean that heads-up play is not that important. If you can win 57 percent of the time when playing for $500,000, the difference between a $1 million first prize and a $500,000 second prize, you will generate a huge edge. You will own 57 percent of that $500,000, meaning you will win $285,000 and your opponent will win $215,000 on average. If you are an expert heads-up player and you manage to get heads-up one time in your life in a major tournament against a mediocre opponent, you will instantly win $60,000 in equity, which is a pretty big deal.

Considerations like ICM go out the window when you're heads-up because there is no added benefit to moving up a payout spot. You both get paid for second place, and you're playing for the diffrence between second and first. If you have an edge and think you cannot find a greater edge later in a heads-up match, you should take it even if it is only slightly better than neutral EV. Also note that if you think your opponent is vastly better than you, which hopefully won't be the case after you finish this book, you can be correct to go all-in with a slightly negative expectation if you expect your opponent to get you all-in with less equity later. I assume here that your skills are at least equal to those of your opponent.

Only two styles work well at heads-up poker: loose-aggressive and super loose-aggressive. This is because most of the time, neither player will make a hand, meaning the person who picks up most of the pots when everyone misses will win a decent amount of money. Suppose you have 50 BBs and raise to 2.5 BBs with 7♠-5♣ from the button. The big blind calls with K♠-7♣. The flop comes Q♠-6♦-2♣. Your opponent checks and you bet 3 BBs. Most opponents will fold in this spot, giving you the pot when the flop doesn't connect with their hand. This demonstrates the power of position in heads-up poker. In tournaments there will usually be an ante involved, which makes a loose- or super loose-aggressive style mandatory if you want to win.

Heads-up poker is different than short-handed poker because the small blind is also the button, meaning the small blind goes first before the flop and last after the flop. The button's edge increases as fewer players are involved in the game, so you should play many more hands from the button and fairly snugly from the big blind, assuming your opponent raises a fairly tight range. The average winning hand can be quite weak when you are heads-up. You should rarely fold top pair, and hands like middle pair can extract maximum value, as most players call down fairly often with bottom pair or ace-high.

Your style of play should depend entirely on your opponent's play. There are four basic types of poker players. Tight-passive players enter very few pots and usually limp in. It's usually correct to raise basically every time from the button and continuation-bet every flop against these players. Most of your profit will come from bluffing them out of small pots. Be quick to get away from your hand if they raise. A good, loose-aggressive player will slowly grind down these players, giving them little chance of winning a heads-up match if they refuse to take a stand.

Most of your value against loose-passive players comes from value-betting relentlessly. Some will call bets on every street with king-high. If this type of player raises on a later street, unless he is creative, which some loose players are, you should respect him and release weaker holdings and even some stronger hands.

Next is the tight-aggressive player. To play tight in a heads-up game is vastly different than at a full table. A tight player in heads-up poker probably raises between 25 and 60 percent of hands from the button. Try to raise more hands than he does from the button and play only strong hands from the big blind. If you and your opponent play strong hands from the big blind the same way, intending to break even in the long run, but you win 75 percent of hands from the button versus his 50 percent from that position, you will win in the long run. If he raises too often, you can re-raise from the big blind with a fairly wide range from time to time, mostly to prevent his becoming a loose-aggressive player. Most tight-aggressive players play decently well post-flop, although some have huge leaks. For example, some will raise pre-flop, continuation-bet every time, and play straightforwardly after that, meaning they will give up with all their bad hands and continue betting with good ones. Try to get to the turn against these players, where you should have a fairly solid idea of their hand range. The best tight-aggressive players will check behind on some turns for pot control and to induce bluffs, so always be wary of them.

Last is loose-aggressive. These players raise between 60 and 100 percent of hands from the button. They can range from being slightly looser than the standard tight-aggressive player to full blown maniacs. I will discuss maniacs first, as they are fairly exploitable. You should generally give a maniac rope with which to hang himself. Do this by raising before the flop with a wide range, which will make him think he can run you over. If you hit a hand like middle pair, be willing to continuation-bet the flop and then go into call-down mode, usually no matter how aggressive the maniac becomes. You can't be scared to go broke against a maniac with hands like middle pair because they are far ahead of his range. You should shy away from raising a maniac on the flop with a strong hand because; unless he's really wild, he will fold most hands that are behind. Tight-aggressive play works better than loose-aggressive against some maniacs because you will want to start with a much better hand than they do on average. If your default strategy, which I will outline later, does not work, be quick to alter it against a difficult opponent. Set traps and let him fall in the hole.

Some loose-aggressive players are good. In fact, they will be your toughest opponents by far. They will aggressively attack small pots but seem to always have a strong hand when a lot of chips go in the middle. If this looks familiar, it is the style I have been advocating throughout this book. You have to quickly figure out these players' leaks and adjust immediately. If they raise all hands before the flop, re-raise them liberally and be willing to five-bet if they four-bet often. Most of these players continuation-bet everytime, hence you should consider check-raising the flop often. Some loose-aggressive players will bet every street unless you put in a raise. They are basically good versions of a maniac, so set traps against them and go into check and call-down mode. Against the players that play a slightly more loose style than the tight-aggressive players, play more aggressively than they do before the flop, which will allow you to win more pots than they do. Against good, aggressive opponents, most heads-up matches will eventually turn into a crap shoot.

You must constantly pay attention to the shortest stack size in a heads-up tournament. If your opponent has 100 BBs and you have 15 BBs, you are playing 15-BB poker. If you have 40 BBs and your opponent has 60 BBs, you are playing 40-BB poker. Sometimes you will have a very big stack when your opponent has a small stack. When this occurs, you must play a short-stack strategy to avoid numerous difficult situations.

As with every type of poker, you must constantly put your opponent on a range of hands. This is a bit more difficult heads-up than at a full table. Most players have a much wider starting range when heads-up, meaning it is tougher to narrow it down to just a few hands. You should get a lot of practice to better deal with this.

You can easily practice heads-up poker online by jumping into a heads-up sitngo. You can play a nine-person sitngo to simulate a nine-handed final table, but it's not the same, as both the stacks and payouts are vastly different at a final table, making nine-handed sitngos decent, but not great practice. Heads-up sitngos are great for practice because the payouts are the same and you will eventually run into every stack-size situation. If you are going to play multi-table tournaments, I suggest you play at least 1,000 heads-up sitngos as soon as possible. Play a loose-aggressive style and actively seek the optimal way to play against each opponent. Start by playing 100 $5 heads-up games and then 100 games at the $10 level. Keep moving up until you find a level that is no longer profitable. If you can't beat the $5 games, stay there until you can beat them for a decent win rate. Keep moving up and you will eventually beat the highest-stakes heads-up games, and you will be well prepared to play heads-up against any opponent in a major multi-table tournament.

Heads-Up Pre-Flop Play

Your heads-up pre-flop strategy should depend almost entirely on your opponent's game plan. If he is playing rather tight, you should fold often from the big blind when he raises, and raise every time from the button. If he is raising every hand, be willing to re-raise with a wide range of hands from the big blind while also playing fairly aggressively from the button. I will outline my general game plan for when I first sit down to play an opponent heads-up with no reads, which will rarely be the case in a tournament because you have been playing the entire final table with your opponent. All information here assumes you are playing fairly deep-stacked. There will be a later section on short-stack heads-up play.

I tend to be fairly loose and aggressive from the small blind. My normal pre-flop raise is between 2 and 2.5 BBs. I will rarely make it more than 2.5 BBs before the flop because I want to be able to continue in the hand cheaply if my opponent re-raises. Also, you shouldn't mind if your opponent calls before the flop because you will have position throughout the hand. I do not vary my raise size based on my hand. I usually raise to 2.5 BBs if I have more than 50 BBs and to 2 BBs with a shorter stack. I will usually raise to 2.5 BBs against opponents that never fold to 2-BB raises until I get down to around 25 BBs, when I switch back to raising to 2 BBs.

I generally raise about 80 percent of hands from the button, which includes basically everything except hands like Q-2, J-3, 9-4 and 7-2. You want a hand that is fairly connected and has some potential. Shy away from hands consisting of a big card and a small card, which have huge reverse implied odds. Consider limping with these hands if your opponent will allow it, but I generally fold them. Speaking of limping, I rarely limp heads-up simply because there is too much value in picking up the blinds and antes before the flop.

If your opponent constantly re-raises or folds to your raises before the flop, raise to a smaller amount so you can call his re-raises and play a 12-BB pot in position. If my opponent tends to re-raise my pre-flop raises. I will raise to 2 BBs with every hand I plan to play, call most re-raises with hands that flop well, like K-Qs, 8-7s, 9-6s, 3-3 and J-10, and four-bet with hands that flop poorly or are very strong, such as A-A, A-K, A-8 and K-4s. Suppose you and your opponent both have 50 BBs and he has re-raised you five times in the last 20 hands. You raise A-10 to 2 BBs and he re-raises to 7 BBs. I would almost certainly go all-in here. Notice that, once again, this simply becomes a math problem. Matches where your opponent plays a loose-aggressive style from the big blind tend to be settled by big all-ins before the flop. Figure out when he is re-raising with a wide range and then apply a lot of pressure.

If your opponent usually folds to your pre-flop raises, then keep raising in position. You will steal a lot of blinds and eventually grind him down. When he decides to play back at you, get out of the way. Suppose you and your opponent both have 50 BBs. Your opponent has been tight for the entire heads-up match. You raise to 2.5 BBs with A-10 and your opponent re-raises to 9 BBs. I would just fold here and continue stealing the blinds. There is no need to gamble with A-10 in this spot because you will eventually easily grind down this opponent.

If your opponent calls often from the big blind, you can either raise to around 3 BBs before the flop in an attempt to gain some fold equity, or raise smaller and assume you will be playing a 4-BB pot in position when you are on the button, which isn't really a bad thing. You will generally win most of your chips from these opponents after the flop, when they tend to call down fairly wide. If they only call bets after the flop when they hit a strong hand, you can continuation-bet every time, as you will pick up about 60 percent of the pots post-flop, for a huge win rate.

You should be fairly tight and aggressive out of position unless your opponent is terrible. Call rarely from the big blind against most opponents because you will be out of position throughout the hand. You are usually better off re-raising or folding before the flop unless you have a hand that flops well, like a small pair or suited connectors. If your opponent raises very few hands from the button, feel free to re-raise hands that are well ahead of his range. If he raises a very wide range, you can re-raise wide as well. Just be careful not to pot-commit yourself with a weak hand.

Suppose you face a loose-aggressive player who raises to 2.5 BBs out of his 40-BB stack. You are in the big blind with K♣-10♠. I will re-raise every time in this spot, usually to around 7 BBs, and fold if he goes all-in. Notice that even in this spot, you must be careful re-raising because you only need to win 42 percent of the time when your opponent pushes. If we assign your opponent the range of 2-2+, A-9+, K-10+, Q-10+, J-10, 9-8s and 8-7s, you will have around 43-percent equity. If he has this range, you are probably better off just calling before the flop, although it is still close. If I had A-J instead of K-10, I would re-raise with the intention of calling if my opponent pushed. Also, if my opponent has been fairly tight, I will still re-raise K-10 before the flop, although I will definitely fold to a push.

Playing heads-up before the flop is really fairly simple. Tend to be loose and aggressive in position. Out of position, fold most weak hands, re-raise with strong hands and hands that are tough to play, like A-Q, A-4 and K-4s, and call with hands that flop well, like 10♣-8♣

and 5♠-5♦. Always put your opponent on a range of hands and make the most +EV decision on every betting round. If you become excellent at determining your opponent's range, you will quickly conquer most players.

Heads-Up Post-Flop Play

Heads-up poker becomes quite difficult after the flop. It is tough to narrow an opponent's range because most players know to continuation-bet often, which decreases the information you get from the most standard play on the flop. Also, neither player will have much of a hand after the flop most of the time, meaning that most bets will be naturally balanced between value bets and bluffs. Value bets are much thinner than when there are more players at the table. As with every other form of poker, figuring out your opponent's range is mandatory if you want to win.

When you raise in position before the flop and your opponent calls, you should continuation-bet almost every time unless he is a calling station. This is because he will miss the flop 66 percent of the time. Some opponents realize that you will miss with the same frequency and will play back at you constantly on the flop. Tend to check behind against these players with your strongest hands like sets, and also with weak hands. You can also pot-control with hands like middle pair, although hands like top pair should usually not be pot-controlled on the flop when heads-up because most opponents will continue with much weaker holdings. You should usually value-bet a hand like middle pair or better on at least two streets, as you almost certainly have the best hand.

Suppose you are heads-up and raise to 2.5 BBs out of your 50-BB stack with K♠-J♦ from the button. The big blind calls and the flop comes J♠-4♦-2♣. When your opponent checks, and he usually will, betting 4 BBs is very standard. Your opponent calls and the turn is 9♣. If your opponent checks, bet again, this time around 10 BBs into the 14-BB pot. If your opponent calls, then push if the river is a safe card. You should probably check if the river is a bad card, like an ace, queen or 10. If you have 10-9 instead of K-J, you should still continuation-bet the flop. When you turn middle pair, betting is usually right because this hand can see a number of bad rivers. Check behind on the river most of the time unless your opponent is a calling station. With A-6 instead of 10-9, bet the flop and consider betting the turn, especially if you know your opponent would call the flop with something like middle pair and fold to further aggression. Feel free to bet the flop and turn with a total bluff like 7-6, but if you're called on the turn, only bet the river if a scare card comes. As you can see, aggression is important when playing heads-up. However, if your opponent plays very straightforwardly after the pre-flop action, be willing to bet once with a trash hand and give up because his check-calls indicate he has a piece of the flop.

If your opponent check-raises on the flop, your play should depend mostly on his playing style. Some players will check-raise the flop only with hands like top pair or better, some with ace-high or better, and some with a wide but balanced range. Pay careful attention to what your opponent shows up with when he makes these plays. Usually, a player who is tight pre-flop will also be tight when it comes to putting a lot of chips in the pot. Loose players tend to be more willing to check-raise with a wide range.

Sometimes the big blind will call before the flop and lead into you on the flop. Most players tend to lead with hands that can't stand much pressure. Because of this, I usually raise these bets and continue firing on later streets. Some players only lead with hands they have no intention of folding. Against these players, just fold to their leads unless you have a strong draw or a strong made hand.

When out of position you will usually be in a fairly large pot, as you will have often re-raised before the flop. When you re-raise before the flop and your opponent calls, you should continuation-bet almost every time, usually between half and 3/5 pot. Tend to fold if you're raised on the flop in these re-raised pots unless you have a strong hand like top pair or you know your opponent is capable of bluffing. If he calls and you have a strong hand like top pair, you should usually check to induce a bluff on the turn if your hand is not too vulnerable to scare cards. If it is, go ahead and bet again on the turn.

Suppose your opponent raises to 2.5 BBs out of a 60-BB stack and you re-raise to 8 BBs from the big blind with 10♠-9♣. The flop comes 10♣-5♠-2♦. Your opponent calls your standard 9-BB continuation bet. Go into check-call mode if the turn is an overcard. Bet again for value if the turn is a blank, with the intention of getting in if a loose, creative opponent raises and folding to someone who is tight and straightforward. If you re-raise with A-6 and the flop comes A-J-4, then continuation-bet the flop and check the turn. Most players will not call down with less than an ace, which means you are either chopping or losing. So, check the turn and value-bet the river if he checks behind. Call down if he bets the turn.

Playing heads-up poker after the flop is all about figuring out when your opponent has a hand he can fold and then applying just enough pressure to get the job done. Stop bluffing as soon as you realize your opponent is most likely not going to fold. Some players will call the flop with anything. Fire a second barrel against these players on the turn. If a player will never fold once he calls the flop, only bet hands that tend to be ahead of his calling range on the flop. You should not run into too many problems playing heads-up if you are constantly thinking.

Heads-Up Short-Stack Play

When you get heads-up in a tournament it's likely that either you or your opponent has a short stack. I usually assume a short stack heads-up to be around 30 BBs or less. When this is the case, most of your post-flop skills are useless and you will be forced to play a solid mathematical pre-flop game. In fact, in two out of my three heads-up confrontations in WPT events, we started with around 75 BBs each but played so long that when the tournament ended, both players had less than 20 BBs. If you can't beat your opponent when you are deep-stacked, you must be prepared to shove very wide when you get short, or he will slowly grind you down.

I suggest you reread the section in *Volume 1* on playing when you have between 15 and 27 BBs. Much of the information applies to heads-up poker except you don't have to worry about players being behind you when you push over a raise. Most players will call with a wider range when heads-up. That shouldn't stop you from going all-in fairly often over a loose raiser. If you know your opponent is loose-aggressive, you should be pushing over his 2.5-BB raises anytime you have less than 25 BBs. If he raises to 2 BBs pre-flop, as I suggest, you should only push over his raises when you have 23 BBs or less. Push only strong hands if your opponent is tight, as you will be able to grind him down by stealing the blinds more often than he does.

Suppose you have 20 BBs and face a player that raises every hand to 2 BBs from the button. If he will only call your all-in with 4-4+, A-7+, K-9+ and Q-10+, then what hands can you push with and still have an edge? Using PokerStove, you can tell this range is something like the top 20 percent of hands. This means he will call us 20 percent of the time. So, we have $(0.8)(3.25) + (0.2)[(x)(40) - 20] = 0$, and $x = 0.175$. The 3.25 is the blinds plus the antes plus the initial raise. This means you only need to have 17.5-percent equity when called to break even. So, you can push with any two cards against an opponent that raises this wide but calls fairly tight, because every hand wins more than 17.5 percent of the time against this range.

Instead, suppose your opponent only raises 50 percent of his hands but calls with the same range, meaning he will now call 40 percent of the time instead of 20 percent. You now have $(0.6)(3.25) + (0.4)[(x)(40) - 20] = 0$, and you need 38-percent equity to break even. Against the calling range of 4-4+, A-7+, K-9+ and Q-10+, you should push something like 2-2+, A-6+, A-2s+ and K-10+, which basically means you should fold weaker hands before the flop if you don't have a lot of pre-flop fold equity and your opponent is playing fairly tight.

Again, I suggest you play around with a poker hand equity calculator and figure out which ranges you should be pushing in each situation against each type of opponent. Studying things like this away from the table will make you much more prepared than most players when the real money is on the line.

Push or fold every hand before the flop when your stack gets down to 12 BBs or less. If you raise to 2 BBs and your opponent pushes, you will usually be getting the correct odds to call anyway with all but the worst hands. Your pushing range should depend directly on your opponent's calling range. Some players will literally blind off to your all-in pushes unless they get a strong hand. Shove against these opponents with any two cards every time from the small blind. If these tight opponents limp a lot from the button, you can push a wide range on them if you expect them to fold often. Notice that if you steal their big blind every time and they let you see a free flop when they are on the button, you will eventually make a hand and stack them. So, don't attack these limps every time because you shouldn't mind them limping.

If your opponent seems likely to call with a fairly wide range, you need to be a little tighter with your pushing requirements, generally pushing hands that have showdown value or that do well against your opponent's calling range. This range would include hands like A-A, A-K, A-2, K-2, 5♠-4♠, 9♠-6♠ and 10♣-9♠. Tend not to push hands with low cards, which perform badly when you're called.

You can figure out which hands you should be pushing if you can estimate your opponent's calling range. Suppose you know your opponent will call your all-in for 10 BBs with 5-5+, A-7+, K-9+ and Q-10+, which is around 20 percent of hands. You will have the equation $(0.8)(1.75) + (0.2)[(x)(20) - 10] = 0$, giving us $x = 0.15$, so you need 15-percent equity when called. So, if a player calls this tight, you should push 100 percent of hands. Even if you have 15 BBs, you only need to win 26 percent of the time, meaning you could still profitably push every hand. Instead, suppose your opponent will call your 10-BB push with something like 2-2+, A-2+, K-2+, Q-9+ and J-10, which is around 40 percent of hands. Now you would have $(0.6)(1.75) + (0.4)[(x)(20) - 10] = 0.37$, meaning you need to push with hands that win 37 percent of the time to break even. So, a profitable pushing range against this opponent, who is much looser than most players, would still be 100 percent of hands. This illustrates that when you get down to 10 BBs or less, you can push basically any two cards against someone that is not crazy and will not call your pushes too wide.

Even though I should be pushing 100 percent of hands against most players when the effective stack size is 10 BBs or less, I still fold the very worst hands like 8-2, 7-3, 6-2, etc. I want my opponent to think I can fold from time to time, which will induce him to fold more often to my pushes. It may also induce him to fold occasionally in the small blind.

Since we know it is profitable to push any two cards from the small blind when someone has 10 BBs or less, what can we do to stop our opponent from pushing 100 percent of the time from the small blind? All we can really do is adjust our calling range. For simplicity, assume our opponent will push only 80 percent of the time, which is probably like most good, real-world opponents. When he goes all-in, there are 11.25 BBs in the pot. We have to call 8.75 more, meaning we need 43-percent equity to call. Plugging in the numbers, we should be calling with 2-2+, A-2+, K-2+, Q-2+, J-6+, J-2s+, 10-7+, 10-6s+, 9-8, 9-6s+ and 8-7s. You may be thinking, "Wow, I am supposed to call with a really wide range of hands." Well, it's true. If your opponent is pushing very wide, you are getting the correct odds to call with basically any decent hand and some junky ones. I tend to cut out the hands with the worst equity, such as Q-2 and J-6, and call slightly tighter. Also, you can play slightly tighter in the big blind if your opponent folds too often from the big blind.

When you are playing the 10-BB push-fold game, never fold a hand like 2-2, A-2, K-6 or Q-J if your opponent is pushing more than half the time. These hands all have around 50 percent equity against a 50-percent pushing range, which is a little tight, meaning they are monster hands against someone that is pushing really wide.

When either you or your opponent gets down to 5 BBs, be prepared to get all-in often. You already know you should push any two cards from the button. We now need to figure out the range with which we should call a 5-BB push. If our opponent is pushing 100 percent of hands, seeing as we need to win 38 percent of the time to break even, we can call with 2-2+, A-2+, K-2+, Q-2+, J-2+, 10-2+, 9-2+, 8-4+, 8-2s+, 7-4+, 7-2s+, 6-5, 6-3s+, 5-4 and 5-3s+. You should call with all but the absolute worst hands if you know your opponent is pushing every hand. If he is pushing 50 percent of hands, you should call with 2-2+, A-2+, K-2+, Q-3+, Q-2s+, J-7, J-3s+, 10-8+, 10-6s+, 9-8, 9-6s+, 8-6s+ and 7-6s. While not quite as wide as before, you should still be calling with all but the worst hands. So, when a player gets down to 5 BBs, don't be scared to call off with any sort of decent hand.

When you are playing this push-fold game for $500,000, you need the guts to push wide and call correctly. If you're lucky enough to get heads-up with a player that calls very tight from the big blind, which some players will, you should rarely call from the big blind when he pushes, and you should push every time from the button. If you are unlucky and have to play someone that pushes 100 percent of hands, don't be scared to hop in there and gamble. If you don't, he will slowly grind you down and steal a huge amount of equity. You will make money in the long run if you make your opponent fold hands when he's getting the correct odds to call. Not too many people want to call a 10-BB push with J-9 with $500,000 on the line. If you constantly put your opponent in this situation, the equity will flow your way.

Some players are confused by what is referred to as the Nash equilibrium chart. This states the effective number of blinds (the lesser of yours and your opponent's) with which you should push with a given hand from the small blind in a heads-up situation if your opponent knows your cards and will only call with hands that have the proper equity against them. Most players look at this chart and see they should push 7-5o only if they have 2.6 BBs or less. They forget that their opponent doesn't know their hand, giving them a huge amount of fold equity, which is why pushing 100 percent of hands for 10 BBs is basically always correct.

The chart is only useful for indicating when you should never fold. For example, if everyone folds to you in the small blind at a full table and you have K-2, you have to push if you have less than 8 BBs. Folding is always a mistake unless you are in an abnormal bubble situation. The chart also lists some hands as being profitable to shove with 20 BBs, such as 5-4s. Some players take this to mean that you should always push with 5-4s from the small blind when action is folded to you and you have 20 BBs or less. The chart actually means that you should never fold the hand when the action is folded to you and you have 20 BBs or less. If you have 20 BBs, you are probably better off raising and folding if you get pushed on unless you are terrible at post-flop poker.

Also notice that pushing A-A from any position in any situation besides the weirdest bubble situations is going to be +EV. That doesn't mean it is the most +EV option. As I stated earlier, you should push every hand in this situation. Because of this, the Nash equilibrium chart is basically irrelevant as long as you know your opponents' calling ranges. Most of the time, your opponents will be calling way too tight, which means you should be pushing any two cards.

Finally, if one player gets down to 10 BBs and the other has 100 BBs, the latter player should not go out of his way to call the short stack's push with any two cards simply to try to end the match. Don't play poorly against a player just because his stack is short. Even if you are really close to winning a title, don't assume you have the match locked up. I have played a few heads-up matches where I had my opponent very low and he came back to win. The most notable was in the $20,000 NBC Heads-up Tournament. We were down to the final eight players and I faced Chris Ferguson, who plays a standard, loose-aggressive heads-up game. I quickly figured out his strategy and picked up a pretty big tell. I had a 7-to-1 chip advantage by the time the blinds got large. From there, he won three coin flips and got it in when he had a bigger pair than I did to beat me. I played a sit-ngo in which I had 13,000 chips and my opponent had 500. He proceeded to win every hand for the rest of the contest, handing me a second-place finish. Crazy things happen in heads-up poker. Keep your cool and play your "A" game all the time and you will succeed in the long run.

Chapter 3

Developing Your Poker Skills

Poker is not just played on the felt. It is played throughout life. In fact, everything you do that is +EV that your opponents do not do will make you money in the long run. Also, everything your opponents do that is −EV that you do not do will also make you money. For example, suppose you lose to an opponent that put all his money in when drawing to two outs going to the river. You really only have two options. You can get upset, yell at the player and curse God for making you so unlucky, or you can muck your cards and get ready for the next hand. If you get upset, you let your opponents know you just took a beat and are most likely on tilt. Giving away this information will cost you money. If you sit there and be quiet, you will gain money because most opponents will flip out whenever they get unlucky. By not getting upset, you have won a battle in the information war.

The rest of this book will teach you how to eat, sleep, breathe and act like a professional poker player. You will find out how to learn, think and live. You will learn how to deal with tilt, which is one of the major reasons why technically sound poker players go broke. You will also learn about tells. It is important to learn to read other players. I will reveal the tells that have won me the most money throughout my career. I will also give you some general tips about how to act and think during a tournament that most players never even consider.

Finally, I will teach you how to be a professional poker player. It is not as easy as playing technically sound poker. You have to learn how to manage your life, which is something most poker players are miserably bad at. Being a professional poker player is a rewarding job that will give you numerous freedoms most jobs simply cannot allow. But being your own boss is tough. You have to learn to balance work and play. Most professional poker players goof off too much and work too little. If you want to stay ahead of them, you have to study and work harder than they do. I will teach you about every aspect of my poker playing life and why the things I do lead to success. Just remember that throughout life, everything you do better than everyone else makes you money and everything you slack on costs you money. Get ready for a lesson on how to be a professional poker player.

Learning

The next few chapters give some guidelines on how to continue learning. Poker is an ever-changing game and this book will eventually become outdated. Also, if every poker player reads this book, you will have to find new ways to adjust to take advantage of their exploitable plays. If you can only do what you are told, you will always be one step behind the best players. You have to be the innovator if you want to stay on top. You have to be the one with the original ideas that work. The next few chapters will point you in the right direction.

Be Open Minded but Skeptical

There are more poker books on the shelves than you can count these days. Unlike basically every other area of interest, you do not have to be accomplished to write a book. You simply have to know how to look intelligent. Because of this, few poker books contain winning information.

Most of the great, older books have become outdated and largely irrelevant because everyone has read them. I read one such book that suggested folding A-K to a middle-position raiser. This is terrible advice for today's games, which are considerably looser than in 1970. Books by well-respected players often suffer because a great player may not be able to transfer his knowledge to written text.

There are a few great poker books, written by well-known players and lesser-known authors. Actively think about everything you read and process all the information before assuming a suggestion is optimal.

An easy way to determine if someone is giving accurate information, especially in poker, is to check out the math behind his statements. If someone says he does something because he feels like it is right or because that it is how he has always played, you should do some research and get a mathematical answer. While some things, like tells, are based on feel and experience, most of the technical aspects of poker are based purely on math and should be verified. For example, folding A-K to someone's 2.5-BB raise, no matter how tight the player, will always be a mistake in non-bubble situations.

Do not listen to everyone you talk to on the various internet forums or in your social group. While many great players are willing to share their insights, most players like to make statements just to make themselves feel important. Research everyone you take advice from. If someone lacks a good track record, don't take his suggestions as undeniable truth.

There is more than one right way to win at the game. It is very possible to win at multi-table tournaments by playing a tight-aggressive, loose-aggressive, or super-loose-aggressive game. The fact that I prefer a standard loose-aggressive game does not mean that those playing another style are wrong. If you analyze all information that comes your way, you will be able to better add additional plays to your game and continue your growth as a player.

Apply What You Learn

While it is excellent that you have picked up this book, it will be of little use if you do not apply what you read. There is a huge difference between reading, understanding and applying. To just skim through a poker book without understanding what you read is basically useless. In high school I would be told to read a book, and I would be tested on my knowledge of what I had read. I would finish reading a passage and have no clue what I had just browsed over. I overcame this problem by taking my time and pondering what I had read, pausing after each section to figure out how one could apply the information to real-world situations. I remember in college reading about how a TV works. I understood the concepts but had no clue how to apply them. While understanding a concept is great, it does you no good if you can't apply the information to real-world problems.

The easiest way to apply knowledge is to take the information in small bits and slowly implement it. Say you read a book on poker tells. Pick a few tells you figure to be the most important and focus on them. If you pay attention to just those few tells long enough, you will eventually learn to focus on them subconsciously and will no longer have to pay attention to them. This will allow you to use your conscious brain power to focus on other tells you have learned that are also important. The same applies to all poker concepts, as well as most of life. Take things slowly, make sure you understand what you are being taught, and learn to apply the vital information you have acquired.

I have taught quite a few amateur poker players how to go from losing at small-stakes to beating the mid-stakes games in only a few hours of coaching. While the basics are fairly easy to pick up, to learn most concepts takes quite a bit of repetition.

One thing that takes time to grasp is how to work with stack sizes. When I play poker, I see all stack sizes in terms of big blinds. I don't see 3,000 chips as 3,000 chips. I see 3,000 chips as 10 big blinds at 150/300, and then play accordingly. I notice this subconsciously, which usually enables me to make a decision in less than a second. This was not a natural talent and I should not expect it from any beginning player. It took me eight years of constant practice and thousands of hours of play to develop this skill. So, realize that some things will take time at first but will eventually become easy.

When I teach students how to play multiple tables online, I never tell them to change from playing one table to 24 tables at a time. It simply is not possible for most people to make such a huge jump overnight. I suggest they add one more table and play two at a time for a week or so until they are comfortable. After a week of playing two tables, I suggest they move to three, then after another week, to four. When you can play eight tables at a time, adding an extra one will take little thought and will come easily. If you add new challenges slowly, they are much easier to accomplish than at one fell swoop.

Have a Clear Mind

When you play a session of poker for a long period of time, your mind will inevitably start to wander. If you have a clear conscience and have nothing bad to think about, you will think about good things, which will help you play your "A" game. I have done good and bad things in my life, and I can tell you with 100-percent certainty that it is much easier to live with yourself when you are a good person. Nothing is worse than having to look over your shoulder or having something bad you did in the past pop into your mind while playing poker. It is similar to the concept that it is easy to tell the truth but tough to tell a lie, because you have to constantly make sure you don't get caught.

I also suggest you do not play poker when you are having arguments with someone close to you, as this will divert your focus from the game. When you show up to play poker and all you can think about is the fight you just had with your girlfriend, poker will not be your main priority.

Numerous professional poker players bet on sports while playing in a poker tournament. I was guilty of this in the past. What happens, especially if your bet is large, is that your focus shifts to the sporting event and away from poker, causing you to miss most of the action at the table.

When I play live tournaments, I force myself at the start of each hand to focus on the cards coming off the deck and pay attention to how everyone appears as they look at their hole cards. This is usually enough to refocus me. My mind gets a short break when the dealer is shuffling the deck between hands. If you fold, continue paying attention to the players in the hand. I usually focus on the players closest to me, as they will be the ones I will play the most pots against. I have recently discovered an audio track that I play on my iPod that is supposed to help you focus. It is basically a series of different sound waves. I am unsure if it actually works, but I have cashed four out of six tournaments since I've started using it, so it can't be too terrible. I also drink a lot of green tea, which helps me to stay calm. Do everything you can to focus on the game at hand. When you go to play poker, think about poker. Anything else will only cost you equity.

Find a Study Group

Probably the most helpful thing I stumbled upon early in my poker career was the Two Plus Two poker forum. This great forum allowed me to read what some of the best players in the game had to say about numerous poker situations and ask any questions I wanted. Now, I don't use the forums too often, as they have grown a lot and much of the advice isn't correct. I currently post quite a bit on the forums of my personal training site, www.FloatTheTurn.com. If you have any questions, feel free to ask.

Also helpful has been my large contact list of players that I talk to about my poker questions. Even if you don't have a huge contact list, there is a ton of free information on the internet. All you have to do is make friends, be sociable and try to soak up as much as you can from people that play the game better than you. If you want to really help your game, talk to people that play slightly higher stakes than you and have a group discussion at least once a week. You can talk about the other players in your games, specific hands, general questions or anything else that comes to mind. Talking out your thoughts and getting feedback is a great way to increase your win rate and move up the ranks faster.

I also find it helpful to have friends that I consider equal or better than me watch me play poker online. I also watch them play, which is quite useful. To be able to ask someone questions in real time and discuss hands as they take place is invaluable. It will teach both of you to think about poker more clearly, assuming you are actually studying and not just goofing off, which tends to happen when poker players get together. Make sure everyone in your group wants to improve.

Learn to Think for Yourself

There seem to be two types of people in the world. Some do what they are told and the rest think for themselves. I am pretty confident that the school and university system in America teaches students to do what they are told, which is not good if you want to be a poker player.

One of the greatest qualities an employee can have is to do what he is told. In poker you are your own boss and you have to figure out what to do on your own. You have to set your schedule, manage your money, work on your game, develop new plays, etc. You should seek help in most of these areas. Relying purely on yourself in the poker world is usually not a good idea. You may need to talk to other players about what you are doing wrong or ask their advice on bank-roll management. However, you can determine most answers by giving a problem some thought.

Poker forums are a great learning tool, but do not rely solely on them. While it's nice that other players say you are playing well, you must be able to determine this for yourself, and if you make it high enough in the poker world, your friends will also be your enemies. It would be foolish to assume your friends would give you optimal information if you were constantly butting heads at the poker table.

Thinking outside the box will also help you in life. I am great at getting things done around my house because I figure out ways to do everything in the least amount of time, whereas many people approach chores randomly. You must also find people to help with things you are not good at, like buying a house or investing your winnings. If you can't figure out if a so-called professional is competent and is looking out for your best interests, you can put yourself in a terrible situation. If you learn to think for yourself, you will be able to deduce the correct play in most situations, both in life and in poker.

Coming Up with New Lines

Most poker players take the same line with each type of hand almost every time. In fact, that is what I suggest doing in *Volume 1*. But you should vary your play so good players can't figure out what you are up to.

One way to do this is to simply take weird lines that make little or no sense. Suppose you raise with 9♥-8♥ and the player on the big blind calls. Assume you are around 200-BBs deep for the following examples. The flop comes J♠-6♥-2♦. Your opponent checks and you make a standard continuation bet. The turn comes the Q♠.

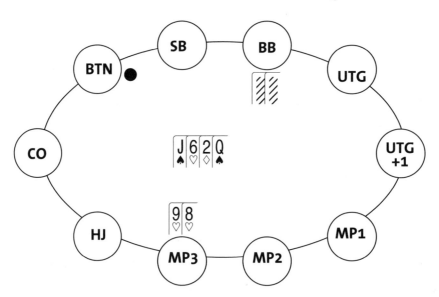

You could make another continuation bet here of around 2/3 pot, but what would happen if you bet 1/3 pot or twice the pot? If you bet 1/3 pot, you should expect to be called often. You can then bet around the size of the pot on the river and almost always get a fold, as most players will assume you made your hand on the turn and bet to sucker them in and try for a large bet on the river. If you bet twice the pot on the turn, most players will be hard pressed to call with a jack or a 6, which are their most likely holdings. It is also almost impossible for them to have a strong hand unless they slow-played a set or hit a queen with exactly Q-J. Both of these plays should work almost every time if used sparingly.

You can also take strong lines that you might not normally take, assuming your opponent will give you credit for a monster. Suppose someone raises and you call with J♠-8♠ on the button. The flop comes K♠-Q♥-8♦. Your opponent makes a standard continuation bet and you call. The turn is the 4♦.

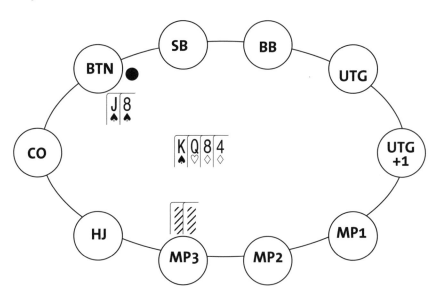

Your opponent makes a standard 2/3-pot turn bet. At this point, you almost certainly have the worst hand. You usually have outs, but aren't getting the right odds to call. Instead of simply folding, you could raise, hoping to force your opponent off a hand like A-K or K-J. Most players will fold to a turn raise with all but the most premium hands. You must know your opponent, as some players will call with A-K but give up if you blast away on the river. You might wonder why you shouldn't call the turn and raise the river if he bets again. If you call the turn and your opponent checks the river, he could easily be check-calling with a hand like top pair. If he bets the river, he could put you on a missed draw and call one more bet. But when you raise the turn, you say right away that you have something good and may be willing to fire a huge bet on the river. You are using a turn raise to commit your opponent to calling a large river bet as well, whereas if you raise the river, he can call knowing that he won't face further pressure.

I was playing the $10,000 WPT event at the Hollywood Casino in Indiana when a pretty weird hand came up. A very good, well-respected player raised from middle position to 500 out of his 40,000 stack and I three-bet on the button to 1,400 with Q♦-9♦. He had been raising a ton of pots but seldom played back when re-raised except by me. I had called his pre-flop raises quite a bit in position and re-raised only once before over about four hours. He called and the flop came A♠-A♣-4♠.

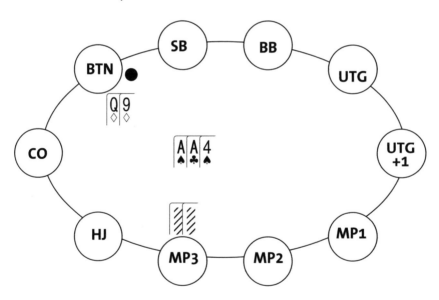

He led out for 1,200. I decided that he likely didn't have an ace because if he did, he would probably take a more standard line and just check. But this player is known to be smart and very tricky, so I couldn't totally count out an ace. If I had an ace though, how would I play it from here? Raising would be silly. He would most likely fold all of his weaker pairs and probably his flush draws, as he knew I probably wouldn't pay him off for too many chips if he hit his flush. So calling was the only option. I could fold, but that was a bit weak and would confirm to him that I was going to let him run me over. Finally, I had a few outs to the queen and 9 just in case he had a 4, allowing me to go into call-down mode if I thought that was optimal.

I called and the turn was the 6♦. He bet 2,600. At this point, I would normally throw out a raise with a good ace for value. If he had an ace, he would certainly bet the turn, but because he bet the flop and turn, I thought he was trying to represent the ace. I had to pick between raising the turn or floating one more time and raising the river. I thought he would find a river raise odd. If I had something like A-J, raising the river wouldn't make much sense because he could call with very few hands that I beat. So, I decided to raise the turn to 8,000. The raise didn't need to be large because the line I took was so powerful. If he called or re-raised, I would have been done with the hand, as he would have to be suicidal to find a call with something like 5-4. He thought for a while and folded.

When you are playing against tough, aggressive, smart opponents, you simply have to combat their weird lines. If you let them get away with every odd play they make, they will win every pot from you. If you see them do something that looks like a play, it probably is, and you should determine how to optimally attack it. You will have no problem with this if you can constantly figure out hand ranges.

Chapter 4

The Mental and Physical Approach

Poker is unlike most games in that you must think about many things besides just playing cards. If you pick the wrong opponents, you will lose money. If you pick the wrong time of day to play, you will cost yourself money. If you play too much, you will decrease the amount of money you can win. We will cover these topics and many others below.

Opportunity Cost

Everything you do in life will cost you something. When you skip your poker session to hang out with friends, not only do pay the cost of going out, but you also forgo the money you would have earned from playing poker.

To understand this concept, think of poker in terms of your hourly rate. If you play a tournament and win $1 million, you didn't actually win a million dollars that weekend. You need to average your wins and losses over the hours you've played. During the year when you won that million dollars, you may have played 1,000 hours of poker and cashed for $500,000 total, after you subtract your buy-ins, meaning you made $500 per hour, not $1 million in a weekend.

Assume you can make $200 an hour playing poker online. If you take a night off and go out with your friends, you may spend four hours at a club and spend $200. So, you spent $200 and you gave up the opportunity to make $800 playing poker, costing yourself $1,000 total. You must decide if taking that time off is worth $1,000.

When I first started grinding sitngos, making that $200 per hour was quite valuable to me. Consequently, my social life was nonexistent. Since then, I have learned about what I will call happiness EV. This is the imaginary dollar value you place on happiness. For example, going out on a date with someone of great interest to you may be worth $20,000. So, except in the rarest situations, you should go out with that person. If you value going out with people you don't particularly care for at $100, you should probably skip that, assuming you can make much more than that playing poker.

I do not recommend that you not have a social life. As you hang out with people less and less, you will notice that you start to miss these social interactions. This will cause the happiness EV you gain from being around people to rise to the point that you no longer care about the money you could be making. Basically, figure out what makes you happy and do that.

You might easily take many of the above concepts the wrong way. Think logically about them. For example, if you play live poker at a casino and your regular game only runs from 6 p.m. until 4 a.m., your time from 4 a.m. until 6 p.m. is worth much less than the time spent playing poker, because the game isn't running. Hence, you should spend your nonworking hours doing things that increase your happiness EV. Poker players that play only tournaments are often great at this. They will play every major tournament but will enjoy life whenever a tournament is not running.

You need to have a well-balanced life, spending time working and also having social interactions. I have seen many poker players become obsessed with making money, only to get burnt out, reducing their hourly rate to zero. I have also seen my peers become so engrossed in nightlife that all they do is party, making their hours spent working drop to zero. So, have a well-balanced life and try to put a value on things. Just make sure those values are realistic.

Game Selection

No matter how well you play, you should expect to lose in the long run if you play with people better than you. For example, if you are the ninth best player in the world and sit in a game with the eight people that are better than you, you should expect to lose. If you are the millionth best player in the world and are playing with the 2 millionth and 3 millionth best players, you should be a pretty big winner. Game selection is usually talked about in reference to cash games, as you do not pick your seat in a tournament. There are, however, a few situations where game selection is key in tournaments.

When playing sitngos, especially at the higher buy-in levels, be careful not to sit in a game full of professionals, as even if you are slightly better than them, you could still lose due to the rake. Avoid playing heads-up sitngos with people you know to be better than or equal to you, as you will both lose the rake.

There are a few ways you can use table selection to your advantage in multi-table tournaments. A few live tournaments, particularly the $5,000 buy-in non-main events in Vegas, are abnormally tough. These tournaments usually have very small fields full of professionals. If you do not have a giant bankroll, I suggest you skip these events. There are similar events online, especially the biggest buy-in events that do not have satellites. The opposite of this is also true. Say you have $10,000 in your bankroll and normally grind $30 to $100 buy-in tournaments online. Every Sunday, a slew of $200 buy-in tournaments with 10,000 players are filled with satellite winners who usually qualify for a few dollars. You should usually play these tournaments, as you will have a huge return on investment (ROI). There are also a few $200 events every Sunday that have no satellite qualifiers. Given the same $10,000 bankroll, avoid these events because your ROI will be fairly low.

You can also use the idea of table selection when you are moved to a table that is unfavorable for you that you know will break soon. I was in this situation at the end of day three in a WPT event at Borgata. Most tables were very soft except for mine, and I knew we would be ending the day and getting a new table draw in around 45 minutes. I decided to not get involved in any big hands and wait until the next day, when I drew a much better table. When this situation arises, just play tight ABC poker and wait for a more favorable situation.

Patience

Patience is important for numerous reasons and can be applied to basically every aspect of your poker game, as well as your life. The main time you need to be patient is when you are getting no playable hands for hours on end. While you can still play a few poor hands profitably as bluffs when you aren't getting many hands, you shouldn't try to run over the table. Also, when you are card dead, don't look frustrated or annoyed with the situation, as people may start to think you are on tilt, greatly decreasing your bluff equity. I remember a few times when I simply got 9-2, 8-4, 7-2, etc., over and over for six hours. I made a point to steal the blinds every once in a while. Eventually you will get a hand to make something happen.

That being said, you should usually not blind off in a tournament. I have only blinded down from 20 BBs to around 5 BBs one time in the last year and that was because every pot was raised in front of me and I had nothing every time. You will usually find something to work with.

Amateurs also lose patience regarding bankroll management. Most players look at the stakes above where they currently play and think they can beat those games. They feel like the only thing holding them back is the size of their bankroll. Some players decide to gamble and move up too quickly, drastically increasing their risk of ruin. While some of these players will move up much faster than normal, most will fail, not only because they are playing on a short bankroll, but because they overestimate their abilities.

One of the most important times to be patient is during a downswing. I have lost 40 tournaments in a row at times. I was playing well, but I lost everytime I got all-in. If you play a lot of poker, you must learn to expect and accept losing for long periods of time. Make sure you are playing correctly when this occurs, not tilting and studying as much as possible. The worst thing to do is to force the action by ramping up the aggression so you are playing basically every hand to the river for all your chips. Instead, relax and realize that variance is the reason why poker is so profitable.

Take Your Time

Once you learn to play fundamentally sound poker, you should know what you are going to do in most situations. Before the action even gets to me, I know what I am going to do in a hand, as pre-flop situations are usually fairly simple. The problem with acting quickly is that when you do need a little time to think, your opponents will know you have some sort of tough decision. For example, you know you are going to raise A-A just about every time, so if you raised it instantly from the button, but you thought for five seconds with 7-4o, your opponents would quickly figure out what was going on.

I generally wait around three seconds before I do anything pre-flop, and eight seconds for post-flop plays. You can change the numbers to suit your needs, as I play faster than most players. It also helps to think about what you are going to do before the action gets to you. Say you flop a flush draw and there are two people in front of you. Figure out what you are going to do if they check to you, if one player bets and the other folds, one player bets and the other calls, or one player bets and the other raises. You will be amazed at how easy this becomes once you get in the habit of thinking during every hand.

Taking a little extra time can also help you make better decisions. Sometimes, just waiting an extra few seconds will let you pick up on a tell you wouldn't have seen if you had acted quickly. I know two professionals that wait until someone gives off a tell before they act. I wouldn't go that far, but it seems like waiting just a little while, especially when the pot gets large on the later betting rounds, is very +EV.

The more you are emotionally connected to your tournament life, the more time you will take and usually, the worse decisions you will make. If you are not emotionally attached to a tournament and you think very logically, thinking everything through is rarely bad. Try to think of every hand you play as just another hand. It is your job to play it optimally.

Dealing with Loss

Losing is never enjoyable. I do a few things to minimize the pain. Most people never give themselves a chance to make it as a poker player because when they lose, they get sad, tilt or quit. The most important thing you can do when playing tournaments for a living is to deny yourself an emotional connection to any tournament. People often talk about their "tournament life" and how it is of the utmost importance to preserve it. They usually blind off, losing any chance of winning a tournament they might have won if they had risked death a few times. I think of a poker tournament as just another of the thousands of games I will play in my life. I probably developed this mentality from massively multi-tabling sitngo tournaments when I was first grinding up my bankroll. When I lost a game, it was no big deal at all. I would just open up another table. Now that I play mostly live tournaments, it is a little different because I have to fly across the country to play another game, but the concept is the same. Hopefully you can see that a tournament should just be a tournament. It should not define you as a person. Losing a string of poker tournaments does not make you a loser at life, and winning a few does not make you a winner at life.

Play well within your bankroll. Players who complain the most about losses are usually playing well above their means. For example, if you have a $1 million bankroll and lose a $10,000 tournament, it really isn't that big of a deal because you still have 99 buy-ins left. If you have a $5,000 bankroll and lose a $1,000 tournament, you've just lost 20 percent of your bankroll, and this can cause great emotional trauma. The solution to this problem is to be smart and play within your bankroll.

Learn to play well and to be confident in your game. I recently lost a tournament that mattered a lot to me. In the WPT main event at Foxwoods, six months after my second WPT title, which I also won at Foxwoods, I busted in 55th place. A win would have given me my third WPT title, made me the first player to win back-to-back main events at the same casino and made me a huge favorite to win the WPT Player of the Year title two years straight. Instead of making history, I lost, but I am fine with the result. I played my "A" game and made good use of every situation. That usually will just not be enough to get the job done. Once you accept that sometimes there just isn't anything else you can do, you will learn to accept losing.

Like most people, poker players do not like to lose. I am certainly in that large group of people. Studying the math behind poker tournaments may help you get accustomed to losing. If you play 1,000 tournaments, even if you make the money frequently, you should only expect to do so around 20 percent of the time, which means you will miss the money 80 percent of the time. I only get in the money around 13 percent of the time, which means 87 percent of the time I walk away with nothing. However, when I do get in the money, I usually have a large chip stack and am a contender to win the tournament.

My last suggestion is to get some experience. It is hard to know what a long losing streak feels like until you have been there. I have lost around $150,000 at poker in two different years. While this seems like a huge amount to lose, I have also won $2 million in two different years, which more than makes up for it. I actually feel lucky that I had a poor first year as a live tournament pro. If I had started off on a huge winning streak, I may not have been able to handle the stress had I started to lose every tournament. Many young players start their careers strong and end up going broke because they have no clue how to handle losing streaks. If you know a losing streak will come at some point, you can handle it when it finally strikes.

Tilt

Most people think of tilt as going crazy and bluffing off your chips when you know it is -EV. I think of tilt as any time I am not playing optimally. There are numerous types of tilt, most of which many professionals are unaware of. Pay close attention to this chapter because tilt is the main reason why technically sound players fail. You will often see what is referred to as a blowup, which is when a pro spews away his chips on TV. That is the person you do not want to be. Some of the biggest winners are not the most technically sound players, but they play their best all the time. I am quite confident that if I had less control over my emotions, I would not be where I am today.

The most obvious type of tilt is what I call standard tilt. This is when you become angry. When you get A-A all-in against 9-3o and lose, it is tough to not be at least a little upset. Less known is what I call happy tilt. This is when you win a few hands in a row, start thinking you are invincible and proceed to play hands you should fold. I have often seen professionals win a few hands and then lose their entire stack. They usually claim they were on a rush, which is when you win a string of hands. The problem with a rush is that you can only see it looking back, not forward, so you should never think about a rush while playing. To me, a rush is just a string of hands in which you run well above expectation, not some mythical stroke of luck where the poker gods favor you, and only you.

The easiest way to minimize your anger, allowing you to play your "A" game, is to never go on tilt. While this may seem difficult, it becomes standard with proper training. When I used to play over 150 sitngo tournaments in a day, there would be times where I would get all the money in good 10 times in a row and lose every time. This alone was enough to desensitize me to tilt. Since most of you probably have no desire to be a sitngo grinder, I will tell you a few other ways to learn to not worry about results.

Standard tilt arises when the results are not those that you want. This can be from being outdrawn, getting the money in poorly, losing a sports bet during a tournament or having an argument with your significant other. When something goes poorly, especially in poker, there is usually no way for you to go back in time and reverse the result. You simply have to live with it. Playing like an idiot certainly will not solve the problem. The only thing that may reverse your loss is patient play.

Assuming you are a good player and get all the money in as a favorite often, I suggest you look at your equity instead of the results when things go poorly. If you win a 1,000-chip pot, you rarely will have had 100-percent equity. Assume you get it in with A-K vs. 2-2 for that 1,000-chip pot. You will win about half the time, which means you will lose the other half of the time. Assuming there is no dead money in the pot, you will break even. Breaking even, whether you win or lose, is nothing to be happy about. That being said, it isn't anything to be too sad about, either. If you get all the money in with 70-percent equity in a 1,000-chip pot and you only put in 500 of those chips, you will gain 200 chips in equity. If you lose the hand, you should not be upset. Instead, you should realize you won 200 chips in equity and be happy. Hopefully this better illustrates why losing when you are a favorite is not a bad thing. Being result-oriented, i.e., being happy when you win a pot and sad when you lose one, is a sure way to either go broke or crazy.

Learn to not let results affect your life. If you lose a pot, you simply lose a pot. You are going to lose a lot of pots throughout your life. If you get upset every time you lose a pot, you are looking at a lifetime of misery. Learn to be detached from this misery and realize that losing is part of the game.

You can also work on tilt control in everyday life. Say someone cuts you off while driving. Yelling, honking and getting upset will do nothing except reinforce those immature behaviors. You really only have two options that produce meaningful results. You can either ram the offender's car with yours, get out of your car and try to kill him, which is probably a bad decision, or you can let it go. You can't take personally what happens to you in life, and especially poker.

Those that take do will make irrational decisions that can cost them their car, life or chip stack.

Become a laid-back person. Some people are quick to get upset. I am lucky because I naturally have a fairly laid-back personality. Not too much bothers me because I realize some things are out of my control and I must accept them the way they are. Many people are the total opposite. Once in a tournament I saw a player get mad because the dealer straightened out his big blind, which was a pile of chips randomly thrown into the pot. The player told the dealer it was not his job and started cursing at him. The dealer called the floorman and the curser got a 10-minute penalty. He came back 10 minutes later and went broke when his 8-3 ran into A-A on an A-7-3-9-J board. Bad beat.

Don't complain when you lose hands because it reinforces the idea that you are unlucky. If anything, you need to reinforce the idea that you are a great poker player and you make +EV plays, not that you are the king of losing big pots. Once you lose a pot, those chips are no longer yours. You simply have to play the stack you are left with. A young kid in a WSOP event called a raise from the small blind; the big blind called as well. The flop came A-7-2. During this hand, the young kid had a huge stack, almost half the chips at the table. He checked, the big blind bet, the initial raiser folded and the young kid called with A-10. The turn was a jack. Both players checked. The river was a 6. The young kid with A-10 bet and the big blind raised. The young player called and lost to 6-6. He instantly flipped out, saying how bad the player with 6-6 was, and how unlucky he was to lose to a player with two outs. He failed to realize that he should have folded the river because few people raise the river here as a bluff, and his top pair, bad kicker was a bluff catcher. He proceeded to go on super-tilt and gave away his entire 300-BB stack within an hour, all the while talking about how unlucky he was. In reality, he simply had no clue how to lose a hand.

Another way people react when they are on standard tilt is to tighten up and only play premium hands. While this is much better than trying to play every hand, it is still bad, as you are no longer playing to the best of your ability. As soon as people notice you are playing overly tight, they will pummel your blinds and put you to a tough decision on every hand you play post-flop. After you lose a big pot, strive to play your standard game.

One of the most powerful plays in poker is to act like you are on tilt when your opponents would be on tilt if they were in your situation. Say your K-K just lost to 9-7o and cost you half your chips. If your next hand is strong, you can raise and re-raise as if you are on tilt. Most opponents will be quite willing to put a large sum of money in with weak hands because they assume their hand is well ahead of your tilting hand range. Little do they know that your range in this spot is fairly tight, as you have a premium hand, and they will be investing their money poorly.

When playing heads-up or short-handed, such as at the very end of a tournament, tilt tends to attack players more quickly than when playing full-handed. This is because you play many more hands per orbit, which means you are going to lose hands more often. Be careful to never let a losing hand bother you. Realize also that short-handed poker is a wild ride. When things go badly, just remember you are playing for a lot of money. Tilting when you have huge sums of money on the line just might be the biggest mistake you can make. Keep your cool and bring home the title.

That pretty much sums up tilt. Every time you're dealt a hand, be ready to accept going broke. When you can do this, you are free to play to the best of your ability without worrying about the results. Resolve to play each and every hand as close to optimally as possible. Once you can play your "A" game basically all the time, you will be on your way to becoming a big winner.

Playing Against Someone on Tilt

When someone takes a bad beat, especially an amateur, you can expect him to be on some form of tilt. Some players go on mild tilt and some go crazy. If someone takes a really bad beat, you can generally expect him to be upset. If you know a player's range will be wide open because of it, you can play hands that would normally be considered marginal.

Say someone in a tournament gets all-in with A-A and loses to A-6 for a 100-BB pot, leaving him with 10 BBs. If he pushes from second position, you would normally be crazy to call with A-7 in the big blind. But in this case I think this is a clear call.

Sometimes situations arise where you are very deep and someone is on tilt. I usually call down if I have something like middle pair or better, as long as the board doesn't get too scary. Say you are 100-BBs deep and your opponent has just lost half his 200-BB stack with A-A vs. A-7. If he raises from middle position, you should call with hands like Q-10 every time in late position. Don't re-raise because you don't want to get pushed on, forcing you off a hand with a lot of equity. Remember that folding is usually the play against opponents that aren't tilting. If the flop is something like K-Q-2 or A-10-2, you should call down every time unless the board gets really scary or he gives off a solid tell that he has a strong hand.

If you think someone is on tilt, you shouldn't be looking to fold. This assumes you know your opponent is actually on tilt. Beware of players that fake being on tilt after losing a hand. If you pay attention to your opponents and figure out how they will react to tilt before it happens, you can find an extraordinarily profitable spot.

Put in Hours but Take Breaks

Playing poker professionally takes numerous skills that most people do not need in their everyday life. One major skill that most people lack is the drive to put in the countless hours that are necessary to get to the top of the game. When I used to grind sitngo tournaments, I would put in 12 hour days every day. Sure, I won lots of money, but I was unhappy and starting to not love poker as I did when I first started playing. I later learned that it is important to have hobbies and a social life. Another problem you might have is that once you get good at poker, you can pretty much do whatever you want. This may cause you to spend all your time doing things besides playing poker. You need to balance work and everything else in healthy amounts.

Coming from a standard job, making a schedule is the best way to make sure you put in your hours. If you know you can put in three two-hour sessions per day, make sure you put in your sessions each day, taking breaks in between. I do not like schedules. I like to play poker whenever I feel like it. Luckily for me, I like to play poker a lot. The only time I have a schedule is when I am playing live tournaments, which require me to show up at a certain time to play. Think of poker as a job. You have to put in hours at your job if you want to make money. Figure out what works for you.

Take short, frequent breaks when you are playing. Most online tournaments give you a five-minute break every hour. Get up, step away from the computer and do something else. Read the newspaper, go outside, make a quick phone call or prepare some food. Anything will do. This will take you mind off poker and allow you to focus much better when you return.

At most live poker tournaments you get a 15-minute break every two hours. I make it a point to get out of the poker area and relax my mind. I often see online kids huddled in a circle, talking about hands they played. While this can often be +EV, discussing poker during your breaks is actually –EV unless someone at your table is giving you a tough time and you don't know how to play against him. I focus significantly better on the game when I let my mind wander freely during breaks. If friends want to talk to you during breaks, feel free, but try not to analyze hands. Try avoiding poker during your breaks for the next month. You might be surprised at the result.

Intuition

Intuition is a funny thing. Some poker professionals swear they just know what to do. Others claim they always make the most mathematically +EV play. I fall somewhere in the middle. I used to be purely a math guy, running the numbers in my head and making a decision. Over the last few years, my brain has started to tell me to make some plays that slightly deviate from math. This is not to say you should make ridiculous call-downs on a hunch or try to see a flop with 9-4o because you feel like you might flop a strong hand. It helps me to define my opponent's range better than I normally would because I can tell when someone is going to get out of line.

I would suggest that 95 percent of poker players go purely by the math. If you always make the mathematically sound play, it is tough to get the money in too poorly in the long run. A lot of poker players like to think they are special, as if God has blessed them with some uncanny ability to know what is going to happen. Obviously, they are lying to themselves, with the possible exception of Phil Ivey. If you know you need to be 45-percent to call in a spot and your hand only figures to have around 35-percent equity, you simply have to make the fold, assuming there are no implied odds at work. Don't call because you have a hunch that your cards are going to come.

Some players make these loose calls and win from time to time. They will continue to make these loose calls, eventually going broke.

You may have heard the saying, "If you think long, you think wrong." While this sounds like a cool concept, it is false. Unless you have played 20,000 hours or more of poker, you probably lack the experience to have any sort of subconscious intuition. You must think through a situation and come to a sound decision. This doesn't mean you should take three minutes every hand. For example, if someone goes all-in for 10 BBs from the small blind and you are in the big blind with 50 BBs and A-9, you generally have a no-brainer call. If you get A-A from third position early in a tournament, you have a no-brainer raise. These, and most decisions in poker, should be automatic. But if you have a tough turn or river decision, take your time and run the numbers in your head. Do not sit there and think, "Does he have A-K or 3-3? I need to make a decision." That just wastes everyone's time. Make sure that you are running numbers and coming up with an optimal decision, and not stalling.

Luck

Luck is an interesting concept. Most people only think about being lucky or unlucky in terms of winning or losing a specific hand. They say if you lose with A-A against K-K you were unlucky. While this may be true, you had to be lucky to get all-in with A-A against K-K in the first place. So, were you equally lucky and unlucky? When you play a tournament, not only do you have to get good hands, but your good hands have to win, and you have to get action with them. Usually only one of the three happens.

In a tournament an aggressive kid raised to 3 BBs out of his 50-BB stack. I re-raised with A-Q to 8 BBs, planning to call if he went all-in.

A tight, old player in the big blind cold-called. The initial raiser then went all-in. The tight player could easily have a monster, so I folded. The tight player also folded. The initial raiser showed A-A and won a medium-sized pot. Had the tight player folded, I would have doubled him up for sure. So, he was unlucky because the tight player decided to randomly call, costing him around 30 BBs. An orbit later, the initial raiser from the last hand got it all-in with 8-8 against A-10 and lost to an opponent that barely had him covered. Had he won an extra 30 BBs from me earlier, he would have still been in the tournament. So, you could argue that the tight player cost the kid his tournament because he cold-called my re-raise with a marginal hand.

Thinking about luck is pretty pointless. You could argue that if the wind blew differently on a specific day, the dealer could have shuffled the cards differently, totally changing the tournament. Obviously, the wind should not affect the way you play a poker tournament. Do not worry about your luck, good or bad. Players constantly talk about being unlucky because they lost with A-K against 10-10. They seem to think they are supposed to win everytime they pick up a decently strong hand. If you think you are unlucky, you will eventually undermine yourself, causing poor play. If anything, you need to think you are lucky. If you are a high-stakes professional poker player, you probably ran well above expectation because if you ran at or below it, you would not be playing at a high level, as your bankroll would be much smaller. Don't worry about luck. Just focus on playing the best poker you can.

Physical

To do anything that requires you to roll out of bed, even things as simple as sitting in a chair and thinking all day, you must be in decent physical shape. Most people don't think of poker as physically strenuous, but it is. Most poker players have very bad spines due to sitting hunched over a poker table all day. This can be easily fixed by learning proper posture. I will mention a few more things in the following sections that will greatly increase your equity over your out-of-shape opponents. Remember, any positive thing you do that your opponents don't do will gain you money in the long run. This includes staying in good physical shape.

Sleeping

I have made the mistake of playing a big tournament with no sleep only once in my life. Needless to say, I did not play well, and I fell asleep at the table a few times. The experience traumatized me, and I vowed to never play tired again. It is quite important to get on a good sleep schedule and change it whenever you will be playing in a different time zone.

I tend to stay on Pacific Time, waking up at around 9 a.m. and going to sleep around midnight. This is because most poker tournaments in the United States are held in the west. If I am going to play on the east coast, I will start to change my sleep schedule a few days in advance, waking up and going to sleep an hour earlier each day. There is nothing worse than being on Pacific Time and having to play a 10 a.m. tournament on the east coast.

Because I like to be fully rested, I rarely play tournaments where I have to totally change my sleep schedule. I recently played the WPT event in Cyprus, where the time difference is 12 hours from Pacific Time. I started getting on the correct sleep schedule early and was fine by the time the tournament rolled around. But I had forgotten that I had to play a big tournament in Atlantic City as soon as I returned to the United States. I was miserable in Atlantic City and played quite poorly. Allow plenty of time to recover if you plan to make overseas trips.

One of the biggest edges in poker comes from playing tired opponents. Some play super-tight and others try to play a lot of giant pots, but either way, they are exploitable and will be looking to donate money. Make sure you are not one of these people by preparing your brain to function well.

Be in Good Shape

My weight changed from 155 to 180 pounds during my first three years of playing poker professionally. I paid no attention to my diet and never worked out. I started to constantly feel lethargic. I began working out about three years ago and now feel much better. I sleep less, which means I have a few more hours to enjoy each day. I am also stronger, which is always a good thing.

I wanted to get in shape primarily to have more endurance at the poker table. I asked my personal trainer to build my endurance and not make me a giant, bulky guy, as they have to eat all the time and most of their muscles aren't actually that strong. They are just bulk. Since I have gotten in shape, I'm able to focus for longer periods of time at the table. My mind doesn't wander as often, which can cost me valuable reads. I also have more endurance than most of my opponents.

Achieving something in the gym somehow increases my confidence in my poker skills. Four years ago, I could barely run a mile. I decided to run a marathon at some point in my life, so I started training. I finished a half-marathon recently and may run the Las Vegas marathon later this year. Unlike poker, there is little variance in physical fitness. If you work hard, you can do quite a lot. If I can go from having trouble running one mile to running 12 with few problems, I can certainly put in the work required to stay at the top of the poker food chain.

An added benefit is that I am probably going to live longer. If I can work out now, gaining one hour of awake time each day (I spend maybe one hour working out and sleep two hours less), I not only gain 365 hours per year but I will also add a few years to my life expectancy. If you enjoy life, this is clearly +EV. It may be weird to think of things such as life expectancy in terms of EV, but it is important to train your mind to think this way. You may find numerous other things in your life you are doing poorly.

Endurance

When you know you will be at a poker tournament where you could play 16 hours straight, you should be prepared to play your best poker for the entire time. Many players arrive tired or become tired toward the end of the day. While I am sure most people go into a tournament playing their best, many quickly fail because they do not practice things away from the table that would help them last through the day.

If you don't get plenty of sleep during the nights before and during a tournament, you are going to get tired at some point. Even with an excellent sleep schedule, I sometimes find myself in a lull at the table. I order a Coke when this happens, and it usually perks me right up. I used to drink Coke all the time, but quit because it is unhealthy. A glass of Coke would do nothing for me before, but now it quickly gets me going again. If you drink lots of caffeine, find something else to wake yourself up, such as energy drinks. Obviously, it is best to not drink anything that is unhealthy, but while you are quitting caffeine, you can use the super-unhealthy energy drinks from time to time, but don't become addicted to them.

Another way I keep going throughout the day is to drink a cup of green tea at every level. If a casino doesn't have green tea, I will bring my own and request a cup of hot water. While it may be all mental, it helps keep me calm and focused. Something about sitting and drinking a nice cup of tea just relaxes me and helps me play my "A" game.

Listening to music or watching TV may help you through the day. I used to listen to music all the time at the poker table, but found I was missing some subtle bits of information. It is useful to learn about your opponents by the way they talk.

Some casinos have televisions located around the tournament room, usually showing sporting events. While watching the games will make the day fly, I suggest you pay attention to poker. Again, never gamble on a sports game that is going on while you are in a tournament. Losing a sports bet could send you into tilt and cost you the tournament. You may also spend most of your time watching the sporting event instead of the poker game.

You are given a break every 90 minutes or so. I usually go to the bathroom and have a little quiet time during breaks to gather my thoughts and to get back to being levelheaded. I make it a point to go into every level with a fresh mindset and try to not worry about the things that happened earlier in the day. Breaking the day up into small chunks tends to make the time pass a little quicker.

As you near the end of a long tournament session, you will hopefully notice everyone around you becoming tired. Realize that while they are tired, you are not. Know that you will make much better decisions than they will. Use this to boost your confidence, as you have prepared for the game better than they have. I won a $500 tournament at Bellagio about three years ago where we started at 1 p.m. and played until 6 a.m. Once we got down to 10 players, I could see people falling asleep and playing poorly. I gave myself a huge edge by simply sitting there and playing my best poker. I became energized by seeing everyone else falling asleep. It was a great feeling.

You can do many things to maintain your focus at the table. While many of them, like drinking caffeine, may be bad for you, they can be useful when used in moderation. Learn what works for you, because endurance is something most poker players lack.

Breathing

Learning to breathe optimally is important for numerous reasons. Just about everyone breathes incorrectly. Their shoulders rise when they inhale. The correct way to breathe is for your stomach to extent outwards when you breathe in, with little to no movement of the shoulders. This helps your body get the most oxygen from the air. I suggest that you learn to breathe this way all the time so that it happens naturally when you play poker.

When you play poker, with all the things going on at the table, the last thing you want to think about is whether you are breathing correctly. If you take long breaths in and out for the first time, you will likely start to feel lightheaded after a few minutes because your brain won't be used to getting so much oxygen. When learning to breathe, concentrate on taking in long, deep breaths for around two minutes at a time. Focus on breathing, and not watching TV or reading this book. If you are like me, you will randomly think about your breathing throughout the day and control it freely. When this happens, take a moment to make sure your brain is getting as much oxygen as possible.

Now that you know how to breathe, what is the point? Filling your body with oxygen is known to reduce stress and increase your body's and mind's performance. Surely you have heard that you should take a deep breath when things are going poorly. Something as simple as breathing can greatly reduce stress. Poker can be one of the most stressful games in the world, so anything you can do to reduce stress can be valuable. Having a brain full of oxygen all day can also help you play more hours and think more clearly throughout your sessions. Many players become visibly tired during the last few hours of each day in a tournament, and just want to get through the day. This is a prime time to gather chips, while many players are giving them away, either by playing too tight or too loose, subsequently making poor decisions throughout each hand. Being able to outlast your opponents is a crucial skill.

Good Posture

Poker players are notorious for their poor posture. Not only will this make you feel bad, sitting in an uncomfortable chair all day, but it will also make your body weak. I sat with terrible posture for years and it is costing me now. I was sitting at home one night when I got a terrible pain in my neck. I had had neck and back pain for a while but this was different. I went to a chiropractor and he showed me x-rays of my spine compared to how it should look. Mine was pretty far from optimal. It turns out my mother knew what she was talking about. Sit up straight and don't hunch forward. You will feel much better in the long run and your spine will thank you.

Nutrition

It is important to eat right and not stuff yourself before a long day at the tables. Many players run to the buffet on dinner break, eager to eat 4,000 calories before heading back to play another four hours of poker. It is well known that eating a heavy meal will make you tired. It will also make it hard to think correctly. I would be willing to bet that players that eat light meals on dinner break do much better than their well-fed opponents during the last few hours of each day. Eat a healthy dinner during your break.

Healthy foods should not be confined to dinner break. You should eat them all the time. I used to eat terrible food at every meal. Once I figured this out, I quickly changed my habits and realized I could play much better poker for many more hours. Remember how I gained 35 pounds during my first few years as a professional poker player? I hit the gym hard and lost 10 of those pounds. Around a year ago, I learned that if you cut all the carb-heavy foods with high glycemic indexes and sugars from your diet, you will lose weight quickly and keep it off. Sure enough, I am now at 145 pounds.

My diet consists of mostly lean meats, low-fat beans and vegetables. I tend to avoid fatty meats, bread, rice, fruit and desserts. People ask why I shy away from fruit, which is supposed to be good. The problem with fruit is that it is full of sugar, and sugar will make you fat.

I allow myself one day per week to eat the things I crave, such as pasta and carrot cake, two of my favorite foods. This keeps my body from becoming accustomed to eating only super healthy foods. If your body gets used to healthy foods, you can gain a lot of weight if you slip up and eat just moderately healthy foods. Changing up your diet once a week will help prevent this.

Since changing my diet and losing a lot of fat, I have become much happier with my body as well as life. Being happy with yourself will help you to play better poker. Eating right is an important part of being physically fit.

Chapter 5

Tells

A tell is a physical action someone takes that, when observed, helps you narrow their range of hands. By the time you look at someone throughout a hand and pay attention to his betting patterns, you should be able to accurately predict a range of hands he can have. There are bet-sizing, subconscious and reverse tells. The next few chapters are not meant to be a definitive work on tells, but they should get you well on your way to reading people accurately.

General Tells

Tells are one of the primary reasons why live poker can be much more profitable than online poker. When I first played live poker, I saw people making weird gestures that I assumed meant something, although I didn't quite know what. Over the last five years, I have discovered a few key tells that are usually accurate and can change an easy fold to an easy call, or vice versa. These tells are powerful because, while most gestures can be faked, these actions are generally controlled by the subconscious, which is quite difficult to harness.

Before you can exploit tells, you have to know how to determine your opponents' baseline behaviors. You have to know what your opponents look like normally in order to tell when something changes. Suppose someone that sits with his feet flat on the ground most of the time suddenly curls his feet under his chair. This is a clear deviation from his baseline behavior. You also need to see a showdown hand in order to determine the reliability of a tell before you invest large sums of money based on it.

By far, the most useful tell I have learned has to do with how often my opponents blink. In general, when people are bluffing, they will blink significantly more than when they have a strong hand. In fact, they usually won't blink much at all when they have a monster. This is because little thought is usually required with a strong hand. When bluffing, you are trying to take a strong line. Blinking is basically always a sign that someone is thinking or that he is trying to shield his eyes from the board because he doesn't like it. Either way, it usually indicates weakness. In order to determine a baseline for blinking, pay a little attention when you get to the table and occasionally during the day and see if anyone is blinking in an odd fashion, and if so, remember that they blink oddly. Most people, however, will blink at a fairly normal rate, which makes spotting fast or slow blinking quite simple.

Blinking is a close second to breathing in usefulness. Fast breathing usually indicates a strong hand and little or no breathing means a bluff. This is because a player who is bluffing doesn't want to do be seen. He hopes that sitting as still as possible will get the job done. It's a little harder to get a baseline on this tell, as it is sometimes tough to see how often people are breathing from across the table. Many people are aware of this tell and may try to reverse it on you. You have to know how sophisticated your opponents are and whether they are capable of using a reverse tell.

The last tell I will discuss in depth concerns what your opponents do with their feet. You can obviously observe this tell only in the people sitting on either side of you. Most people don't even realize that their feet move while they are in a hand. A player with his feet out comfortably usually has a strong hand; if they are tucked back, as if trying to get away from the table, the player has a weak hand. Again, having a good baseline is important here, as some people will sit with their feet curled back all day and never move them from that position. This tell is useless against those players. However, when you find someone whose foot movements are correlated to his hand strength, it is like printing money.

A few other tells are not quite as reliable but are still worth mentioning. Someone who is shaking uncontrollably almost certainly has a strong hand. This is similar to the breathing tell. This could also be because a player is new to poker and is nervous. A player who rubs his face or covers his mouth during a hand is usually weak. Again, he is trying to shield himself from the bad things going on at the table. He usually has a monster hand if he puts his hands up like the steeple of a church, with his elbows on the table. In general, anything that greatly defies gravity, such as fingers and arms straight up in the air, indicates a strong hand. The same goes for standing up at the table. A player who stares at you is usually weak, whereas he is strong when looking away from the table. A player who makes stupid faces, as if he is thinking hard about a hand, usually has a strong hand unless he is overly straightforward. Finally, a fast pulse almost always indicates a strong hand.

There are many tells, not just relating to the face. If you study each of your opponents, you will usually find something. Be sure to confirm that a tell is accurate before investing a lot of money based on it. Be wary of reverse tells from good professionals. They might induce you to go all-in when you should fold instead.

Initial Reads

When you first sit down at a poker table, there will almost always be someone you don't know, and you might not know anyone. When this happens, you have to rely on predetermined reads based on how your opponents look and act. While the following may be incorrect about any particular person, it can be quite useful in making initial reads. Stereotypes are usually only useful during the first few levels of play. There is no replacement for sound observation. Please do not be offended by any of the information below. If you are a poker player, you need to have thick skin.

The typical player you will see at the poker table will be the rich, old, white man. This type of player usually plays tighter than he should and will most likely overvalue hands like A-K and big pairs, investing too much money post-flop when the situation suggests otherwise. Go out of your way to abuse this player's blinds and make many stabs post-flop, as he will give up most marginal hands to continued aggression. If this player is willing to put a lot of chips in the pot, you need to have a strong hand to continue, as you will usually be looking at top pair, top kicker or better.

Then there are the Asian players. They generally come in two types. The first type, usually an amateur, is super-loose and aggressive. He has no problem re-raising with any two cards pre-flop and will bluff whenever you show weakness. To combat him, just check and call down anytime you make a good middle pair or better. The other type, probably a professional, is fairly tight and aggressive. He picks his spots very well and can occasionally run a giant bluff. Usually though, when the pot gets large, he will have the near nuts. He will probably take his time and act as if he plans to play numerous hands, especially pre-flop, hoping to give the false impression that he is playing many hands. Try to play small posts against this guy, and realize that you need a strong hand to stick around when the pot gets large.

Next is the growing number of online players. They are easy to spot, as they are usually young, although there are a few older guys out there that are also online grinders. These players can be either loose or tight, but are almost always aggressive. They also tend to have little or no control over their tells, as they are used to sitting in front of a computer screen all day, where they have no reason to conceal them. I usually try to play small pots with them and use my reading abilities to pick up pots whenever it becomes clear that they want to give it up. I make it a point to not fold big hands to the most aggressive online players because they are usually trying to push me off my hand.

The next group is the ladies. While women can range from great to terrible, most amateur females are tight and passive. Once they're involved in a hand, they usually go into call-down mode, basically never folding a hand like middle pair. Play aggressively against them, but be willing to put on the brakes if you see that your bluffs are going to fail.

The professionals are by far the toughest to play against. They can be any race or gender, and usually carry themselves confidently. You can generally pinpoint them by the way they talk and handle their chips. I will discuss this more in the next section.

It is important to recognize your own demographic group and how each player type will view you. For example, if you are older, you should expect the young players to go out of their way to push you around. If you anticipate this, you can make big call-downs with hands like top pair and knock out some of the more aggressive players fairly early in a tournament. If you are a young online player, most other players will eventually get fed up with your constant aggression and play back at you. If you can figure out when to tighten up, you will have a huge edge.

Never play weakly against any specific demographic. If a player is sitting at your table, you should have a strong desire to utterly destroy that person. You should not be looking to give someone a free ride because of who he is or what he looks like. Some demographics that are soft-played constantly are women, elderly players and pros.

You can also generate initial reads on a player based on how he talks at the table. Someone who uses the words "set" and "trips" incorrectly is usually a weaker player. (A set is a pair in your hand that matches a board card; trips is a pair on the board that matches a card in your hand.) You can also tell by the way he talks about hands. If he leaves out vital information, like stack size or image concerns, he is usually not that good.

One of the quickest ways to pinpoint a super-weak player is by the way he stacks his chips. I make stacks of chips that all have the same value, such as $25, $100, $500 and $1,000, plus a stack of all the larger-valued chips. Most weak players keep their chips in short, unorganized stacks. Better players tend to keep their chips in stacks of 20, or at least an even number.

While you can initially assign one of these numerous stereotypes to players, you should have specific reads on players after the first few levels of play. No set of general guidelines will ever be as valuable as accurate observation.

Having No Tells

Now that you can spot the most powerful tells, you need to ensure that you don't hand out your own tells. There are two ways to do this, and I am only good at one of them. The first, which I am not too good at, is to constantly talk and move your body, making it impossible to isolate tells among all the information you're giving out. The other method, which is simple and effective, is to make no movements at all. You only need to be still while you are in a hand. Once you have folded, your actions no longer matter.

The hand starts as soon as you look at your cards. Once you know what you have, you should make no unnecessary movements. The easiest way is to have one hand on each side of your chip stack with your cards in front of them. I usually look at my cards rather quickly, as I want to protect them from peering eyes as much as possible. Remember your cards, as looking back at them during the hand could reveal information about your hand's strength. Do not look at your hand and do what I call "thinking with your face." This is when you move your face as if talking to yourself. Your face should remain perfectly still to avoid facial tells.

Place your bets using smooth, repeatable motions. Do not talk or move your face in any way during a hand. Weak players may grimace when the fourth card of the same suit comes on the river, usually indicating they don't like that card too much. Some players will rise up from a slouch when a great card for them hits the board. Learn to keep your emotions from affecting your facial expressions and gestures. This is hard to learn because most people are taught to show their emotions. One simple way to greatly reduce your stress is to play for an amount of money that is fairly meaningless to you. It will also help if you realize that one hand is nothing in the grand scheme of things and if you play well, things will turn out just fine.

Try to breathe and blink at a steady pace. Your opponent can't learn much if you move no part of your body that you can control. So, learn to give off no information from the two most common motions, those of breathing and blinking. To do this, simply blink and breathe at a constant rate. Blink a little more than normally so your eyes don't get dry. Take fast, deep breaths so that your chest and stomach don't rise or fall too much.

Do not touch your chips unless you plan to use them. Many players shuffle their chips constantly during a hand, only to fumble them or allow me to see their hand shaking nervously. Leave your chips alone. The same goes for your cards. Don't move them back and forth or look at them on every street. All in all, if you move as little as possible and regulate your body's natural functions, you should have not just an excellent poker face, but a total poker body.

Do Not Give Away Free Information

Besides not giving off tells, it is important not to give away other useful information. This includes not revealing your cards after a hand. You should have no desire to show your opponents that you bluffed them or you had the nuts; you don't want your opponents to learn about your betting patterns or physical mannerisms. So, don't show your cards.

There are a few times when you can show your cards, primarily when the information is irrelevant. For example, if you raise with A-A in the cutoff and everyone folds, they all know you raised A-A in this spot, so no one gains information if you show your cards. The only side effect of showing your big hands when you steal the blinds is that people may play a little tighter against you, allowing you to steal a bit more in the future. I tend to show a few of my big hands early in a tournament, hoping to get a little more credit from my opponents later, when blind stealing becomes more important.

Another time to show your cards is when you know it will put some-one on tilt. This mostly happens when you bluff someone. Most peo-ple, when shown a bluff, feel like an idiot or compliment your nice bluff. They don't go on tilt too often unless they are playing way over their heads. So, showing your bluff usually is not worth the risk of letting your opponents know your betting patterns when you are bluffing. You can also show your cards to someone you are being friendly with, usually on your left, so he will play back at you less often. In general, there are very few spots where showing everyone your hand is +EV.

The Hand isn't Over Until it's Over

Don't let anyone know if you intend to fold. You can do many things to let them know you no longer have interest in a hand. Say you raise A♥-J♥ and someone calls from late position. It comes J♠-4♠-2♠. If you bet and he calls, don't let him know you are unhappy when the turn comes a spade. Say the turn is the 8♠. If you look visibly sad, your opponent will probably bet every time you check to him. Instead, if you look like you are contemplating a bet, as you would with a weak flush, but then check, he may check behind on the turn and the river, giving you a free showdown and the pot.

Don't act like you plan to fold before it's your turn to act. I have been guilty of this and realize it was very bad etiquette, and it hurts you in the long run. Say a player raises, someone calls and you call on the button with 7♠-6♠. The flop comes A-K-4. If the first person bets and the second player is thinking about calling, don't act as if you have no intention of calling. Act as if nothing has happened and you are waiting for the second player to act. You know you are going to fold, but you should not let the second player know this. Also, before the first player bets, do not let the other players know you missed the flop because you could check the hand down and run off a pair or trips and win the pot. Notice if you had 4♦-4♣ instead of 7♠-6♠, you would not lose interest in the hand because you flopped a monster. If you are known to ignore a hand when you plan to fold, then your opponents will know you have at least a decent hand when you pay attention. You will get much more value out of your strong hands if you act as if you are going to have a decision in every hand.

Weak players often look at their hand pre-flop before the action gets to them. Say you are on the button with K♠-5♣. You would normally fold this to a raise but if everyone folds to you, you should consider raising to steal the blinds. If you look at your hand as soon as you get it and act uninterested, most observant players will know you have a weak hand if you raise when everyone folds to you. I saw a great example of this in a WSOP event. A young kid, who always telegraphed if he was going to play his hand, looked at his hand as if he was going to fold. Everyone folded to him on the button and he raised. I had K-J in the small blind and re-raised, as I figured he would fold every time. He surprised me by going all-in. I made what I think is an easy call, as I was confident with my read, and he had 7-2. I won the hand and a nice pot.

Always watch for players that telegraph their actions before it is their turn to act. Sometimes if you wait around five seconds, even the most stone-faced players will get annoyed and let you know if they want you to fold or raise. Pay attention next time you play poker and you will be at amazed at how often these tells occur.

Take Useful Notes

Online players often spend a decent amount of time taking notes only to refer to them later and have no clue what they mean. I also see people write notes like "total idiot", but that really doesn't tell you what your opponent does that makes him an idiot. He could be a huge calling station or someone that bluffs way too often. You need a method to take notes on players that gives you as much specific information as possible.

After a hand is over, I usually type how the hand played out in the notes box. It will usually look something like "limpcalls nr w 3-3 oop, check pushes 9-4-2 when short." What this means is that my opponent limped with 3-3 and called out of position once I raised. The flop came 9-4-2. He checked, I made a continuation bet and he went all-in for his short stack, which usually means he started the hand with 20 to 30 BBs. This note would also mean there were no other players in the hand, as they were not mentioned. You can make your notes as long or as short as you desire. Just make sure they give all the relevant information and are easy to read later when you need them.

In live tournaments, you should constantly take mental notes about what goes on during hands, especially when you aren't involved in them. You should be able to clearly assess what is going on because you are not emotionally involved. Note who was in the hand, as someone may play quite differently against you than against another player. A few years back, I decided I was going to write actual notes about each player in live poker tournaments. This took too much effort and diverted my attention from the game because I was constantly scribbling on my notepad. For live poker, unless your memory is really bad, I suggest you stick to mental notes. You need to look for every ounce of information you can about your opponents all the time, as that insight may help you win your opponent's stack later on, in that tournament or another one.

Raise the Same Amount Every Time

Don't provide information with your bet sizing. The easiest way to do this is to raise the same amount every time before the flop. I always raise between 2 and 3 BBs before the flop, depending on everyone's stack size. The exact number doesn't really matter as long as you raise to the same amount everytime. It doesn't matter if you raise to 2,000 or 2,100 at 400/800. Obviously if there are limpers or raisers in front of me, I will not raise to 2.5 BBs, as that would be really −EV. Basically, I raise the same amount in each pre-flop situation.

I usually make my continuation bets the same size as well. By the time the pot gets to the turn and river, you will usually be able to vary your bet size a little more, as you will not make it to too many turns and your opponent will not have much information about the way you play the later streets. Because your opponent will have a tiny sample size when it comes to seeing your turn and river bets, you can vary your bets based on what you want them to do. You can usually vary your bet sizes a bit more against weak players than against professionals. Minimize the bet-sizing tells against competent players and you will be on your way to being one of the toughest players.

Bet-Sizing Tells

The number of chips someone bets on any given street can provide valuable information about his hand strength. These tells can be used against basically every player because everyone has to bet at some point. Players generally fall into three categories. They either bet large with their strong hands and small with their weak hands, they bet small with their strong hands and large with their weak hands, or they vary their bet sizes in such a way that makes them tough to play against.

You generally want to make larger bets with your strong hands and smaller bets with your weak hands. Despite this, you should bet all your hands the same, especially pre-flop and on the flop. My betting strategy is outlined in *Volume 1*. Keeping your early-round bet sizing the same will keep things simple and eliminate bet-sizing tells. Your opponents will have seen so few of your hands on the turn that you can vary your bet sizes based on the strength of your hand at that point.

Amateurs give off a few generic bet-sizing tells. If a player opens with a raise to 5 BBs pre-flop when he normally raises to around 2.5 to 3 BBs, he usually have J-J or 10-10. Some players mix in A-K or Q-Q. Players do this because they don't want to be outdrawn. Instead, they turn their hand face-up and let their opponents play optimally. Weak players will also put a lot of chips at risk with a hand like top pair when there is a flush draw on the board. They will make huge all-in raises over a normal bet because they fear being outdrawn. Against these players, you can be confident calling off with a hand like top pair, top kicker or better. Some players will always lead into the pre-flop raiser with hands like middle or bottom pair to find out where they are at. When this type of player leads into you, it is almost always correct to raise with weak hands and slow-play hands like top pair, as these players will generally fold to a raise but continue betting if you call. Your opponents want to be told they have the worst hand. Be sure to give them the bad news and force them to throw away the best hand.

As you can see, there are numerous ways to exploit bet-sizing tells. Pay attention to every bet that goes onto the felt. It will drastically increase your win rate.

Timing Tells

Timing tells are usually used online, where no other reads are available, but they can also be useful in live tournaments. Probably the most common timing tell is to quickly call with a hand for which that seems to be the only viable option. This usually occurs with some sort of draw, as most weak players are scared to raise with a draw. They also usually call fairly quickly with hands like top pair, bad kicker because they know they aren't going to fold or raise, leaving a call as the only option. People usually take a little longer when they have a hand that is either a call or fold, or a raise or call. Some players take almost the same amount of time whenever it's their turn to act. Any significant change in the amount of time they think about a hand is a good sign that they have a tough decision. You can usually couple this tell with a tell listed in the "General Tells" section to figure out if his hand is strong or weak. As always, it is important to have a solid baseline on a player's tells before putting significant money into play.

Busy Tells

A player who is preoccupied with anything besides poker is much more likely to fold marginal hands. Because of this, if he is getting a massage, ordering a cocktail, talking to a friend on the rail or actively watching a sporting event, he is much less likely to make a play at you. If someone raises while distracted, assuming he is not a great player, you should usually respect that raise. You should also go out of your way to raise the blinds of these distracted people because they will usually give you the pot with little resistance. I have seen a few great examples where players basically turned their hands face-up because something rather important was going on.

The most memorable example happened in a $5,000 tournament at Bellagio. Someone raised from early position. Right about at this time, the cocktail waitress brought someone a hot green tea and proceeded to spill it all over the table. It also happened to get all over the cards of the player who ordered the drink. When the action got to him, he looked at his soaking wet cards and re-raised. The initial raiser went all-in with 9-9 and the player with the soaked cards called with A-A. When sitting at the table with soaked cards, the last thing you are thinking about is making a play on an early-position raiser. If someone is preoccupied with something like hot tea on his cards, he is basically never going to run a big bluff. Folding 9-9, or even J-J or A-K, is an easy play in this situation.

Now that we know players that raise when busy usually have a hand, we need to find a way to exploit this. When I get very deep in a tournament, I sometimes make a point to get a massage. Most players go into a lull when being massaged, folding most weak hands. Instead, I raise and re-raise much more aggressively than normal. When the cocktail waitress brings me a drink, I usually make a point to raise with air and act like the waitress is distracting me from a huge hand. It is amazing how often this works because people just "know" you must have a hand to raise when you are doing something important like tipping a waitress.

Chip Placement

The way players place their chips in a pot can give you a huge amount of information about the strength of their hand. You would be shocked at how often some people splash the pot with a weak hand or set them in nice and neat with a strong one. This type of tell is a little tougher to generalize, as everyone puts their chips in the pot differently. Watch how people put their chips in the pot and see what type of hands they turn up. For example, if someone bluffs on the river by throwing a random handful of chips in the pot and you later see him count out some exact number and nicely set them in the pot with a strong hand, you can be pretty certain he will do that in similar situations.

I will now explain the meanings of some basic chip motions. Most people try to act weak when they are strong and strong when they are weak. When they put a stack in the pot rather meekly, they usually have a strong hand. When they spew chips into the pot, they usually are weak. Another odd thing people do is throw the chips toward you when they are weak and away from you when they are strong. These are just a few things people can do, but you should look for anything and everything when trying to pick up on someone's tendencies.

I try to always put my chips in the pot in the same way. I count out the chips in the staging area and place them, in one big pile, up to 20 chips high, into the pot. The dealer will usually break down the stack to make sure it is the right amount. Some players may get slightly annoyed at this, as it takes an extra second, but the longer you have your hand out there stacking and restacking your chips, the more likely you are to knock a stack over or start shaking from exhaustion, as it really does take a decent amount of endurance to sit still during a 10-minute hand.

Chip Tricks

Performing chip tricks during a hand when you are bored may pass time or make you feel cool, but it will almost always cost you money. When you are in a hand, you want to do everything in your power to provide no information about your hand. If your opponent is staring you down and you randomly grab a pile of chips and start playing with them, it may give away something about the strength of your hand. One well-known pro usually shuffles chips when he is weak. That makes him easy to play against, at least if you know he has this tell.

In general, playing with chips is a pacifying behavior, which means people do it when they are trying to make themselves feel comfortable, usually when they have a weak hand. See if your opponent's hand shakes while he plays with chips. It is usually a dead giveaway about his hand.

While I shuffle chips when I am not in a hand, I never even consider it once I've been dealt cards. I only touch my chips when it is time to bet them. This is the optimal play for almost everyone. To give away as little information as possible, you should be still. Playing with chips is the opposite.

Poker Gear Tells

When you show up at a poker tournament, always pay attention to who is wearing poker clothes from their favorite online site or casino. These players usually think they are good poker players but aren't. They tend to have a decent amount of experience, so they will usually not be the worst players at the table. Professional poker players don't brand themselves to a site for free because if you are known to be a player at only one specific site, once you do well in a few tournaments, other poker sites may have no interest in sponsoring you. Never wear poker attire unless you are paid to wear it. It will give professional players an initial read on you that may cost you equity as soon as you sit down at the table.

Tells Based on Who You Associate With

If you see someone talking to a specific demographic he doesn't belong to, he probably plays like the people in that group.

I was playing with an older player who I thought played decently well, although I hadn't played enough hands with him to know for sure. I noticed though, that every 15 minutes or so, a different young online player would come up and talk to him. I asked around and learned that the older player was a high-stakes online tournament professional that backs quite a few players. If all the kids didn't constantly come up to the table, I would have assumed he was just a semi-competent older man.

Another time I was playing with an older Frenchman who I thought played decently well, but not great. Everyone that came up to him was also French and older, which led me to believe he was probably just a random guy from France. I ended up knocking him out when he overvalued a weak top-pair hand. If I had not seen him talking to other players that were not professionals, I may have missed a value bet on the river, costing me the opportunity to stack him.

Giving Off Reverse Tells

While I usually advocate giving off no information during a hand, there are a few spots where I will throw out a reverse tell. I only do this when I have a monster hand and greatly need a call. I don't give off reverse tells often because they would quickly lose their effectiveness. Your opponent will pick up the tell you are going to represent and know what it means, so perfect spots to throw out the reverse tell don't come up too often.

During the Foxwoods World Poker Finals WPT event I won, I gave off probably my most memorable reverse tell to date. There was a hand where Bill Gazes, a well-respected, very smart pro, raised from the button, Alex Bolotin, another respected, rather aggressive pro, re-raised and I went all-in from the big blind for around 40 BBs. Bill folded fairly quickly and Alex thought for around three minutes before folding. I sat perfectly still while he was thinking. About an hour later, David Pham, one of the most aggressive and best players on the circuit, raised from the cutoff. Bill Gazes re-raised on the button, and I went all-in with K-K for around 50 BBs. David quickly folded and Bill thought for quite some time before giving me the "okay, I'm going to fold" look. As soon as he started getting his cards ready to muck, I took my hand from the felt and put it on my mouth. All professionals know that this indicates a bluff. Bill put his cards back down, thought for another 30 seconds or so and called with A-Q. I later talked to Bill about this and he said he didn't remember me doing it, which I am sure is the truth. That does not mean his subconscious did not pick up this move. I am confident that, had I not made that play, I would have not had the stack that allowed me to win my second WPT title.

Hollywooding

Hollywooding is when a player takes an exorbitant amount of time to try to trick his opponent into thinking he has something he doesn't have. I rarely engage in fake thinking or acting as if I am scared. I take around the same amount of time for every decision. While this may give up a little equity against the weakest opponents, I think it is optimal overall.

For example, someone limps from first position, you raise with 9-9 in middle position and he goes all-in. But first he acts as if he is in pain or deep thought for a few minutes, like he's agonizing over the decision. Unless you are getting 2-to-1 or better to call, you should almost certainly fold. You have two great concepts working for you here. Your opponent limped from first position, which is what weak players do with big hands, and he put on a show.

Another example of hollywooding is what is referred to as "the speech." This is when your opponent goes all-in and then starts talking to you once he realizes you are going to fold. If your opponent sees you are about to fold and he is bluffing, he will just let you fold and pick up the pot. On top of that, most people can't hold any sort of conversation while bluffing. Because of this, when someone opens his mouth, he usually has a strong hand. The opposite may be true if your opponent thinks you are about to call. Sometimes I will get the correct amount of chips in my hand as if I am going to call and act like I am about to put them in the pot. If he starts talking just as you seem ready to put them in, you should almost certainly call, because he wants you to fold.

As stated earlier, I never put on a show or talk during a hand. Against even semi-competent players, it will usually only hurt you. If your opponents have no clue at all, you can consider it. If it works in your specific game or against a specific opponent, don't be scared to use it.

Looking Back At Your Hand

As stated before, you should only look at your hand once. Sometimes though, great opportunities come up where you can trick your opponent into thinking you have something you don't. Someone who looks back at his hand usually is either checking what suits he has or seeing if he actually has a monster.

Say someone raises pre-flop, you call and the board comes J♥-5♥-2♥. If your opponent looks back at his hand, you can be pretty sure he has only one heart because most players remember if they have A♥-10♥ but don't remember which card is a heart if they have Ax-10♥ or A♥-10x. So, you can be fairly confident getting all the money in if you have two pair or better here because your opponent likely doesn't have a flush.

If you are playing against a competent opponent that knows about this tell, you can put a hurt on him by looking at your cards when you know you have a flush, because he will assume you have a flush draw. Again, don't make these plays against world-class players, but only players that are competent but not great.

The other time people look back at their cards is when they hit an unlikely hand, like top set. So, if someone raises from early position, the flop comes A-7-3 and he looks back at his hand, he almost certainly has A-A, 7-7 or 3-3 and wants to be sure he didn't misread his hand.

Some opponents look at their hand quite often, sometimes on every street. Ignore these types of tells against these opponents because the information you get is usually irrelevant. To be sure you are not giving off these tells, only look at your cards at the start of the hand. Practice memorizing your cards so you don't leak away money by looking back at your hand.

World-Class Players

I usually only look for subconscious tells against a world-class player, such as his foot position or blinking rate. I am talking about a true world-class player, not someone with a small win rate, which describes most professional poker players. If a world-class player thinks for a long time about a decision or talks to you during a hand, you should not let it affect your decisions. These players are excellent at figuring which false tells you will fall for, and will employ them when necessary. One of my favorite false tells to throw out against great players is to hold my breath when I have a strong hand, because most players don't breathe when they bluff. Notice I said great players, not world-class ones. Against the world-class players, I do everything the same every time. Most world-class players have a large bag of tricks used to separate weaker professionals from their money. Don't fall for them.

Hand Reading

Throughout this section on tells, I have taught you how to spot both weakness and strength by the way your opponents act. While it is great to know your opponent is weak, it doesn't do much good if you don't know how to apply this information. You must learn to accurately narrow your opponent's range based on your reads while only discounting certain hands from his range in order to make up for the times you are wrong, which you will be from time to time.

Suppose you raise K♠-K♣ from middle position to 3 BBs out of your 100-BB stack and the player on the button, a loose-aggressive player known for bluffing, calls. The two of you see a flop of A♦-9♠-4♣. You continuation-bet 4 BBs and your opponent calls. At this point, your opponent gives off a tell that you believe is a sign of extreme weakness. The turn is the 2♣. You need to figure out if your opponent will raise a turn bet or will only bluff if you check. Assume you are unsure about your opponent's tendencies. In this spot, I would check to induce a bluff. You will be in a tricky spot if you bet and he raises because, unless you are totally sure of your read, which will rarely be the case, you will sometimes face a better hand in a huge pot. If you check to induce a bluff, you can still get to a fairly cheap showdown, greatly reducing variance. Notice that to check-raise the turn wouldn't make sense with any hand you decided to check the turn with except for a stone bluff because if you check-raise, your opponent will most likely fold, which we don't want because he is usually drawing thin. So, you check and your opponent bets 9 BBs. You call and the river is the 10♦. Again, leading here will usually result in a fold or raise. You don't want to face a large river raise with a weak made hand, so you check. Your opponent bets 20 BBs. You have a clear call because you induced bluffs the entire way partially because your opponent displayed a tell of weakness. Even though you can't beat any ace, you should still call if you are confident in your read. Some players get to this river with K-K and fold to the last bet. This is usually a huge disaster because, as played, your line looks so weak that your aggressive opponent will do everything in his power to take you off your hand.

Sometimes your opponent may show up with a hand like A-3 in the above example. Even though you read him for being very weak, he was actually only mildly weak. The fact that a player thinks he is weak doesn't mean he has total air. Be careful when determining his range.

When you make this call-down and are wrong, go back and figure out where you made your mistake. You will probably need to work on your reading ability. Only make big plays based on a read if you are confident it is correct. Many players go with their consistently incorrect reads in huge pots, costing their tournament lives. These players would be better off going against their reads.

If you are unsure about the meaniong of an opponent's behavior, simply ignore it. Most live players read hands so poorly that they would be better off playing blindfolded. Your win rate can skyrocket if you invest a lot of time playing live poker and figuring out what the most standard tells convey. But don't prematurely assume you are a mindreader.

Chapter 6

Practical Tips for Tournament Play

This collection of tips has taken me years to figure out. I will cover all the subtle things you can do in and around poker tournaments that will greatly increase your edge. I will discuss a wide range of topics such as sunglasses, berating bad players and slowing down the game. Understand all these topics and you will have a huge headstart.

Protect your Hand

It should go without saying that you must ensure that no one else can see your cards. Even at huge buy-in events, you see people who do not know how to look at their cards without showing them to their neighbors.

Practice protecting your cards by sitting around a table with a friend and taking turns looking at your hands. Have your friend sit on either side of you so he can tell you if there is any angle at which he can sit and see your hand. If he can see your hand, you aren't looking at it correctly. Practice different ways of looking at your hand until you get it right.

I should also talk about using card protectors to cover your cards once you look at them. Card protectors, when used by nonthinking opponents, can lead to hugely profitable tells. Some players always cover their hand when they plan on playing it and some only cover monster hands. I suggest not using a card protector. I never have and never will. As I mentioned before, anything extra you do can give away information.

When you are in the 1 or 10 seat, hold onto your cards so the dealer doesn't take them by accident. I have seen this happen several times, and it usually causes a huge argument. I stick my arms out slightly on either side of my cards, almost boxing them in, with the only opening facing toward the center of the table. On rare occasions a dealer will tell me he can't see my cards. I put them out a little further so they can be easily seen, but I have never had my hand taken by accident and have never used a card protector. If you don't mind getting scolded by a dealer occasionally, this is the best way to go.

When to Look at your Hand

There is always some debate about when you should look at your cards. Many players suggest you not look at your cards until the action gets to you, so that opponents acting before you can't get a read on you. This is a little silly because, if you have a decent poker face, looking at your cards should not change the way you look. I suppose if you are lazy and act as if you have folded once you look at a weak hand, then you should wait to look at your cards, but this book is not about playing lazy poker. One other problem is that everyone gets to watch you look at your cards. In general, you don't want anyone looking at you, and you slow the game down while you look at your hand.

If you look at your cards as soon as you get them, you may give off some tiny tell that great players will pick up on. You may breathe differently with a big hand, not turn your head with a big hand, and so forth. No one's poker face is perfect, which is really the main reason to not look at your cards as soon as you get them. One other interesting thing to consider is that if you are looking at your cards, you can't look at anyone else while they are looking at their cards. Clearly, you want to pick up reads on opponents while they are checking out their cards, which is another reason to wait until the action is on you before you look at your hand.

I mix up when I look at my hand. It discourages people from watching me. Sometimes I wait for the action to get to me and sometimes I look as soon as I get my cards. I wait to look at my cards when I am in the blinds, button or cutoff. When someone raises in front of me, I will usually look at my cards if I'm not in the blinds. Sometimes I will look at the first card as soon as I get it and the second card once the action is on me. Look at your cards fairly quickly and don't look at them again. The more time you spend looking at your hand, the more time your opponents can watch you look at your hand. Mix it up and maintain a solid poker face until you have folded your hand.

When You Think a Card Flashes

A dealer will occasionally pitch a card in a way that allows some players to briefly see it, although it doesn't land face up. Flip the card up, especially if it's yours. Sometimes the dealer may not see the card flash. Say, "This card flashed," as soon as it hits your hands, and flip it up. Don't give anyone the option to say, "No, it didn't." I have never had a problem doing this. The dealer will give you another card after the deal is complete, so you have two cards. If the floor comes over and says your hand is dead, which would shock me, realize you would rather your hand be dead hand than your opponents know one of your cards.

This spot that can only be +EV. If you flip up the card, you get a new card your opponents don't know. If you keep the card, your opponents may know your hand. There is nothing bad that can come from flipping up your card, making it a purely +EV decision.

I have seen players receive an ace, then see another ace flash up on the way to them as their second card. They usually go nuts because they would have had aces. But dealer mistakes shouldn't bother you. They are going to affect everyone equally over time. Don't be concerned because you got the bad end of the deal this time. It happens. Realize that cards are random. Instead of A-A this time, you will just have to play the powerful A-4.

Look Left

When it's your turn to act, either before or after the flop, pay close attention to the players to your left. They will often clearly indicate their intentions before you ever decide how to play your hand.

Suppose everyone folds to you and you have 9♠-7♣ in the cutoff. You could either raise or fold this hand, depending on what is going on at the table. Once the action gets to you, look left and see if the players are reaching for chips or are acting like they are going to fold. If you see the button eager to muck his hand and the small blind watching the TV, feel free to raise. If you see the button staring forward and the small blind staring at you, especially if this is not normal behavior for them, fold without a second thought.

Pay attention to how each player on your left holds his cards when he intends to play a hand. Try to figure out where he looks when he is going to play. Some players will stare intently at the action when they have a playable hand and some will look straight forward, as if trying to hide their odd behavior. If you can figure out when someone is going to play his hand, you can fold your marginal hands and save a lot of chips.

Checking in the Dark

Phil Hellmuth popularized a move referred to as "checking in the dark." His logic is that if you check before the flop comes, your opponent will have no information on whether you hit. The only problem is that you forfeit the option to steal or take the initiative against certain opponents. On some flops, leading is almost always better than check-calling or check-raising. Giving up this option is a mistake.

While the way Phil does it isn't too terrible, amateurs take it to a new level by checking in the dark on multiple streets or pre-flop. I have seen players check in the dark throughout an entire hand. Giving up the option to bet throughout an entire hand is awful. I have seen other players check in the dark from the big blind. While this may not cost you a lot of money, you will occasionally find yourself in the big blind with A-A in a 3-BB pot instead of a 10-BB pot, costing you the opportunity to stack your opponent.

Checking in the dark is just another form of fancy play syndrome. Don't do anything too fancy, especially when it takes away your options.

Betting Weird Amounts

Against a player that tends to be curious, you should strongly consider making a bet that is sized a little oddly to arouse that curiosity.

Against these players, when I want to get called, instead of making a standard bet of say, 42,000, I will bet 42,375. Throwing out a whole pile of chips will entice them to call. When you want them to fold, bet something that looks bland, like 40,000. This works extremely well with a big pot on the river against a weak player that you think plans to fold. Throwing out an extra 475 chips could induce him to make a crying call.

Some players always use weird bet sizes. Be concerned when they bet a round number. In general, once you figure out what types of hands correspond to a player's odd and normal bets, you can be fairly confident that he will play the same way in the future. I don't bet odd amounts in every situation because it causes me to move more. Remember that you want to move as little as possible. Betting weird amounts also slows down the game because the dealer will have to count your bet.

I tend to make normal sized bets all the time against good, thinking opponents. Most good players can think through these situations and will often make the correct decision. Do the same thing every-time and they will never be able to out-think you.

Do Not Worry About the Average Stack

Tournament players often worry about whether they have more than the average chip count. Some take this so far as to raise when-ever they have less than the average stack, regardless of their hand or position. Clearly, this is a huge leak. Some weak players will tighten up significantly if they get a large stack. They feel safe and then they blind off all their chips instead of trying to grow a large stack to win the tournament. Your play should not depend at all on how your stack compares to others.

In a tournament, especially early on, you should only be concerned with how many big blinds you and everyone else at your table have. That is all that really matters. At a final table, you may find one player running away with the chip lead. The average doesn't matter in this situation because everyone except the huge chip leader will have less than that. Usually, you will see more players with less than the average chip stack than with more. This is because a player can have more than twice the average stack but you can never have a negative chip stack. Really, worrying about the average chip stack is as frivolous as worrying about if the weather is going to be above or below the average temperature for the last 100 years. It is just irrelevant information that weak players like to think about to justify their poor play.

When Your Bluff is Called

When you bluff on the river and your opponent calls, you have two options. You can either turn your hand up or you can muck. In my opinion, mucking is always wrong. When someone calls my bluff, I turn my hand up proudly. If you act timidly, the players at the table will assume you are embarrassed by your play. When you turn up the bluff proudly, it shows them you have the heart to make a bluff and are not concerned that everyone knows it. This is one way you can make money even when you lose, by striking fear in your opponents. Also, if you muck your hand, your opponent doesn't have to show his hand, which means you fail to see what he called with. Sometimes you will be shocked that an opponent only called with the second nuts, or you may be surprised to find that he called with king-high. Be proud of your plays. They are what make you successful at poker.

Players will occasionally muck the winning hand after seeing your bluff. I once saw a player bet the river with 7♥-6♥ on a J♥-5♥-4♣-2♠-K♦

board. His opponent called and the bluffer proudly flipped up the nut low. His opponent looked at the board for around 15 seconds, shook his head and mucked his cards.

You do not want to be known as a habitual mucker. Some players always muck on the river when caught bluffing. The danger of this was displayed in an online video in which Roland de Wolfe mucked the winning hand on the river when Tobias Reinkemeier called his bluff with queen-high, knowing he could probably only win the hand if Roland mucked, which he is known to do often. Roland bet on the river and Tobias called. Roland acted timid and said he was bluffing and acted like he was going to fold his hand. Tobias just sat there, as he didn't have to show his hand unless Roland turned his hand up. At this point Roland showed a king but didn't show the other card. The hand is technically not face up until both cards are turned up. After a while he mucked the other card and Tobias turned up queen-high while raking in a huge pot. Mucking the winner even once in your career will cost you a huge amount of equity.

When the Big Blind is Sitting Out

From time to time, the player in the big blind will be away from the table, which means the big blind is dead money in the pot. Most aggressive players try to pick up that dead money. If you are smart about this, it can make you a lot of money.

If you are in early position, tend to raise with only a slightly looser than normal range. I would not go nuts, raising any two cards, as you have to worry about the rest of the table. From middle and late position, feel free to raise a wide range, assuming your table is tight and will not play back at you.

If your table is fairly aggressive and will play back at you, you need to be careful because you will probably get re-raised, especially if you raise from middle or late position. When an aggressive player re-raises, figure out his range and play accordingly. This is tricky because some players will vastly widen their range and some won't widen their range at all. Losing this leveling war can cost you a lot of chips.

My most memorable such hand occurred in a $15,000 WPT event at Bellagio. The blinds were fairly large but everyone still had 200 BBs or so, as Bellagio starts everyone with a ton of chips. The big blind was sitting out. I raised from the cutoff with A-J to 2.5 BBs, which is obviously a standard raise. John Juanda re-raised to 8 BBs from the button. I figured he was playing back at me so I four-bet to 23 BBs. He instantly made it 70 BBs. At this point, I had to decide if he was making a play or simply had a hand. I remembered a hand in another tournament in which he put way too many chips in a pot with 3-3, so I figured he was capable of making a play. I decided to push for my 200-BB stack. He instantly folded. I was happy. Notice how this could have easily gone terribly wrong if he had actually had a strong hand. Maybe I got lucky.

Sometimes a substantial number of players haven't shown up yet when play begins at a table. Raise as many pots as possible when this is the case. At most WSOP events, only four or five players per table show up at the start of most of the larger buy-in events. This is a great time to raise and pick up a few tiny blinds. If someone plays back at you, just get out of the way in most cases.

Chopping

When you get down to a few players, especially in a smaller tournament, most players want to split the money. Unless they give you a great deal, you should almost never chop. If your opponents are scared to gamble for large sums of money and you aren't, you have a huge edge. Assuming you play well, you should have a decent edge before you even start playing for the big money.

Most casinos try to help with chopping but use incorrect formulas to determine how much each player should get. They divide each player's stack by the number of chips in play to determine his percentage of the remaining prize pool. Everyone is guaranteed the lowest payout remaining, so that money is taken off. This grossly favors the large stacks.

Suppose there are 100,000 chips in play. Three players remain, holding 80,000, 15,000 and 5,000 chips, respectively. First place is $100,000, second is $50,000 and third is $25,000. So, the player with 80,000 chips owns 80 percent of the $100,000 in contested money, plus $25,000 guaranteed, according to this formula. This player would then get $105,000 if he made this deal, which is more than first place pays. This should demonstrate how silly this method is. That being said, if you are the large stack and everyone wants to make a deal, insist on using this formula because it will give you much more equity than you deserve.

The only accurate way to determine the proper payouts is to use the Individual Chip Model. Remember that from before? While ICM has its flaws, such as assuming everyone plays equally well, it will determine an accurate chop. In the example above, the chip leader, with 80,000 chips, should get $89,580, the middle stack, with 25,000 chips, should get $51,450 and the player with only 5,000 chips should get $33,970. These numbers are determined by computing the percentage of the time each player will finish in each spot, and averaging the numbers. You can search online for a simple tournament poker ICM calculator. If you have a short stack, you should demand to chop using ICM. If no one has a clue what you are talking about, you are better off playing.

I have chopped twice in the distant past. The first time was in the Sunday Million, the biggest online tournament of the week. We were down to four players and I was the short stack. We looked at the numbers based on ICM. I asked for $10,000 on top of my fair share. Everyone agreed and I picked up $10,000 simply by asking for it. The second time I was heads-up against a well-known tournament pro. He agreed to give me $3,500 more than I should have gotten if we split the prize based on chip stacks, which is the only way to do it when you are heads-up. I accepted and was $3,500 richer.

On the bubble in smaller tournaments, someone always seems to ask if everyone will throw in some money for the person that bubbles. Never do this unless you are the shortest stack. The bubble is one of the most profitable situations in poker. Use that time to build your stack, not give money away.

Pot-Limit Holdem

Pot-limit holdem is the closet relative to no-limit holdem, and these two types of holdem tournaments are played almost the same way. The main difference is that there are never antes in pot-limit holdem tournaments. You should play significantly tighter throughout the tournament because there is never a need to gamble. Also, you can only make a pot-sized bet on every street, which means you can't go all-in before the flop unless you have 3.5 BBs or less. There are a few tricks you can use in pot-limit holdem that do not work in no-limit.

Since you can't go all-in before the flop unless you have 3.5 BBs or less, you should be willing to blind down a bit lower than suggested in the "Playing Poker" section of *Volume 1*. For example, if you have J♠-8♣ on the button with 10 BBs in no-limit holdem, you should go all-in if everyone folds before you. If you raise to 3.5 BBs in pot-limit holdem and someone calls, you will be in a tough spot after the flop when you miss, which will happen around 65 percent of the time.

Just fold these hands instead. Be a bit more willing to blind down and wait until you have a hand with showdown value or can push when someone raises in front of you.

You also can consider limping the button, especially when everyone has between 25 and 50 BBs. If you raise to 3 BBs, your opponents can re-raise enough to make you fold most hands. If you limp instead, they can only raise to 4 BBs before the flop, so you can always see a fairly cheap flop in position.

You can raise less before the flop in pot-limit holdem because there are no antes. My standard raise in pot-limit holdem is around 2.25 BBs throughout the tournament. When antes are involved, players know they have to make plays from time to time in order to keep afloat. In pot-limit holdem, even if you steal the blinds only once in 12 hands or so, it is tough to lose too many chips. This is one of the reasons why tight play is profitable in these events.

Most people play pot-limit holdem exactly like no-limit holdem, meaning they are constantly raising and re-raising. When you en- counter this type of player, simply wait for a hand and bust him. In no-limit holdem, you can be pretty happy with a hand like middle pair against an overly aggressive player. In pot-limit holdem, I sug- gest waiting for a slightly better hand, like top pair. Again this is be- cause blinding down a little doesn't drastically erode your stack.

To summarize, play pot-limit holdem tournaments much tighter than no-limit. While the games look and feel the same, they are not.

Do Not Slow Down the Game

Nothing is worse for your EV in a tournament than to be stuck at a table full of slow players. If you know you make some amount of eq- uity per tournament, you can figure out how much you make per hand. If that number is positive, you should play as many hands as possible during each level of a tournament. If you make $1 per hand and play 40 hands per hour, you bring in $40 per hour on average. If you play 60 hands per hour, you instantly get a 50-percent raise. Giving yourself a hefty raise simply by playing faster is a great play that every profitable player should implement.

A few years back I got stuck at a table full of players that all had slightly less than an average stack on the second day of a $1,500 WSOP event. They all knew we would get in the money within an hour, so they decided to play as slowly as possible to make sure everyone at the table made some money. They didn't realize that playing that slowly caused everyone's 2/3 average stack dwindled down to 1/3 average, reducing everyone's chances of winning the tournament. After I lost, I went back to check on how everyone at my table did. Only one of them lasted more than four hours after we got in the money. Because everyone was so short, they were forced to go all-in with weak hands. While we all got our money back, none of us had a chance to win the tournament, costing us loads of equity.

Show Up on Time

It is important to arrive on time to play poker tournaments, especially if you are a good deep-stacked player. Most tournaments start you with a decently large chip stack, and most amateurs have no clue how to play with a deep stack. If you skip the first few levels of a tournament, you miss a chance to get a huge number of big blinds all-in with an opponent drawing slim or even dead.

Some players claim that if they show up late, some of the field has already been knocked out and they can never go broke early. While there is some value in just surviving in a tournament, you will have fewer chips than everyone else at your table and some of the weak players will have already lost their entire stack. If you play better than your opponents, you will stack them more often than they stack you. I estimate that of the times you double up or go broke, 66 percent of the time when you show up on time you will have doubled up by the time the late registration period ends and 33 percent of the time you will be out. This alone proves that showing up on time is +EV.

Players also say that showing up late allows them to sleep a few extra hours, enabling them to be more alert in the later levels of a tournament. If you want more sleep, go to bed earlier. I take off the day before every major tournament I play to make sure I am well rested. If you can't play 12 hours of poker at a high level, you need to work on your game. Most tournaments require entrants to play no more than 12 hours a day, so that is all the stamina you need. Pretty much everyone can put in 12 hours if necessary.

Interestingly enough, some of the players that arrive late are the better players, which is one more great reason to show up on time. You will get to play with weak players for a few hours. The only possible reason to show up late is if your time is worth more to you than the money you stand to win in the first few hours of a tournament. If you are a billionaire, playing poker for a few hours to profit $3,000 on average probably doesn't seem that appealing. You may rather show up late and get into a flip for $10,000. If that is the case, then do whatever you want. Show up on time if you want to maximize your expectation for a tournament.

Confirm the Action if You Miss It

If you are in a hand and are confused about the action, ask the dealer. Sometimes a player will check without making much of a motion. If you wear headphones, someone may say "all-in" or "check" and you won't hear it. If you have even a little doubt about what happened, ask the dealer.

Occasionally a player wearing headphones will have the nuts and someone will say something that he doesn't hear. He knows the player said something but doesn't know what. The correct play is to say, "Is the action on me?" Don't say something like "Call!!!" because you thought the player said he was all-in.

A pretty crazy situation came up at the 2010 WSOP main event where an overly loud, annoying player went all-in on the river. The player facing a decision for all his chips was known for being slightly controversial but not overly shady. The annoying player was trash talking the other guy, which probably annoyed him. After about five minutes, the annoying player called for a clock, meaning the controversial player had one minute left to think about his hand. By that time, a crowd of media personnel and numerous onlookers had surrounded the table. With one second left, the controversial player said something which was inaudible to most people. The annoying player proudly flipped up his hand, saying "I got the nuts!" The controversial player then said that he had folded. This caused a huge uproar because the controversial player basically pulled a huge angle on the annoying player. A player sitting next to the controversial player actually said that he had called. The floor person could not confirm what had happened. Had the annoying player simply asked the dealer if the controversial player had called, he probably would have been awarded the player's stack. Instead, it was ruled a fold and he missed out on $20,000 in equity.

Whenever you ask what the action is, do it with a strong voice. If you sound overly excited, people will know you have a monster. If you sound disgusted, they will think you have a weak hand. As with all situations where you give away information, make sure the information is irrelevant. If you miss action, make sure you know what is going on. Failing to do so can cost you huge amounts of equity.

Carry a Bag

Carry some sort of bag when you play a tournament, especially ones with long days. I usually carry a backup iPod, headphones, a book or two, a jacket, sunglasses, water, some food, paper and a pen. Take whatever you may need throughout a day. You may need nothing. If that is the case, don't take anything. I usually don't need anything from my bag, but it is better to be safe than sorry.

It is of the utmost importance to put nothing extraordinarily important in your bag. Twice in my poker career, I have seen a player walk off and forget his bag, only to have someone take it. Both times the player came back and no one had a clue what was going on. Both players had large sums of money in their bags. Setting yourself up to lose that kind of money is always -EV. Keep your money on your person; you will never leave yourself behind. Don't put expensive accessories in the bag, either. If someone stole my bag, it might cost me $200 to replace everything in it. Be smart. Prepare ahead but don't prepare poorly.

How to Stack Your Chips

You might think the way you stack your chips shouldn't matter, but it does. Some players keep their chips in a random pile, forcing them to dig through them everytime they plan to put money in the pot. This slows down the game and allows other players to pick up tells. You want your motions to be as smooth and fast as possible while still looking natural.

Some players keep their chips in one stack, with the largest chips on the bottom. The player must then dig through his stack to find the correct chips. I once saw a player who would shake like crazy when digging through his stack if he had a large hand and would smoothly go through his stack when weak. I wonder how much money he would save if he just stacked his chips so they were easy to access.

When you start a tournament, you will usually have eight $25 chips, eight $100 chips and some chips for larger amounts. To set up your stack like mine, start with your stack the way the casino probably gave you the chips, with the smallest on top and the largest on the bottom. Place your chips in three stacks, in order from left to right: $25, $100 and everything larger. You can then access any amount with ease. Since your stacks are ordered from smallest to largest, you can grab your chips without even looking at your stack, but don't try this until you are comfortable with the layout of your chips. One mistake could cost you a lot of money.

As your stack grows, you will have to devise new ways to arrange your chips. I stack chips with the same denomination until I have around 30 of them, at which time I will make adjacent piles of 20 and 10 chips. So, if I have 18 $25 chips, 38 $100 chips and six $500 chips, I will make four stacks in this order: 18 $25 chips, 18 $100 chips, 20 $100 chips and six $500 chips. If I have 50 $100 chips instead of 38, I will have two stacks of 20 $100 chips, with the other 10 sitting on top of those two stacks. Once the stack on top gets to around 25 chips, I will put 20 of them in front of the other two stacks of 20, making a triangle, with the remaining five $100 chips sitting on top. I will do this for every denomination until I have a big, triangular arrangement.

Put your big chips on the bottom of your stack when you go on break. A thief could easily walk by your stack and take a large chip if it's sitting on top of your stack. I have heard of this happening at least twice in my career.

Making Change

Someone in a live tournament will often run out of small chips and ask for change. Go ahead and make change if it will leave you with a decent number of small chips. Motion toward another player if making change would leave you short of small chips.

Instead of asking for change, a player will sometimes throw a big chip in the pot and state his action. The dealer may ask someone to make change. Give the dealer change if you can. If there is enough change in the pot, players can take back the difference.

You may ask why all of this matters. Sometimes players get protective about their chip stack and refuse to make change, which drastically slows down the game. Some players collect all the small-denomination chips and refuse to make change for anyone. They do this to build a large, intimidating stack, but they cost themselves equity by missing out on playing a few hands at each level. If you don't like money and want everyone to hate you, collect all the small chips and don't let anyone have them.

Do Not Put Chips in Your Pocket

You will have to change tables from time to time in every tournament. When this happens, you will usually be told to not put your chips in your pocket. Despite this, every year at the WSOP, someone puts his chips in his pocket. This player is always disqualified because he broke the rules. Forfeiting all your equity is very –EV. Listen to the rules the floor man tells you and keep your chips out of your pocket.

Sunglasses

There has been much talk about banning sunglasses among high-stakes poker players. I think sunglasses are good for the game, and a ban just might push poker back into the dead age of the 1980s.

The first and main reason why sunglasses are good for poker is that they give new players confidence to hop into games they normally wouldn't play. Being stared down by a tough player is hard even with glasses. If I couldn't wear sunglasses, I simply wouldn't play with some players unless forced to. Most of the weaker players in major tournaments wear sunglasses. If you ban them, half of those players might not play because they won't enjoy the game. If you remove half the weak players from major tournaments, you'll be left with a bunch of pros paying the rake.

In addition to boosting confidence, sunglasses help players reduce their tells. Some players like to think poker is a game about staring people down, getting a read on them and going with it. Some think it's about math and using logic to figure out what is going on. The math guys tend to prefer sunglasses because they don't rely on tells, which they don't find as useful as logic. The feel guys cry about sunglasses because it reduces their edge. I think of myself as a mix of both types. Having common sense, though, I wear sunglasses in every major tournament I play. If you give me a weapon that will cut my opponents' edge in half, I will use it. It's as simple as that. Most online players that have moved to live poker wear sunglasses because they realize that not wearing them can only be −EV. I like making +EV decisions, so I wear them. Not giving off tells to the guys that have no clue how math applies to poker makes me happy. The fact that the feel players realize their edge is diminishing is not a reason to give them what they want. Maybe they will be forced to become better players.

Sunglasses also allow you to observe a player without his knowledge. You should rarely look at the person who is thinking about making a big call on the river, which is where most people look. You should look at the guy that made the bet. A good player will be looking at the bettor, not the caller. If you are a weaker player, or even a good one, you don't want to let the bettor know you are trying to pick up his tells. If you have to stare right at him, he will realize this and do things to throw you off in the future.

A lot of players, especially older ones, complain that sunglasses hurt their eyes because they are so dark. Thankfully, in today's world, sunglasses don't have to be dark. You can pick up a great pair of mirrored, basically 100-percent see-through glasses from www.BlueSharkOptics.com. They are fairly inexpensive and work very well.

If you ban sunglasses, where do you draw the line? Will we ban iPods next year? Maybe the next year, you won't be able to order drinks at the table because they're spilled all over from time to time. Maybe you will be forced to wear a suit and tie to make the game look more formal and reputable. Taking away the players' right to do something is rarely good because the people who make the rules rarely know when to stop.

The idea of cheating with sunglasses has also been brought up. Honestly, anyone who would mark cards when the penalty is jail time has mental problems. If you think someone is cheating with their glasses, ask to try them on and see if you notice marks on the cards. As far as I know, I have only been cheated in a poker game once, and that was in a private home game. Sunglasses were not involved. Cheating simply does not go on in high-stakes poker games because the penalty is much too high.

Some say that sunglasses are bad for TV. This simply isn't true. Weak players play in televised events because they have a chance to do well. If they stop making final tables because of huge eye tells, this will diminish the concept that anyone can win a major tournament. If you want the general public to watch and play poker, you have to let them make the final table and occasionally win.

I am all for sunglasses. This is not because they are magical or special. I know they give me an edge. It's that simple. I wear sunglasses in every major event I play, and I suggest you do the same.

Headphones

I wore headphones until a friend told me how much value I was missing. Picking up on small things can hugely increase your equity in a tournament. Who's on tilt because his wife made him mad on the phone? Who really wants to get in the money? Who doesn't care about money? If you have your ears open, you will hear these things. If you wear headphones, you won't. People say that with headphones they can play longer because the brain is occupied by music instead of players' ramblings. I agree, but it is worth toughing it out to pick up equity from knowing what is going on. It took me about a month to get used to playing without headphones. I only wear them now if the players at my table are talking cluelessly, which usually annoys me pretty nicely. I keep a set of headphones in my bag but rarely use them.

Treat People Well

When you go to a casino, your goal should be to make everyone there happy. This includes players, dealers, floor supervisors, cocktail waitresses, janitors and anyone else in your vicinity. If you want to make money playing poker, you need a place to play. Think of the casino as your workplace. When you show up, you make some money. If the casino is happy, you are happy. Players often complain about the casino and the way they run their tournaments. You should do the opposite.

If you treat the dealers poorly, they may quit, which means the poker room will be short on dealers, which means it may cost them more money to hire replacements, which will make tournaments less profitable for them, which may cause them to stop running tournaments altogether. This may seem farfetched, but if enough people are rude to the dealers, it could happen. You should want the dealers to be happy. It's not fun playing at a table when the dealer clearly doesn't want to be there. When you make it deep in a tournament, leave the dealers some money. I like to make sure the dealers get about 3.5 percent of the prize pool. Most tournaments take 3 percent off the top, meaning I will leave an additional 0.5 percent of my cash.

If you are rude to a floor supervisor, he may become disgruntled and do a poor job, which will also cost you money. The floor supervisors usually go over the top to make the players happy. If you treat them well, they will usually get you whatever you ask for. If you need a discounted or free hotel room, ask the floor supervisors and they will either get it for you or point you in the right direction. You can also ask for food comps, which can come to thousands of dollars annually. Tip the floor staff very well. They are the people that get the job done and make sure that you are treated like royalty.

Treat the service people well. If you upset a cocktail waitress, she may avoid your table. If you are rude to the janitor, he may leave the casino floor strewn with trash.

Finally, treat the other players well. Tournaments don't run if they don't enter. You may think you can profit by treating the good players poorly, but you need them to show up because weaker players like to know they can win a large first prize. In order to have a large first prize, you need a lot of players. Also, you don't want to be mean to the amateurs because they might quit playing altogether.

I try to live by the golden rule: treat others as you would like to be treated. I like to be treated well, so I must treat everyone else well. In my mind, there is no other option. Remember that even if someone is not in your circle of friends, he still deserves respect.

Do Not Berate Poor Play

Berating the bad players might be one of the biggest mental problems I had to overcome. Losing when you are a huge favorite is never fun. Poker would be much less profitable if no one ever brutally sucked out on you, as weak players would stop playing and the games would become unbeatable. To overcome my anger at the weaker players, I had to realize that my ROI would be considerably lower without them.

There are two main reasons for not telling players how bad they are. First, if you go off on them too harshly, they may quit and never play again. Second, you may motivate them to play better. So, you either lose a dead-money player or turn a bad player into a decent one.

Berating players can also create a table dynamic that will put you in tough situations. The other players may or may not think you are on tilt and may or may not play differently against you than normal. You want to have a clear idea of how your opponents will play against you. Clouding that vision can cause you to make mistakes. You want to make as few mistakes as possible, especially when a mistake can cost you your tournament life. If you tell someone he is a terrible player, he may play differently against you. He may try to beat you in every pot or make big folds to show you how good he is. Either way, it will make your reads incorrect.

I now do better than just ignoring bad beats. I'm nice to the weak players. I have heard that the late Chip Reese was the best at making high rollers want to play with him, because they didn't mind losing to him. Making weak players want to play with you should help you to enjoy a long and profitable poker career.

Quite often, especially at smaller buy-in tournaments, I will see a semi-competent player berate a poor player. Wanting to keep the poor player happy, I usually look at his tormentor and shake my head in disgust. This usually gets my point across.

Do Not Fear the Pros

If playing with professionals gets your heart rate up and your pre-flop raise percentage down, you are probably scared of playing with them. The pros are just like you, only with more experience and skill. They are not poker gods that always make the right decision.

Players often avoid playing hands against certain pros, fearing they will be outplayed. If the greatest poker player in the world raises from middle position and you have A-K on the button, you should never fold. In fact, if you think someone plays well post-flop, you should usually re-raise with the intention of getting all-in if the stacks aren't too deep. What actually makes most pros good is that they steal more pots than the average player. Because of this, you should actually want to play more hands with the loose-aggressive pros, usually by applying maximum pressure. This is obviously not true against the tighter pros.

Some players are on the other extreme, always trying to outplay the pros. Don't go out of your way to put a play on a world-class player so you can tell your friends how you outplayed a pro. This will just cost you equity. If telling your friends a story is worth risking the loss of a tournament, go ahead and try it.

Just play your standard, tight-aggressive "A" game against the top players. Don't play overly tight and don't go out of your way to play pots with them. Most pros expect amateurs to play too tight or too loose. Playing right in the middle will throw them off their game.

If you are a pro and people already fear you, you have to optimally adjust to each player. I am in an interesting situation where most, but not all, tournament players know who I am. I have to figure out if people are going after me, staying out of my way, or just thinking I am another random, young kid. If you are someone like Phil Ivey, everyone knows you, so they will generally play either too tight or too loose.

I pay attention to who is looking at me more intently than I think is normal. Someone might mention that he is at a tough table, which indicates he might know me. Once you determine who knows you, try to determine whether they will play tight or loose against you, then play accordingly and take their chips.

Table Talk

Table talk is the practice of talking to your opponent in a hand to get information out of him. I personally don't ask my opponents too many questions at all because I give people enough credit to answer in a manner that might level me into playing my hand incorrectly. The main time I talk to the players is during the WSOP, where the worst players in the world come to play.

When someone talks to you in a hand, simply ignore him. This denies him any information. Do this every time; your silence could be a tell if you normally talk during a hand. I remember a hand on ESPN where Phil Hellmuth had something like A-K on K-x-x and folded to a guy that had A-A because the guy basically told Phil he had A-A.

Clearly, this was a huge mistake. He probably would have stacked Phil if he had just sat there and said nothing.

Players generally tell the truth in a stressful situation. I saw a great example of this on the bubble of a $1,500 WSOP event where I raised with A♠-Q♠ and someone went all-in for 15 BBs. I would normally call here but as I was counting my chips to see what I would have left, the player said, "I have two aces. If you want to gamble, call." I folded and he flipped up A-A, saving me a decent number of chips.

Most players aren't too quick to think of smart things to say when they are worried about going broke. If they tend to jumble their words or act overly nervous, they are usually bluffing. Also, when two players are talking and one of them instantly stops talking when he looks at his cards, he usually has a big hand. Once I had A-J in middle position and a player who had been talking nonstop suddenly shut his mouth. I folded and he showed up with K-K.

Table talk can also provide information in online poker. You should generally not type much of anything in the chat box. I only reply when a student is talking to me or if someone says "nice hand." If you lose a big pot, the last thing you want to do is to type gibberish about your bad luck or your opponent's poor play. This will tell everyone that you are probably on tilt. Also, if you play lots of tables at once, distracting yourself by typing in a chat box will only cost you equity and give you less time to make decisions on other tables. Don't talk while you are in a hand. It can only cost you money in the long run.

Do Not Talk Strategy at the Table

Sometimes a player will ask your opinion about a hand. Say as little as possible; you don't want players to know you think about the game. I must be decently well-known because people ask my opinion often. I usually dumb down my answer and often give totally incorrect information. Some players see what I am doing and others don't. Until people are constantly trying to talk to you, I suggest you keep the strategy talk at the table to a minimum.

I am more than happy to talk about poker away from the table with friends. Talking to other players is one of the best ways to improve. But when you talk about strategy at the table, you are basically giving everyone a free lesson. Poker lessons are meant to be expensive. Make a point to keep it that way.

Chapter 7

Etiquette

This chapter will deal with a few poker etiquette issues that are breached all the time. If you are going to play a game, you need to know the unspoken rules as well as the formal ones. Not knowing these rules not only makes you look uninformed, but it may cause someone to take offense.

Do Not Talk to the Person you Just Beat

When you beat someone for a big pot, the worst thing you can do is to talk to him afterwards. Someone who loses a pot either wants to sit and fume over the hand or think it through. He doesn't want to be talked to. It's even worse to berate a player after he loses.

I had the pleasure of losing a big hand with J-J against a semi-competent regular tournament player who had A-Q. We had talked before the hand about his business and how using it could benefit me. He berated me after we got it all-in and he hit a queen to beat me, saying I should have known he had a big hand and folded. After this, I certainly will not be giving him any business, not because he beat me in a hand, but because he has no clue about how to treat people after something bad happens to them.

The moral of that story is to leave people alone after you beat them in a big pot because you really don't want to make people hate you. It is nice to go to sleep at night knowing you didn't upset anyone. That is not what poker is about.

Excessive Celebration

Not much annoys more than to get sucked out on and then have to watch someone run around and scream about how good he is at poker. But my displeasure isn't reason enough to write about it. Besides slowing the game down and causing a scene, excessive celebration lets people know you are emotionally attached to the game. You want opponents to fear you because you have no respect for money. If you get excited when you win a pot, you let them know they should not fear you.

Excessive celebration can also adversely affect the person that lost the hand. If a weak player loses a big hand, he doesn't care to watch someone celebrate having taken his money. It is another form of berating him.

I am trying to come up with some counterpoints as to why celebrating is good and I can't come up with many. It is good when someone wins to act like he cares. Some players celebrate because it makes them feel good to belittle their opponents. I am obviously not in that camp. I am quite opposed to excessive celebration, and I hope you will be, too.

Know What You are Talking About

I was playing a $1,000 tournament at Venetian when I heard a few players discussing a WPT final table that was also being played that day. They concluded that it started at 1:00 p.m., even though I knew it started at 4:30. They determined that Phil Hellmuth was second in chips at the final table when he actually busted in seventh place. They said Mike and Vince would not be there, but they would. One player provided most of the erroneous information.

This player either thought he was giving accurate information or was blatantly lying. He probably thought he knew what he was talking about. If you do not know the answer to a question, you should not feel obliged to make something up. If you don't know the answer, just say so.

I have been to a few poker seminars whose instructor clearly did not know what he was talking about. One "professional" actually said, "If you get ace-king in middle position and raise, if someone reraises, you should probably fold because you have a drawing hand and are behind all pairs." That is just silly, but people were there listening and taking in that information as if it was the truth. If you are getting information from someone claiming to be a professional, make sure he actually is a professional. As it turns out, the player giving the seminar had won his last tournament in 1986. Please don't be like this person, giving out blatantly false information.

Rapping the Table

I have no clue how knocking on the table started, but it is supposed to mean "nice hand". So, when someone wins a nice pot off you, it is acceptable, although fishy, to lightly rap or pat the table in the winning player's general direction. I see this misused frequently.

When you win a hand, you should not talk to the player you just beat. You certainly should not tell them "nice hand." I would bet 25 percent of amateur players rap the table when they win a hand. If you don't want to look like a jerk, don't rap the table when you win a pot. Just sit there and stack your chips. Imagine what would happen if you busted someone and said, "Nice hand, buddy," as he was leaving the table. That would be a fun situation.

Telling the All-In Player "Good Luck"

When someone goes all-in, you don't need to say anything to him, especially if you aren't involved in the hand. I almost exclusively see weak players wish the all-in player good luck, effectively telling an opponent that they hope they lose. I think this is because the worst thing that can happen to a weak player that is playing well above his bankroll is to bust out of a big tournament. He thinks everyone is in the same boat and doesn't want anyone else to go through that pain. I hate to break it to you, but everyone except one lucky person is going to go broke in each and every tournament. Next time someone goes all-in, don't tell him "good luck". You might as well be telling the other player, "I hope you lose."

Talking During the Hand

You already know that you shouldn't talk when you are in a hand. What about when you're not in a hand? Only talk to the players on either side of you and on either side of them, as long as one of the players in the hand is not sitting between you. If you have to talk around someone in a hand, be quiet and talk later. Nothing is worse than thinking about a big decision while someone rambles in your ear. The courteous and respectful thing to do is to be quiet and let the player think about his hand.

Don't talk about the cards you folded while the hand is going on. For example, if the 2 and 3 seats are in a hand and I am in the 7 seat talking to the 8 seat, even though they can't hear me, I should not say anything about the current hand. I should not even whisper it. You should take this one step further. Say someone raises, I call and someone re-raises. The first player thinks for a while before calling and I fold 10-10, which I would never do. If it comes 10-4-2, I shouldn't throw my hands up in the air and act as if I just lost out on a lot of money. This would tell the other players that I folded something that would have connected well with the flop, which could only be a set.

Similarly, you know you will check-fold if someone raises, someone calls, you call with 9♠-8♠ on the button and the flop comes A-K-2. Don't let everyone know this, such as by uncapping your cards, drinking your drink or talking to your neighbor. Just sit there as if you plan to play the hand.

It all comes down to showing respect to fellow players and letting them play the game as it was meant to be played.

Do Not Reveal Your Cards

Assuming you play well, you should never have a desire to show a neighboring player your hand. You will often see players, especially at low stakes, show the players on either side of them a decent, but obviously beaten hand when they fold. This gives those players information the rest of the table doesn't have, and may cause the other players to think you are colluding with your neighbors.

For example, say you raise with A-K from middle position and both blinds call. The flop comes 9-5-3. The small blind checks and the big blind bets. Some players in this spot will show the A-K to their neighbors and fold. Now the small blind knows you probably had big cards, which takes a few hands out of the big blind's range. Also, everyone that saw your hand will now know you can fold A-K in that situation, which probably means you are a straightforward player. They may also realize you are probably on semi-tilt because you didn't want to fold a hand that was probably behind. All in all, nothing good comes from this. Simply fold your hand and get ready for the next one.

Make Chips Easy for the Dealer to See

Before the flop, especially with antes in play, the dealer will sometimes have a tough time telling who has anted and who hasn't. To avoid confusion, which can slow down the game tremendously, make sure your chips are easy for the dealer to see. An example will better illustrate this.

Suppose you are playing 250/500-50 in the small blind. Some players will put out a big stack of 12 $25 chips. The dealer will have to break down your pile of chips and then take out your ante. Some players put out four $25 chips and two $100 chips in one pile. Again, the dealer will have to try to find your ante. Some players will throw out three $100 chips, causing the dealer to make change to get your ante. Make sure your ante is visibly in front of your blinds. This eliminates any confusion.

Some players put their ante on top of the dealer button. This can cause the dealer to totally miss your ante or drag the entire pile, along with the dealer button, into the pot, again causing confusion.

This may seem like nitpicking, but these things slow down the game. Even if you play only one less hand per level, you will miss out on a ton of hands every year. If you play 500 fewer hands per year at $1 profit per hand, you've forfeited $500 per year by putting your chips into the pot in a confusing manner.

Chapter 8

Going Pro

At some point you may consider becoming a professional poker player. If you have to ask if you are ready, you probably aren't. Becoming a professional is a major decision that will drastically change your life, as you will no longer have a stable job. If you have a good job and make plenty of money, you probably should not even consider becoming a professional poker player because you are already financially secure. Poker makes a great hobby and can even bring in a significant amount of money on the side. I know a few successful businesspeople that make over $100,000 at their jobs and bring in an additional $100,000 a year playing poker. If you have a family to support, you should strongly consider keeping your day job because it would be terrible to let your family down. The decision is easier if you are young and no one depends on you.

I decided to become a professional when I was 18. I was a college student working at a job that paid $10/hour. I lived with my parents at the time. So, I had no bills and a rather low-paying job. I had grinded my bankroll up to around $20,000 by playing $200 sitngos and felt invincible. I quit my job and started grinding full-time. I dropped out of college and eventually grew my bankroll to around

$60,000. I decided it was time to put $20,000 down on a condo and move out of my parents' house. This created some bills, as I now had to pay out around $1,500 each month for living expenses. I then went on a downswing, leaving me with around $10,000 in my bankroll. I was on thin ice, as I had no money set aside for living expenses if things continued to go poorly. I moved down in stakes and played numerous hours. I eventually emerged from the rut and got to where I am today.

I made a few huge errors when I decided to go pro. I could have become just another failed poker player if my situation had gotten much worse. First, I only had 100 buy-ins for my regular game, which isn't nearly enough if you are going to have no other source of income. Since going broke was not an option, I should have waited until I had around 200 buy-ins, or $40,000.

I had no money set aside for living expenses. This was huge mistake number two. I was not used to paying $1,500 per month for living expenses, which made it much tougher to make a profit.

Once I got up to $60,000, I decided to put a third of my net worth down on a condo. This was huge mistake number three. Once I had a decent bankroll, I decided to put a third of it into an investment from which I couldn't withdraw for a long period of time. Condos in general are a bad idea because they usually charge a monthly association fee which can add up to thousands of dollars per year. I am just now learning how bad that is, as I rent out two condos and have to pay a decent chunk of the rent money in association fees and taxes.

Notice that I would have been in fine shape if I had lost $30,000 out of a $60,000 bankroll, still having $30,000. I had to move down to smaller games when I lost $30,000 out of $40,000, which probably cost me a decent amount of equity. If I broke even for a while, I would have gone broke because I had set aside nothing for living expenses. I also would have gone broke if I had run much worse with my remaining $10,000 bankroll. I was pretty lucky to make it out of there alive.

I did not mention dropping out of college in my list of mistakes. This was a great decision. Most people go to college either to get a degree or to hang out with people. I wanted to be a poker player, so I didn't need a degree. I didn't have many friends in college because most of my close friends from high school had moved away. Having a degree to fall back on if poker goes poorly is very +EV. I quit college about two years before I would graduate. I probably would have finished if that time had been much less. I have seen a few world-class online players drop out with only six months left, which seems crazy. Sometimes you just have to bite the bullet and finish school. I'm constantly asked if I ever plan to go back and finish my degree. My answer is a solid "No". A degree really has no value to me, and I don't want to have to show up to class and take tests. It's as simple as that. Nevertheless, I suggest everyone in college finish their degree before becoming a professional poker player.

Before you consider going pro, grind up a bankroll and play a limit where you can make around three times your current salary. You need a huge sample size to know your actual win rate, so play around 3,000 tournaments, 5,000 sitngos, or 200,000 hands in cash games before you consider quitting your job. Next, determine your living expenses for the next six months. Set aside $3,000 if you are a young kid living off $500 per month. Set aside $30,000 if you have a family and spend $5,000 per month. You can then consider quitting your job and going pro.

You also should consider what happens if you go broke. The decision to go pro is easier if you know you can get your job back. If you can't return to your job or get one that pays at least remotely similarly, you should seriously consider that before quitting. You also need to think about how you will grow your bankroll while still paying your bills. If you are grinding out $30/hour playing $30 sitngos, you will probably make around $4,500 per month, assuming you have a 5-percent ROI and play 3,000 games in a month. If you have a $30,000 bankroll and want to move to the $50 games, you will only be able to add $1,500 to your bankroll each month if you have $3,000 per month in bills. This means it will take you a year before you have enough money to move up. The solution is to either keep your living expenses low or to not go pro until you are playing at a high enough level that your living expenses do not matter.

You should also save money every month. Somewhere down the road you will need money, and if you set aside some amount every month, you will have it. This is tougher for multi-table tournament players than for those who play sitngos or cash games, who generally have more consistent winnings. I set aside money everytime I win a big tournament. However you decide to do it, plan for the future.

There is a lot to think about when deciding whether to go pro, but it really comes down to a few simple questions. How much am I actually making from poker? What will happen if I go broke? Will going broke adversely affect anyone else? Do I have enough money to grow my bankroll while paying bills and saving money? You can consider going pro if you have good answers to all these questions.

Do Not Overestimate Yourself

I have seen countless poker players that could beat $1,000 tournaments move up to $10,000 tournaments and get crushed. Moving up and playing with tougher competition is a way to get better, but it certainly is not a way to keep your bankroll intact. While most players are confident in their abilities, the truly great players realize there is something to learn every time they sit at the table.

When I play tournaments with buy-ins around $500, I see a lot of young players that think they are the greatest in the world. When they talk about poker, it is clear they know the jargon, and it is also clear they have no clue what they are talking about. These people tend to play well beyond their bankroll and eventually go broke, as I rarely see any of them in $10,000 buy-in events for long. They are not as good as they think.

The nature of poker tournaments greatly influences players to think they are better than they are. If you beat 500 people in a $500 tournament, assuming you know nothing about math, you will probably assume you are better than most of those 500 people. This couldn't be farther from the truth. On any given day, as long as you are aggressive, you have a chance to win any poker tournament. That does not mean you have any business playing in the largest games.

You can evaluate your level of play by watching training videos by the best players in the game. If their play differs significantly from yours, you are probably not that good. The level of tournaments that you win is a decent indication of your skill level. If you have been playing $500 tournaments for years and only have one win, you are probably playing too high. Similarly, if you play $10 tournaments and win one every week, you are probably playing too low. I know a pretty good player who plays for small stakes because he likes having a consistent win rate. He thinks he is a world-class player because he can beat $3 tournaments with ease. Needless to say, beating $3 tournaments does not make you God's gift to poker.

Note where the money comes from in high-stakes tournaments. Most weak tournament players are the big winners in their home games. They beat up on the really bad players in their local games and come to Vegas to play with the professionals, usually to be sent home with only a story to tell. Being able to beat a home game does not qualify you for high-buy-in tournaments.

Keeping their ego in check is a constant struggle for some people. I was fortunate enough to be wired with the realization that I am not the best poker player in the world. I have a long way to go, but with study and practice, eventually I will be at the very top. Even if you get to the top, there is always someone right on your heels. Be humble and accept that you do not know everything there is to know about poker.

Do Not Try to be Macho

Amateurs tend to think poker is a game about who has the most guts. They think that the person that makes the biggest bluff or the grandest all-in should win the money at the end of the day. Most professionals know this couldn't be farther from the truth. While playing aggressively will help you become a winner, you also must be patient, selective, cunning and manipulative, which is much different than bullying everyone around and spewing chips into the pot.

Don't become obsessed with beating a player you think is bullying you. You will play too many pots, trying to flop too many decent hands. You may put too many chips in the pot with a hand like a weak top pair. This soon leads to tilt and from there, you are doomed.

The smartest, easiest thing to do is to play your "A" game and don't try to show how courageous you are. If you keep a level head, you can sit back and slowly, but surely pick off the players that are constantly trying to out-play each other.

Do Not Set Silly Goals

Players often set goals that are silly because they can't control the outcome. For example, some players say they want to win $10,000 per month. Clearly, if you make $200/hour, you need to play 50 hours on average to make $10,000. This appears to be simple, but you could easily lose $200/hour over those specific 50 hours. Setting monetary goals, especially in the short run, will only cause you to play poorly. If the end of the month is coming and you have only won $7,000, you may gamble hard to try to reach that $10,000 goal, costing yourself a decent amount of equity.

Another silly goal is to move up to a certain buy-in level by a given time. This is similar to the monetary goals because usually your bankroll determines the level you can play. If you currently play $20 tournaments with a $2,000 bankroll and decide that you want to be playing the $50 tournaments in three months, you are basically telling yourself you want to win $3,000 over the next three months and have enough skill to beat the $50 games.

Another goal that makes sense initially but fails in the end, at least for me, is to say you will play a certain number of hours each month. While setting a schedule and sticking to is seems fine, if you are playing poorly, you are probably better off spending some time away from poker. Say you decide to play 160 hours per month but end up playing only 120 hours of good poker. If you play the next 40 hours on tilt, you will be giving back much of what you won in the first 120 hours.

There are some good goals to have. First, have a goal to not go on tilt. When you feel tilt creeping up on you, recognize it and make sure it doesn't affect your game. Another great goal is to always play your "A" game. If you are drifting into autopilot and playing suboptimally, correct yourself instantly. Try to be happy in your life. You may have heard the saying, "Attitude is everything". Well, it is true. A lot of poker players are miserable in life. Avoiding this will greatly increase your expectation.

When set a goal, make sure it is one that is not subject to variance. Then, make sure the goal is reasonable and will help you become a better player.

Do Not Pity Yourself

I have heard players, especially young online guys that are known for being smarter than the average person, constantly complain about their luck. First off, if you are a professional poker player, I can almost guarantee you ran at least at neutral EV during the start of your career. In fact, poker players often run really hot when they first start playing, only to later learn that they actually are not great players. This alone should temper the desire to complain about bad luck.

When some people lose a big hand, they get upset and focus on their bad luck. Instead, they should realize they made a +EV play that didn't work out. Losing a hand should not cause pain. It is true that misery loves company. If you aren't miserable, you will have no desire to voice your pain to everyone. In fact, you shouldn't even feel pain.

I instantly lose a level of respect for a player who complains about a bad beat, especially if he does it to get sympathy. We have all lost to unfortunate situations. It happens. I don't view any standard bad beat, such as losing with A-A on an A-7-7 board, as that unlucky. It happens to all of us, so there is no reason to get upset. If you are not prepared to deal with variance, poker may not be the game for you. You will be much happier when you realize you are going to lose hands when you have a lot of equity. If losing doesn't cause you pain, you will have no reason to get upset, which will allow you to play much better poker in the long run.

Be a Good Person

My conscience beats me up when I've done something wrong. I have done enough bad things in my short life to learn that I play much better when I have a clear conscience. I know a few players that constantly do things that I would consider bad, but it appears not to bother them at all. If you don't mind playing while having to worry if someone is thinking about killing you because you just screwed them over, then I guess this section isn't for you. Actually, it is common sense that you should not do bad things.

Once you start living a good life, you can do a few other things to help others to have better lives. First, you can donate money. While I have not donated a huge sum of money, I have donated some. It is always a great feeling to know others are going to have a slightly better life because of my donation. You can also donate your time. There are many great causes out there that need people to help. You can find something you care about and support that cause. You can also give back to other poker players. This book and my online coaching videos are forms of that. Not much makes me happier than to hear someone who has watched my poker videos tell me that because of me, he has made it as a poker player. Doing good things simply makes you feel good. If you feel good, you will play better poker.

Leaks

Poker players, and people in general, would have much more money if they could plug their leaks. These can range from super-expensive meals to drugs. While it is important to spend your money on things you enjoy, spending all your money on any specific thing is usually a bad idea.

The top leak for most professional poker players is probably casino gambling. You have to have some level of degeneracy to be a high-stakes poker player. I mean, you have to be a little crazy to put up $25,000 to play a game for a few days, right? Obviously, levels of degeneracy differ from person to person. Some poker players can play $10 blackjack while they play $10,000 buy-in tournaments. This isn't much of a leak. Some people play $10,000 hands of baccarat when they play $10,000 tournaments. This will keep these players near broke for most of their careers.

Even if you are smart about it, you will lose perhaps 1 percent at casino gambling, which means you will lose $1 for every $100 you bet. While this doesn't look like much, if you play 100 hands per hour at $10,000 each, you can expect to lose $10,000 per hour. That will put a hurt on anyone's bankroll.

Sports betting was my major leak. While I thought my bets had a positive expectation, betting $1,000 per game with an edge of perhaps 0.5 percent will result in huge swings. Unless you are willing to devote $300,000 to a bankroll, you are almost certain to lose a lot of money in any sample of bets that isn't huge. My best advice is to never, and I mean never, play any game a casino offers besides poker. This includes sometimes +EV games like sports betting and blackjack because even if your edge is positive, it won't be most of the time. The simple solution is to stay away.

Another major leak of poker players is partying, drinking and drugs. Lucky for me, my parents taught me from an early age to not drink or do drugs. Also lucky for me, I don't like the loud environments of clubs. Many poker players feel like they are living the cool life by spending $10,000 at a club every other night. While there is nothing wrong with hanging out with your friends and having a drink, it will cause huge problems in every aspect of your life if done to excess. I think most people feel like going to a club is a way to be hip and hang out with friends. Once you get a lot of money, like most poker players, you feel like you can afford to spend a huge amount of money everytime you go out. In the long run, this will cost you a large percentage of your bankroll.

If you can drink in moderation, you should have no problem. But most people can't drink in moderation. As for drugs, putting anything into your body that can kill you is just plain dumb. You should avoid anything that can greatly increase your chance of death. This includes smoking, doing drugs, driving cars really fast, robbing banks, etc. My advice is to not start in the first place.

One final monetary leak is what I will call "living the high life," i.e., having to have the nicest things possible. I do not have a huge house or a super nice car. I do have a fairly nice house and a fairly nice car. Quite a few poker players win a tournament for $1 million and assume they will make $1 million per year for the rest of their lives. They get a loan on a $5 million house, fully expecting to pay it off in 20 years. They find that paying a mortgage is tougher than they thought, especially if it is for a decent amount of their income. The same goes for buying a car, going on vacations or eating nice food. I love great food as much as anyone, and this may be a borderline leak for me. Spending $200 for a meal once every two weeks is basically negligible if you make $20,000 per month. If you eat $200 meals every day, like a few of my friends do, that quickly adds up to $6,000 per month, which is 33 percent of their monthly income. While working hard and making money does allow you to have nice things, make sure you don't live well beyond your means, as your actual salary is hard to predict in poker.

Now, let's talk about leaks that don't actually cost money. Most people call these hobbies. When done in excess, they will suck up numerous hours that you could have spent playing poker. My number one time spender, which I have to constantly monitor, is watching television and playing video games. I group these together because they are both spent sitting in front of the TV. When poker is going poorly for me, I will take a day off and watch a TV series. While this seems harmless, I am losing an entire work day. A few years back, I played no poker for a month and just watched TV. Clearly, that is a problem. While you do need to take breaks from poker, don't become a professional TV watcher. This concept can be applied to pretty much anything that can be done in excess, such as hiking, fishing, sleeping or watching sports.

Learn how to spot leaks in your life. Anything that consumes a lot of your time or money is probably a leak. If you're running to the sports book every day like I used to, placing a bet you don't actually have the bankroll for, you have a leak. Once you find a leak, you have to admit that you have a problem and become determined to plug the leak. You may need to talk to your friends or get professional help if your problem is big enough. There is nothing wrong with asking for help.

It is important to spend your money on things you like and your time on things you enjoy doing. After all, one of the major benefits of playing poker for a living is the freedom to do what you want. However, it is of the utmost importance to preserve your bankroll. Leaks will eventually suck it dry and leave you broke.

Poker is a Numbers Game

If losing a string of hands bothers you, either you need to change your mindset or realize that poker may not be for you. When you play poker, you have to think in terms of your ROI. For example, I used to play $200 sitngos for a living. You can lose $200, or you can win $200, $400 or $800. These look like big numbers, but on average I won around $10 per game. So, if I played 1,000 games, I knew I would win about $10,000 on average. If I played 10 games, I could easily be up or down $2,000. If I wanted consistent results, I had to play a lot of games. So, I tried to play at least 2,000 sitngos every month to ensure that I won consistently each month. In contrast, people who play one or two games per day will have big swings over long periods of time. To deal with this, you have to put in lots of hours and play lots of games.

Poker has huge short-run variance. I have played around 55 WPT tournaments. I have two titles, four final tables and 13 cashes with an ROI right around 900 percent. Does this mean I am the greatest player ever? In the WSOP, I have played around 150 tournaments with one final table, 11 cashes, and a -70 percent ROI. Does this mean I am the worst player ever? My ROI is about 400 percent over all the live tournaments I have played, which means I've gotten back $400 for every $100 I've invested. But if you compare the WSOP and WPT, you see two very different pictures.

The best high-stakes online multi-table tournament players hope to have around an 80 percent ROI, i.e., they expect to win $80 every-time they play a $100 tournament. If they only played two $100 tournaments per day, they would make $160 per day on average, which isn't that much money. They have to play 15 $100 tourna-ments per day, bringing in $1,200, which isn't too shabby.

When you sit down at a tournament, the prize pool shouldn't affect your thinking. Professionals often talk about skipping tournaments because first place is only $300,000, or go well out of their way to play in a tournament with a $5 million prize pool. If your ROI is the same in both tournaments, which may or may not be true, you should play both of them, assuming the travel rake isn't too high. Poker is a numbers game. If you put in a lot of volume, you stand to win at a fairly consistent rate in the long run.

Have a Large Skill Set

There are two main types of poker players: those that play only holdem and those that play every game. I used to be only a holdem player but I have branched out to PLO, PLO8 and the stud games. Holdem players usually play either all forms of holdem or only one type. The types include limit, pot-limit and no-limit, and holdem can also be broken down into tournaments, sitngos and cash games.

If you want to play poker tournaments for a living, you need to know most aspects of holdem. Large buy-in multi-table tournaments usually start you off with 200 big blinds or more, which means that standard middle-stacked tournament theory goes out the window. A deep-stacked tournament starts out basically as a cash game with a little more emphasis on not going broke, since you can't rebuy. It becomes a sitngo when you reach the final table. If you have no sitngo experience, you will encounter situations where you are clueless. At times you will play very short-handed, such as on the money and final-table bubbles, and at the final table. To be a successful tournament player, you need to be a winner at both full-ring and short-handed cash games, sitngos and tournaments.

There is also value, which I admittedly miss, from playing all the other games. Numerous pros think I am crazy for not being adept at the stud games. The only time these skills really come into play is during the WSOP, where tournaments are played in every poker format. Most non-holdem tournaments get a small field, making it significantly easier to win a bracelet, even if you are only break-even against the field. This is why becoming competent at the other games is next on my list of things to do.

It is tough to learn a new game. Once you have plenty of money in your bankroll and can devote some time to learning another game, I see nothing wrong with going for it. I have been spending most of my free time lately learning to play six-handed cash games. My nine-handed game is near optimal but my six-handed play is a little shaky. I am starting to see that six-handed poker has much more variance and, despite what I initially thought, I am actually pretty good at it. Once I feel confident in my short-handed no-limit game, I plan to learn Omaha 8 or better to the best of my ability. I am already fairly competent at it, but would like to be world-class. Spend at least a week playing a new game online, which will force you to learn the fundamentals. You may play your normal game three weeks in a month to pay the bills and devote one week to learning your new game. I suggest you first learn to play holdem, as this is the most played game by far and likely will be for a long time.

Of course, you should learn a game decently well before playing at the level of your regular game. I know a few great no-limit holdem players that have seen a weak player in an Omaha game. They assumed a weak holdem player was also a weak Omaha player, which may or may not be true. They usually got in the game, lost a few buy-ins and quit. Just because there is a bad player in a game does not mean you are better than that bad player or the other pros at the table. Make sure you know a game before playing it for high stakes.

You should always be moving up or branching out, either increasing your hourly rate or your skill set. There is nothing worse than remaining stagnant in the ever-evolving game of poker.

Know the Game You are Playing

When I first started playing live tournaments, it only made sense to play my normal strategy. The problem was that my normal strategy was used to beat sitngo tournaments, not multi-table tournaments. While they both involve no-limit holdem and are played until one person has all the chips, they require different skill sets and strategies. A sitngo strategy is too tight for a large multi-table tournament. You need to make the top 1 percent of the field in a multi-table tournament to make a big score, whereas in a sitngo, you are happy to just get in the top 30 percent. Clearly, you should use different strategies to achieve these goals. You need to know the proper strategy to beat the game you are playing. You certainly would not play seven-card stud as you would no-limit holdem. The same applies to the cash-game and tournament forms of no-limit holdem. Do not assume you know how to play tournaments because you know how to play cash games or sitngos.

Tournaments are quite interesting because you need a large skill set to do well. You must have sound strategies for both deep and short stacks. It is important to put in numerous hours at each form of the game. To improve my game, I put in countless hours at 100-BB cash games, turbo sitngos and heads-up sitngos. Even with all my experience, I still find myself in tricky spots, especially when I have around 40 BBs, as there are basically no games where you play with that stack size. If you work hard at the numerous forms of no-limit holdem, you will be well on your way to beating tournaments.

Play a Game with a Future

While most people enjoy playing no-limit holdem, a few prefer lesser known games like razz or seven-card stud. There is a reason why these games are not as popular as holdem. These games usually require too much skill, causing weaker players to go broke too fast. Other times, the game just isn't enjoyable. A few people only play specific types of games, like pot-limit Omaha sitngos, which run at small levels but never at the higher levels, which is where you have to play to make a living. I suggest you do not play games that do not run at a high level because if you become a winner, your skills will have a fairly low value, whereas the equivalent skill at something like Texas holdem will be worth quite a bit.

At the time of this writing, I see only three viable games to learn. First is no-limit holdem, which is where most of the tournament and cash-game action takes place, and which will likely continue to dominate for a long time to come.

Second is pot-limit Omaha. This game is quickly catching on as the second most popular cash game. Omaha has huge variance. This is normally not good for pros, but it fools the weaker players into thinking they are winners, causing them to stick around for a long time.

The third option is to learn the new eight-game mixed format that has started to run online. It's obviously quite difficult to learn eight games instead of just one. The high-stakes action seems to be headed this way, as the limit and no-limit players all think they have a big enough edge in their preferred game to make up for their disadvantage in the other games. I can tell you, if you are good at PLO and no-limit holdem, you will have an edge in these games, even if you are a small loser in the limit games.

Play in Soft Games

Decent poker players often try to make a living at games that are just a little too tough for them. There is a level that each competent poker player can beat. I, for example, can beat basically any tournament, whereas one of my students may only be able to beat $500 tournaments. If they play higher than $500 tournaments, they should expect to lose money. Another example would be if you are the tenth best cash game player in the world and you are playing with the nine people that are better than you. Even though you are tenth in the world, you should expect to lose. On the other hand, you would have a huge edge if you decided to play with the 101st to 109th best players.

There is one main reason to play in games you can't beat. If you can beat $50 tournaments, you will probably break even or be only a tiny loser at $100 tournaments, which makes playing them only a tiny mistake in terms of dollar equity. Playing these games still may be

+EV because you will hopefully learn from the better players. There are cheaper forms of practice, such as reading books or watching training videos, but we all would like to move up sometime. Basically, you should play in games you can beat if you want to make money, and play in tougher games if you want to gain experience. Just realize that playing in those tougher games will cost you equity.

The Long Run

People talk about the long run in poker, but few know what they are talking about. When playing live poker, you can frequently tell who cares about the long run and who is short-term result-oriented. People who get upset about a bad beat are usually result-oriented. Players who realize poker is a long-run game are usually the biggest winners.

Players say things like, "I got all-in with ace-king and lost to ace-queen. Either poker is rigged or I am the most unlucky person ever." I hope you see how this is just silly. I hear players say, "I had a losing month. I must be pretty bad at the game." Even world-class players have losing months. I have had two losing years out of six in live tournaments, and I play more hands than 99 percent of poker players. My results are a bit skewed because my two losing years were -$150,000 and two of my winning years were +$1.5 million.

If you don't play often, you should expect long losing streaks. I may play 150 live poker tournaments over the course of a year. While this may sound like a lot, if I grinded online, I would play 150 tournaments in a few days. You will reach the long run much faster online than live. A good sample size for tournaments is around 2,000 games. Obviously, the number of players in each tournament will affect this figure. If you play sitngos, I suggest you play around 5,000 games at a given level before you determine your ROI. For cash games, you probably need to play 200,000 hands before you claim your win rate. As you can see, even my six years of playing live tournaments isn't what I would consider a decent sample size. If I don't have a representative sample size, most people will be nowhere close.

You are going to get bad beats over and over again throughout your poker career. It seems like most people think they are 100-percent to win when they get it all-in with A-K vs. A-Q and get upset when they lose. When you are 70 percent to win, you are only going to win 70 percent of the time, not 100 percent. Also, when you get all-in with 30-percent equity, you are going to win sometimes. You should not feel bad when you suck out. When you lose 10 times in a row when you are 70 percent to win, you must realize it is just variance. Variance is what makes poker profitable. If the weak players never won, they would quickly stop playing. It is actually the bad beats, which so many players complain about, that make poker such a profitable game. The sooner you realize this, the sooner you will be on your way to being a great player.

I should also mention the silly idea of streaks, as they are really just variance. Sometimes, you are going to win 10 sessions in a row. This does not mean you should move up in stakes, unless your bankroll dictates it. Also, if you win a few hands in a row at the poker table, it does not mean you should try to see the flop with your next hand, no matter what it is. Variance causes the cards to do funny things sometimes. You only see these streaks in hindsight. All you can do is play each hand optimally. Spend more time paying attention to the game and less trying to find that mythical hot streak.

Bankroll

Bankroll management has been the downfall of many great players. Two of my students failed because they refused to listen to me about bankroll management. I tend to put a little too much emphasis on survival because I have no way to refill my bankroll if I go broke. Note that your bankroll is not all the money you have to your name. It is the money you have set aside to play poker. I suggest that every serious player set aside at least six months' worth of money, aside from his bankroll, to pay bills. There are a few times, however, when you can gamble quite a bit more than most people consider.

To make things simple, I would always keep 100 buy-ins for tournaments, 50 buy-ins for full-ring cash games and 80 buy-ins for 6-max cash games. Having any less than that greatly increases your risk of ruin. If you are playing for a living and have no way to refill your bankroll if you go broke, you should keep much more than I suggest. You will need an even larger bankroll as you move to higher-stakes games, where your ROI will be lower. You will also need a larger bankroll if you play a game with higher variance, like pot-limit Omaha. Again, if you do not mind going broke, feel free to lower the numbers, but not too much. For example, I suggest a $10,000 bankroll if you want to play $1-$2 no-limit full-ring games with a buy in of $200. This may seem absurdly high, but it is necessary to avoid going broke.

The main time bankroll management goes out the window is when you can play in a tournament full of weak players. This happens every week in the large Sunday tournaments online and during the WSOP. If you normally play $2 tournaments, there is a $10 tournament on PokerStars that is one of the best tournaments of the week. If you normally play $50 tournaments, each site has a huge $200 or so buy-in tournament that is full of online qualifiers. The World Series of Poker Main Event is a great example of a tournament that every competent player should try to attend. If you win, not only do you get a huge amount of prize money, but you are a lock to be sponsored by an online site, which could easily be worth more than the prize money. If you normally play $1,000 tournaments live, it would be criminal to not play the $10,000 WSOP main event. Basically, you should look to play tournaments where the average player is much weaker than normal for that buy-in level.

The other time you may want to gamble is when you win a satellite into a big tournament. Clearly, if you have $30,000 to your name and you win your way into a $10,000 buy in tournament, it would usually be wise to sell the seat and add the $10,000 to your bankroll. However, if that extra $10,000 will not really change things for you, it may be worth playing in a large tournament because if you do well, an extra $1 million would be life-changing. Make sure you have adequate practice at live poker before jumping into a large buy-in tournament. If you are -EV in the game, which most satellite winners are, I would always suggest selling the seat and continuing to play your standard game.

Another situation occurs when cash games that are higher than your normal game are super soft. This happens frequently at the $200/$400 no-limit cash games online, where successful business-people want to play with the best poker players in the world. If you normally play $25/50 no-limit and have a $2 million bankroll you have grinded up over the past three years, it would be criminal to not play the $500/$1,000 game when there is a very bad player at the table, even if you are slightly worse than the other four professionals at the table. Basically, you will have about a 60-percent chance of winning. Do not be scared to lose a few buy-ins. I have watched great players lose one buy-in and then quit even though they are still very +EV in a game.

Let's talk now about how to grow your bankroll. If you have $1,000 and want to play tournaments, you should be playing $10 tournaments. If you run well for a while and grow your bankroll to $2,000, you can play $20 tournaments. It is fine to move up a level before you have 100 buy-ins. Once you get up to around $2,500, give yourself about 10 buyins to play $30 games. If they go well, you will move up faster. As you move up, so will your bankroll requirement, as the games will be tougher and your ROI lower. Once you get up to around $5,000, you can start playing the $50 tournaments, but you shouldn't become a regular at the $100 games until you have around $12,000. You should usually move down a limit when you have only 50 buy-ins at your current limit. So, if you are playing $20 games and your bankroll gets down to $1,000, move down to $10 games. Don't be ashamed or embarrassed about this. Everyone goes through a stretch when they are forced to move down. The players that refuse to move down when things go poorly are the ones that end up broke.

Downswings

It has been said that the next best thing to winning at gambling is losing at gambling. Whoever said that clearly did not play poker for a living. Downswings either build a player's character or break him. If you play long enough, you will eventually hit a stretch when you run worse than you ever thought possible.

Professional poker players often run hot at the start of their career. If they had run poorly, they would have gone broke and never become pros. I went through a yearlong downswing when I first played live poker. It seemed like I lost everytime I got all-in. I lost about $150,000 of the money I had won grinding sitngos online, which was quite depressing. I would have gone broke at live tournaments if I hadn't started with a huge bankroll. I kept my head up and eventually started winning. I often see a player launch his career by winning a tournament and eventually run poorly, losing most of his winnings and finally going broke.

While downswings are quite common, most players never learn to accept them. You must realize that you are not going to win at poker tournaments everytime, or even most of the time. You will experience long periods when you win nothing. I eventually realized that if I won all the time, the weaker players would never win. If there were no weak players we would all be out of a job.

My friend Mike Matusow often talks about the rising stars of poker getting humbled. This is what happens when someone runs overly hot for a year or so and then goes on a multiple-year downswing. It seems like there is a new star in the poker world every year that later fizzles out and goes broke. Most of these players are not as good as they think, which gives them the false confidence necessary to play in the biggest games in the world. They usually end up failing. The true test of time is how a player handles the roughest times in his career, when he fails to win for a long period of time. I have been lucky to survive two fairly large downswings. If you realize that downswings will eventually come, you can prepare for the drought.

When I am on a large downswing, I try to do things I enjoy. This could be working out, reading books, hiking, watching TV, talking to friends about poker hands or taking a vacation. I generally have little problem with tilt, so I just keep playing my normal poker schedule. If you have even the slightest problem with tilt, I suggest you take a little time off and refocus on playing optimally. Many players remain in downswings much longer than they should because when they run poorly, they start playing poorly. When you are losing, you should not alter your style in an attempt to get even or lose less. Just play your normal game and keep calm. Assuming you play optimally, which may or may not be the case during a long losing stretch, you will find yourself winning again in no time.

The Rake

Poker is a zero-sum game, which means a dollar is won for every dollar lost. However, you will pay some sort of rake basically anywhere you play poker. This is usually a small percentage of each pot or tournament buy-in. Because of this, only a small number of poker players win a significant amount in the long run.

The rake in a tournament is usually a percentage of the buy-in, which generally decreases as the buy-in increases. For example, the standard $50 tournament in Vegas is $50 + $15, with the $15 going to the house. The standard $500 tournament charges $40 rake and the standard $10,000 tournament charges $300. The $3 online sitngos charge $.40, which is pretty high by online standards. The $6 games charge $.50. I suggest you start at the $6 level because of this much lower rake.

If you play cash games, you need to know how much the house is going to charge. For example, you pay 5 percent of each pot, up to $4 per hand, in most Vegas $2/$5 no-limit games. You are expected to tip the dealer around $1 when you win a pot, so the total rake comes out to around $5 per big hand you win and $3 for a small pot. Once you move higher than $2/$5 no-limit, you usually pay a fixed amount per half hour to sit at the table. At $5/$10 no-limit, it is $6 per half hour, so you pay $12 per hour plus dealer tips, which will come out to around $18 per hour. The rake is uncapped in most European countries. I played at a place in Europe that charged 3 percent per hand at $10/$20 no-limit. There were probably two pots per hour where the house took $150 or more. Even though the players were awful, I thought I would not be a huge winner simply because of the rake.

There is also travel rake, i.e., expenses for traveling to play poker. I paid $5,000 for hotel rooms and airplane flights on that European trip. That means I had to have at least 50-percent ROI to break even, which very few poker players will have. This is one of the main reasons I rarely travel overseas to play in tournaments. The rake is just too high. However, if the players are much worse overseas, to the point where your ROI goes up more than the rake, it becomes +EV to travel to those games. A great example of this is the World Series of Poker. Basically every professional poker player in the world comes to Vegas each year to play in these events because there are more weak players in one place than any other time of the year. Note also that you have to spend quite a bit of time traveling to these events. You could spend that time playing poker or enjoying life.

Recently there were two sets of tournaments going on at the same time, one in London and the other in America. There were around $50,000 worth of events in London over a month. In America there were $10,000 worth of events over a two-week period. It would cost $7,000 to go to London for the month. The cost of staying in America was $1,000, as all hotel rooms were comped. Staying in America meant I could see my family for a week, as they lived near one of the tournaments. I also needed to sit down and spend some quality time writing this book, which couldn't be done if I went to London.

I estimated I would have a 50-percent ROI in London because the tournaments had tough fields and I would be playing on a poor sleep schedule, for a profit of $25,000 minus the $7,000 travel rake, giving me $18,000 profit for the month. In America I would have perhaps a 150-percent ROI; the fields were super soft because most good players were in London. I would make $14,000 minus the $1,000 travel rake, for a $14,000 profit with the added benefits of seeing my family, not having to change sleep schedules and getting to work on my book. After running the numbers, staying in America made the most sense.

Going to London could have been the correct play had I highly valued going to London or playing big events with great players. If two choices have a similar ROI, I tend to go with the one that will make me happiest.

So, what can you do about the rake? If you play online, you can get rakeback, which returns a percentage of your rake, usually around 30 percent. When I grinded sitngos, I would regularly get $10,000 per month in rakeback. When you play a lot of $200 + $15 sitngos, it adds up fast. I would usually win $10,000 per month from playing the games and get another $10,000 from rakeback. If you play in casinos, you can ask for a discounted room rate (the poker rate) which is usually no more than $100 per night even at the nicest casinos. You can also ask for food comps. Most poker rooms have reward programs that give you $2 or so per hour while you are at the poker table. If you talk to, and tip, the tournament directors, they will almost always hook you up. Tournament directors can also get you cheap package deals for events where few players are expected.

Despite the rake, poker is a very profitable game. But do everything in your power to keep the rake low. A penny saved really is a penny earned in this business.

Hourly Rate

I've always been lax about figuring out my hourly rate at tournaments because I know they are worth my time. If you are not sure, you need to keep records on the hours you play and figure out what you're making on an hourly basis.

Poker tournaments, especially live ones, take a long time. For the big ones, you often have to fly across America the day before the event and fly home afterwards. Be sure to include this time in your calculations, especially if you tend to waste time while on an airplane. You should also count time that you spend driving or studying tournaments, as you could spending that time doing something else. This is a lot to keep track of, but you need to do it if you are serious about figuring out your earn rate. Most poker players would be shocked at how little they actually make once they add all this together.

Suppose you are a decent cash-game player and can make $100 per hour at a local casino with no time investment except a 15-minute drive to and from the casino each day. Despite this, you want to play tournaments. Maybe you value being on TV or having the recognition of your peers. There are many things you should consider before making the switch. You estimate you could switch to tournaments right now and make $50 per hour. You also think it will take about 50 hours of studying tournaments to increase your earnings rate to $100 per hour. So, you have to give away 50 hours to gain this skill. You can spend your free time, away from your normal $100-per-hour cash game, to study tournament poker. You can watch less television or sleep a little less. You can take one day off from your cash game every week, giving up about $800 in equity, and use that time to play and study tournaments. You can spend perhaps four hours of that time playing tournaments and four hours studying, which means you will lose $600 in equity, because you will profit $200 from tournaments, and you will get closer to being able to make $100 per hour from tournaments. You don't have to totally change your life overnight. Try to find creative ways to play your normal game while learning a new one.

Suppose you have a job you don't really enjoy that pays $50 per hour for an unlimited number of hours. You can play poker, a game you love, and make $40 per hour. Finally, your favorite thing in the world to do is to relax on the beach, which you can do whenever you want. You have to find the optimal balance between dollar EV and happiness EV. Clearly, you can't relax on the beach all the time if you need to make money. If you can't quit your job and get it back later, you should probably keep your job. You also need to consider your bankroll and savings when determining how much you should play poker. Also, is the enjoyment you get from poker worth losing $10 per hour compared to your job? You have to answer all these questions to determine how to spend your life. Think things out clearly; otherwise you could end up in a mess.

I make some fairly poor decisions in these situations. About once every six months, I am randomly at a casino where there is a small buy-in poker tournament starting soon. The most recent was a $500 tournament at a local casino that was going on at the same time as the WSOP. I had no more WSOP events that day, so I figured I might as well play this tournament for fun. I failed to take numerous things into account. First, would I be happy if I won? Probably not, as first place was around $6,000. Would I be sad if I lost? Probably, because losing is never fun. Did I have other things to take care of? Yes. I had spent the previous two weeks playing WSOP events and I had numerous errands to perform. Would going to bed early and relaxing at home help me in the future WSOP events? Yes, because I was worn out from playing constantly for the last two weeks. All in all, playing this $500 tournament was a huge leak even though I made about $800 in equity from it. Just because something will make you money does not mean it is the correct choice.

Spots You Should Not Pass Up

Situations come up all the time in everyday life that are either slightly -EV, neutral EV, or highly +EV. A great example is when you are lost while driving and trying to get somewhere quickly. Say you are at a spot where you can either go left or right. Unfortunately for you, you are not sure which way to go. Fortunately, there is a store right at the fork in the road where you can ask for directions. You can guess the correct route, possibly going well out of your way, or you can take two minutes to ask for directions. Giving up two minutes to ensure you are going the right way is a much better play than losing 15 minutes by going the wrong way half the time. You can express it in a simple equation.

There are many spots in poker where you can gather free information that can be quite helpful. Say you have the nuts and you think your opponent said, "I'm all-in," but are unsure what, if anything, was said. In this spot, I will wait a few seconds for the dealer to react. If the dealer does nothing, I will just sit there. If the dealer looks in my direction, I will calmly ask the dealer what the player said. If the dealer confirms that he is all-in, I will obviously call as fast as possible, but if the dealer says that the player said nothing, I will continue to wait for my opponent to take his action. The other, much worse option in this situation is to quickly say, "Call," and turn my hand face-up. Clearly, if the other player has taken no action, you have just given up the opportunity to win an extra bet on the river.

Don't pass up an offer from a much better player to help you improve your game. Do whatever you can to get as much information from him as possible. If you are around poker players a lot, someone may offer to back you in a game much larger than your regular game. Take these opportunities if you are not giving up much by skipping your regular game, as you can only gain from them, ignoring the problems that sometimes arise between backers and the players they bankroll. This is similar to situations where you take a shot at a larger cash game, except your only options now are to break even or win.

Players often get up and walk around while a tournament is in progress, choosing to not even look at the hands being dealt to them. It should be clear that if you are better than your opponents, you should be playing and not walking around, unless you have tilt issues that are resolved by walking around or are dealing with business that is more important than the tournament. When you are away from the table, you not only miss hands that you would normally play, but you also miss watching everyone else play their hands. A wealth of knowledge is available just by paying attention to the action at the table. You may see an obvious tell that could later gain you lots of chips, or you may miss the fact that someone is on tilt and ready to give away his stack. I almost always show up on time to a tournament because of this.

I lost with A-A, K-K and A-K within the first 30 minutes of a $25,000 WPT main event at Bellagio. Because we started with 1,000 BBs, it only cost me one-fourth of my stack, but I was still mildly tilting. I decided to get up and grab some food. The blinds were very small, so blinding off for an hour was basically irrelevant. The only thing I missed was the opportunity to pick up tells, which I would have a hard time doing, given my mental state. So, while being away from the table can be acceptable in some situations, they are few and far between.

In both poker and life, look for situations that cost you nothing but can pay off greatly. In my opinion, the only thing better than usually being +EV is always being +EV.

Other Sources of Income

Every professional poker player should find ways to make money outside of the game. This can come from any source, as long as it is fairly consistent. Most of us have bills, and if you can have enough income every month to pay those, you can concentrate much better on poker because there will be less pressure to win.

Quite a few players are endorsed by online poker sites. The deals these players get range from great to terrible. Sadly, most of the deals aren't worth too much money and if they are, most players don't have the skills to make them pay off. A few top players get a chunk of money each year to play tournaments. Clearly this is ideal because you don't have to pay for buy-ins, making any cashes pure profit. These deals only go to players that the general public loves, which excludes almost everyone.

Another way to bring in income is from coaching. I love coaching because it brings in variance-free money and allows me to help players to improve their game. Make sure you know what you are teaching;

you don't want to take someone's money and give them incorrect information.

I've invested in real estate each time I've won a big tournament. Now, I bring in a little money each month through rental houses. I hired a management company for all the hands-on work, so all I do is collect a rent check each month. You can also do this by investing in businesses. Make sure you know what you are investing in before putting all your money into it. You could lose money on your investment, and you risk locking up a large portion of your bankroll, which could prevent you from playing your normal games.

However you decide to bring in extra money, make sure there is a low risk of loss. You don't want to put a lot of money in something, fully expecting a nice monthly check, only to lose it all. Be creative when finding outside income sources. I am sure there are great opportunities that I have never thought about. Make sure you still have time to play poker, as some businesses require a lot of time. Finally, make sure you don't have to worry about where the money comes from. A bad day in business could easily sink into your mind, causing you to play bad poker.

Have a Retirement Fund

Unlike people in regular jobs, poker players have to set up their own retirement funds. Most of us do not want to have to play poker until we die. In order to retire, you need to start saving now. Every year, I put as much money as I can into my retirement fund. This money is taxed at a much lower rate than normal, which reduces my tax bill. As an aside, pay your taxes. Failing to do so will catch up to you at some point.

Your poker abilities will likely start to diminish around age 60. At this point, you will either have to move down, which means you will make less money, or you can retire. If you have $5 million in your retirement fund, which isn't too tough to do if you are putting $40,000 towards your retirement every year, you can retire and live the rest of your life doing basically whatever you want. If instead of putting money into a retirement account, you spend it on partying; you will have to work until the day you die. This all goes back to planning ahead. If you plan ahead, you will do much better than everyone else.

You should probably avoid keeping your money in dollars, at least for now, because the U.S. government is currently printing dollars as fast as it can. This decreases the value of your dollars. Suppose there are one million dollars in the world and a gallon of gas costs $1. Each dollar is worth one gallon. If the government prints one million more dollars, the price of a gallon of gas will almost certainly rise to $2. Your dollars lose value as more enter the marketplace. For this reason, at least under current economic conditions, I suggest you invest your money in commodities, like oil and food, or precious metals, like gold and silver. For the foreseeable future, people will drive cars and have to eat. As for gold and silver, there is very little left on the planet that is yet to be mined, meaning all that we currently have on earth is all there ever will be. Also, silver is constantly used in numerous industries. Did you know there is actually less silver on earth than gold now? This is because we have used it up. Eventually, the price of silver has to rise simply because we are running out of it. In a year, these suggestions could easily be obsolete, so make sure you are well educated before you invest your money.

Coaching

I suggest you hire a coach, especially if you are actively trying to improve your game, which you should be. Your coach should be someone you respect that plays at a slightly higher level than you. Obviously, your coach should be a winning player. I have had at least four coaches, as well as numerous mentors. The difference between a coach and a mentor, in my opinion, is that the coach spends a lot of time with you working on your game, whereas a mentor is more like a friend who will answer any questions you have. I also discuss concepts with numerous poker friends all the time.

I have spent around $20,000 on coaching and it has been well worth it. One of my first coaching experiences was at sitngos. I was a solid winner at the $200 sitngos but my win rate had started declining. This was mostly due to the weaker players going broke. I had to improve in order to continue playing the highest buy-in games. I paid a player $5,000 for 10 hours of coaching. Even though his advice was basically "push more and call less," it was well worth it. Even if I increased my ROI by just 1 percent, or $2 per game, I would pay off the coaching over 2,500 games, which was how many I played every month. You can pay a large sum of money for coaching, but given the number of games you play, the money is almost insignificant.

One of my other coaching experiences was in preparation for the NBC heads-up tournament the first year I played it. Even though I was a small winner at $1,000 buy-in heads-up games online over a large sample, I hired one of the best thinkers in the game to help me, even though he normally played the $100 heads-up game. We worked on my game quite a bit and I ended up taking fifth place out of 64 people, cashing for $75,000. While it is tough to tell if spending $2,000 for his coaching was worth it, as I might have taken fifth place without it, notice that I break even if I increase my ROI by 10 percent of the $20,000 buy-in. Even if I break even on this tournament, I have this knowledge to use in the future, making hiring a coach an easy decision.

The last coaching experience I will mention here was with Bill Seymour, an older player that used to regularly play on the tournament circuit. Bill was my first coach, and we continue to talk from time to time. He helped me with my tilt issues, which plagued me in my younger days. He also helped me think about life and poker in a way that helped me to become less emotionally involved. He didn't teach me too much about the technical aspects of poker, but he helped me with the mental side of the game.

I have had a wide range of coaches, and if I had to do it again, I would go out of my way to find more. Spending a little money to get a winning player's perspective is almost always worth it.

I recently started coaching players. I had always shied away from coaching because I didn't think it was worth my time, but it has been a rewarding experience. I'm happy anytime a student tells me he won something because of the instruction I gave him. Also, when you coach someone, you learn a lot about your own game because you are forced to talk out your thought process. Sometimes I will find myself saying something that doesn't make much sense; I quickly correct myself and learn about leaks in my own game. Consider coaching a few hours each week once you get to a level where you feel the information you could give a player would improve his quality of life.

Many "coaches" are actually losing players that prey on unsuspecting players that will do anything to improve their game. At Bellagio, I was playing a $10/$20 no-limit cash game one night and an older player was talking to another player at the table about how he was a poker coach. He then min-raised A-A before the flop out of his 50-BB stack, which was laughable right off the bat because most good players like to have at least a semi-deep stack in a soft no-limit game. Three players called and the flop came 9♣-8♣-2♠. Everyone checked to the coach, who bet 4 BBs. The big blind check-raised all-in and the coach instantly called. The big blind had 9♠-8♠ and busted the coach. The coach went nuts on the guy, telling him how bad his call was before the flop with 9♠-8♠, and stormed out of the room.

Clearly, this guy is not someone you want helping you with your game.

When looking for a coach, find someone you can verify is a winner, and talk to some of his past students. If someone is a new coach, unless he is an excellent player, you should generally shy away from him because a lot of poker players can play well but can't explain their thought process. There are also numerous sites online where coaches post ads. In general, I only get coaching from people I know are good. A great coach usually doesn't need to post ads because his schedule is full. Ask a past student what he likes about the coach and what the coach did to improve his game. The most important thing is to confirm that the coach is actually good at poker. Paying a fraud to coach you is a huge mistake that could make your game worse.

There are many training sites on the internet with videos in which great players explain how they play poker. Even if you can afford a private coach, I suggest you sign up to a few of these sites and watch videos that pertain to the game you are trying to learn. I watch around 90 minutes of training videos everyday. I also own and operate a training site, www.FloatTheTurn.com, where I teach students how to win at basically every form of tournament poker.

Do Not Loan Money

When it comes to loaning money, the poker world is unlike any other. Most poker players constantly loan and borrow money. This is usually because it is tough to get large amounts of cash from one place to another. Some players loan money to other players simply because they don't know how to say "No." Making a lot of loans for small amounts will quickly add up if you fail to collect.

I was recently in a tournament when a player that was clearly trying to scrounge up enough money to enter stood behind a player at my table while he was in a hand. The player lost the pot and the guy asked him for $500. He was told to go away. He came back about 30 minutes later and told the player that refused him that he had come up with enough to play the event and he hoped he got to bust him. The player later told the table that the guy asking for money owed him $10,000. He also said he barely knew anything about the guy but he saw him around a lot. While this may be enough for some people to loan someone $10,000, it is not nearly enough for me.

I have been pretty lucky when loaning money. I have loaned out a significant amount of money twice and gotten it back both times. I have made a few smaller loans and failed to collect on about half of those. Loaning money is a terrible idea. Some players say that they have to be willing to loan money if they ever want to get a loan themselves. While this may be true, if you manage your bankroll well, you should never need a loan.

The only time I need a loan is when I hear about an event and can't get to the bank or my box at Bellagio. I count on a close group of friends to front me the money. I am always available to front money for them as well. All these friends are in great financial shape and we all pay back the money as soon as possible. Once you know you can trust someone, lending him small amounts for short periods of time is never a problem. However, it takes a lot to gain my trust, and only about six players truly have it.

This situation also comes up online because most poker players don't like keeping a large sum of money online. It is not uncommon for a player to lose his bankroll online. From time to time, someone I barely know will get in touch with me right before a tournament starts and ask me to send him money, saying he will pay me back next time he sees me. Unless he is in my close group of friends, he has no shot at getting money from me. There's no problem at all if he wants to give me money in person and then have me send it online. Unless I have cash in hand, I never send money to anyone except my group of close friends.

I may seem a little stingy with my money, but it keeps me from just handing it to someone else. If you plan your poker trips well and keep track of your bankroll, you should rarely need a loan. If you never need a loan, you should probably never give one.

Find Ways to Solve Problems

Throughout life and poker, you will run into problems. The smart people always find solutions while everyone else is complaining. Everytime I find a much better play than everyone else, it makes me happy because I know I just gained some equity.

The room where the WSOP is played is known to be very cold. This year they made it even colder. I would estimate that some sections were around 45 degrees Fahrenheit. Players were constantly complaining to the floor person, asking him to warm up the room, which he apparently could not do. Instead of complaining, I put on my jacket, which I took with me because I knew it was going to be cold, and I ordered a hot tea, which tends to keep me warm. While everyone else was shivering and complaining, I was playing my "A" game.

Another problem occurs at most Bellagio tournaments, where you can only buy into tournaments with chips. This is done to keep tournament registration lines short, and probably also to induce players to keep their money in Bellagio chips, in hopes that they will gamble more. This results in a huge line at the main cage to convert cash into chips just before a tournament starts. Most players stand in line for up to 30 minutes. They fail to realize that there is more than one place at Bellagio to change cash into chips. The poker room has a cage where this can be done, and there is never a line. When I know there is going to be a line at the main cage, my first stop is the poker room cage.

At some casinos, where there is only one cage or I don't know the layout, I may be forced to wait in a long line to convert chips to cash. When this happens, I watch poker videos on my iPhone instead of standing around doing nothing. I absolutely hate wasting time, so I use that time doing productive things, like studying poker.

All this really boils down to is thinking outside the box. If you run into a problem, instead of complaining about it, try to fix it. If you can't fix it, find ways to deal with it.

Differences Between Live and Online Poker

At every tournament I seem to hear a debate as to whether online or live poker is tougher. Here is the answer. Online is significantly tougher than live poker at an equivalent buy-in. This is because people play for much more money live than online. The smallest tournament you will find in most major casinos will have a buy-in of around $65. The smallest you will find online is one cent. Those playing purely for fun play much smaller online than live. In general, a $65 live tournament will be about as tough as a $10 tournament online.

I am sure you have heard players complain that they can't beat online poker. This is because they do not play a fundamentally sound game. When you play live poker, you can actually play much worse because the average $50 player live is much worse than his online counterpart. These players also lose faster online because they can play much more quickly than they do live. You can easily play numerous tournaments per day online whereas you can only play one or two live. Because of this, losing streaks feel more brutal online.

There are a few other differences. First, you have fewer reads online. When playing live, you can read your opponent's tells. Online, you only have timing tells and bet-sizing tells. This means you have to play a fundamentally sound game online, whereas you can get away with playing suboptimally live if you read players well. The blinds usually increase faster in online tournaments, forcing you to gamble sooner. Always know the structure of a tournament before you play it. You don't have to study every level, but know about how fast you need to gamble in order to have a chance to win.

You can also multi-table online. This will usually increase the win rate of a winning player, but it will take concentration away from any individual table. If you get to where you can play 24 tables at a time, as I often do, you will find yourself playing on autopilot. In live poker, you only have to pay attention to one table, and you should always be gathering reads on players. Again, reads matter less in online poker. You play more hands per hour online. This makes it easier to tilt because you can lose hands more often. If it only takes three losing hands in 30 minutes to make you tilt off your stack, you will do so much more often online than live.

I suggest you start online before playing live because it will force you to learn fundamentally sound play. You will also get many more hands of experience per hour than at live poker. The only problem you will have when transitioning to live poker is learning how to gather reads, which will come with time. If you can beat the tougher games online, you should have no problem beating live poker, even at much higher stakes than you normally play online.

Online Tournaments

Unlike live tournaments, you can play numerous online tournaments at a time, which means you have to pay attention to your stack size on each table, as well as how deep-stacked you are in each event. In the higher buy-in online tournaments, ranging from $100 to $1,000, you will usually face very tough competition, similar to a $10,000 live event. If you are going to be an online tournament professional, you had better know how to play technically sound poker.

Every Sunday, basically every online site runs satellites to a large buy-in event. These create hugely profitable situations. Satellites are God's way of giving back to professional poker players, as it allows players into large-buy-in tournaments when they have no business playing in them. If you have a $7,000 bankroll, I see no problem at all in playing one of these $200 events every Sunday. If you run hot for 16 hours, you can walk away $250,000 richer.

I play Sunday tournaments about twice per month. When I play on Sunday, I tend to play every $100 or higher buy-in event or higher across the major sites. Playing only one or two events is usually a waste of time. In fact, I would venture to say it is tough to ever make it in the long run playing online tournaments if you only play one or two tables at a time. I guess if you don't really care about making money and are playing purely for fun, feel free to play one table, but if you are playing poker to make money, you need to play as many games as possible. Failing to do this is giving away too much equity.

How to Multi-Table

The biggest advantage of online poker is the ability to play more than one table at a time. When I first played poker, my friend Dave "Raptor" Benefield introduced me to the concept of playing more than one table at a time, and I gave it a try. At the time, the sites would only let you play four tables at a time, which I quickly mastered. If you win $30 per hour per table, you will win $120 per hour if you play four at a time, assuming playing more tables does not discount your win rate. This is a pretty easy way to get a hefty raise. Eventually the online sites allowed us to play 16 tables at a time, which gave us even a bigger raise. Your win rate per table will start to drop off at this point. Suppose you normally have a 10-percent ROI in sitngos while playing four tables but only a 5-percent ROI when playing 16 tables. If you play $10 games, you will make $4 per hour 4-tabling, assuming you play one set of games per hour, and $8 per hour while 16-tabling. Despite winning half as much per table, 16-tabling clearly makes more money.

I have taught numerous students. Some were capable of multi-tabling as soon as I met them and some required a lot of work. If you are used to playing one table at a time, try to play two the next time and stick with that for around a week. At that point, you can add a third table and play that for a week. Next, add a fourth table, and so on. When you play multiple tables, once you make your action on a table, you can't sit there and watch. You have to move your focus to another table, where the action will be on you.

I suggest you tile your tables, which will make it easier to pay attention to each one. When you tile your tables, you will have one table in each corner of your monitor, with no tables overlapping. Once you exceed nine tables, cascading them, which is overlapping the tables starting with the first table in the top-left corner of your monitor and the last at the bottom-right corner, is probably a bit easier if you are playing on one monitor. You can still tile them if you have multiple monitors. If you put in enough time, multi-tabling will become second nature. When I play poker online now, I almost always play at least six tables at a time, and that is barely enough to keep my attention.

If you get accustomed to playing a huge number of tables at a time, you may find live poker boring. I combat this by making it a point to pay attention to every detail of the table. I am constantly updating everyone's stack size in my head and trying to pick up tells. If your brain can focus on 16 tables at a time online, it can focus on every aspect of your live poker table, which in time will make you a strong live player.

It Takes a Year to Adjust to Live Poker

Every year a fresh batch of 21-year-old online players think they will take the poker world by storm. Most go home with their tails between their legs. They may be great online, but they fail to adjust.

Things went terribly when I turned 21 and moved from online to live poker. Plays I would make online simply did not work in the live arena. I would assume a player was weak, try to bluff him off his hand and be called down by a set. Player's ranges are different in live poker. Failure to adjust to this is why online players fail at live poker.

You can pick up tells on opponents at live poker, and they can pick up tells on you. Most online players think tells are overrated. They act with their normal mannerisms and think it's impossible to give away useful information. This is the main reason why I like playing with young online players. While they take aggressive lines, which is normally good, they are huge tell boxes, so it is easy to know when they have a weak or strong hand. If I know they are bluffing, I will make a hand like middle pair and call down. These young players usually go crazy when I bust them with a weak hand, wondering how I made the big call. They tell me how far I was behind their range and how I was spewing equity by calling. They fail to realize that their range was made up entirely of bluffs. When you know someone is bluffing 100 percent of the time, it is pretty easy to call down with middle pair.

Online players also have a problem focusing while playing only one table. They get bored when they go from playing 1,000 hands per hour to 30, allowing them to get fancy and spew off their chips. They are missing the forest because of the trees. You only play 30 hands per hour, but a huge amount of information is conveyed every hand. Learning everyone's mannerisms and playing styles takes as much concentration as playing 24 tables at a time, in my opinion. They fail to acknowledge all this information.

Hopefully, after reading this short chapter, the online players will avoid the traps I fell into. It took me an entire year to figure out these things. Maybe now they will only lose for a month instead of a year.

Know How to Play Short-handed

Nine or ten people play at a table in most major tournaments. While you should be able to play well at a full table, you also must be able to play with fewer people at the table. The deeper you get in a tournament, the fewer people will be at your table, meaning you will have to play short-handed. You will usually be shorthanded when playing for the most money during a tournament. Some examples are on the final-table bubble, from 11 players to 10, the TV final-table bubble, from seven to six, and for the title, from two to one.

There are times when I am sitting at a good table in a tournament, maybe with one other professional and eight weak players. We will lose a weaker player and the professional will get a floor person to bring someone to fill that seat as soon as possible. I suggest you keep quiet and keep the table a little short. Gaining an extra bad player doesn't do much for you, as the table is still weak, whereas your equity will be greatly diminished if you gain a professional player. In this spot, if the replaced player is a pro, there will be three pros and seven amateurs, or 30 percent pros, and if it is an amateur, there will be two pros and eight amateurs, or 20 percent pros. If you just leave the seat empty, there will be two pros and seven amateurs, or 22 percent pros. You are much better off taking the 22 percent than gambling on getting another amateur.

It also pays to be good at short-handed poker when a bad player wants action in a cash game but doesn't want to wait for a seat to open in a full game. When you see this situation arise, offer to start a new table with the weak player, in which case you will be the only one with the opportunity to take his money. You may be quickly joined by other players, but that is still not too bad. You just want to play as many hands as possible with the weak player, giving you a great shot to gain lots of equity.

There are many ways to practice short-handed poker, and playing online might be the best. While the higher-stakes short-handed games are quite tough and aggressive, the lower stakes are quite similar to what you will encounter in live poker. You can also play in the short-handed capped games, where you can practice playing with shorter stacks. Finally, you can play sitngos, where you will have the opportunity to play full-handed, short-handed and even heads-up in the same sitting. If you plan to play mostly tournaments, I suggest you play a lot of sitngos simply because they are the closest thing you can get to being at a final table without actually having to make it there. One of the reasons I do so well when I make a final table is that I have more experience than basically everyone in the world at playing sitngos. No matter how you choose to practice, make sure you are well versed in short-handed poker, as it could be the difference between first and seventh place.

Soft Large-Buy-In Tournaments

There are a slew of tournaments each year that most pros make a point to attend. Their fields are made up mostly of satellite qualifiers. Currently, the largest such tournaments are the World Series of Poker, which will be discussed in depth in the next chapter, and tournaments run by online sites.

Basically every large online site sponsors a tournament each year. PokerStars runs numerous tournament series, the most notable being the European Poker Tour. This circuit takes place mostly in Europe but also in the Bahamas. These events are widely considered to be the softest large-buy-in events of the year because so many players get in for relatively little money. I actually met a guy in the Bahamas who won his seat to the $10,000 event for $1 and could not afford to eat at the resort where the tournament took place. Instead, he was eating ramen noodles. Clearly, someone who is eating ramen noodles every meal for a week probably won't be playing his "A" game.

These tournaments are interesting because just getting in the money is a huge ROI for many players. If you got into the tournament for $100, cashing for the minimum of $15,000 feels like a huge win. You can abuse the bubble much more than normal in these tournaments. Figure out who is hurting for money at your table and abuse his blinds once you get anywhere near the bubble.

If you win a satellite into one of these events, go ahead and play it if you have a decent bankroll. If you have $2,000 to your name and win a $12,000 package, I suggest you take the money, as a $14,000 bankroll is worth much more than a $2,000 bankroll. If you have $50,000 to your name, I say gamble it up and try to hit it big.

World Series of Poker

The WSOP is widely regarded, especially by amateurs, as the top tournament series of the year. Most poker players dream of winning a bracelet, which is awarded to the winner of each event. What they don't realize is that the WSOP has gone from being the top tournament series to a huge moneymaking scheme by Harrah's, as every event charges a huge rake. But every pro, myself included, still shows up to play as many events as possible, chasing that gold bracelet.

The way I see it, the WSOP is divided into four sets of tournaments. There are the small-buy-in no-limit holdem events, which range in price from $1,000 to $2,500 and attract from 1,000 to 6,000 entrants. There is also a group of small-buy-in events featuring games like pot-limit Omaha, seven-card stud and 2-7 triple draw. These tournaments usually get much smaller fields than the holdem events, making them prime opportunities for the pros to win a bracelet. There are the big-buy-in events, most with a $10,000 buy in, besides the $50,000 mixed game tournament. These are played in various games as well, like pot-limit holdem, limit holdem, 2-7 no-limit and seven-card stud. These events usually get only around 150 to 500 entrants, also making them prime choices for the top pros that are playing purely to win bracelets.

Finally, there is the Main Event. In most players' eyes this event crowns the best poker player of the year. Obviously, this is ridiculous. In order to win this tournament, which has drawn as many as 8,773 entrants, you have to be extraordinarily lucky for eight solid days of play. But this is by far the large-buy-in tournament with the weakest field, due to the huge number of players that get in cheaply through satellites. Most pros estimate their ROI to be 1,000 percent in this tournament, which means they expect to cash for $100,000 on average each year. While the pros have a huge edge, any one person is still a huge long shot to win this event.

The structures of the WSOP events vary from year to year, but are usually fairly poor, given the size of the buy-ins. This is mostly because the fields are so large that with great structures, each event would take two weeks to complete. Except for the Main Event, the

$10,000 events usually have abnormally poor structures, which makes little sense to me. The Main Event is known for its excellent structure, usually starting players with 200 big blinds and having 120-minute levels. As far as I know, besides WPT events, this is the slowest structure of any tournament, which is one of the reasons why it has such prestige.

Most pros play as many events as they can during the WSOP, mostly because the fields are full of weak players. I play most holdem events, limit and pot-limit included, plus some PLO tournaments. I also play a few mixed-game events if I have nothing else going on. Most pros that are out only to win bracelets play as many of the non-holdem events as possible, as these have the smallest fields. If your goal is to only win bracelets, I suggest you do that.

Sadly, bracelets have lost much of the prestige they had in the past. Twenty years ago the WSOP had maybe 10 events, making each one special. Now there are 57 events, meaning they will give out around 600 bracelets over the next 10 years. There certainly is value in winning a bracelet though, at least as long as the general public thinks winning a bracelet is significant. In my opinion, the only bracelets that actually mean you are good at poker are the ones you win by playing against mostly professional players, like in the larger buy-in events that only get 300 or so people. However, most people that win a tournament with 5,000 players either have some skill or are quite lucky for a few days. The WSOP has been compared to a room of 8,192 monkeys flipping coins in a heads-up bracket. One monkey out of the 8,192 will win 13 coin flips and be world champion of coin flipping that year.

When planning for the WSOP, I expect to show up most every day to play something. I make a point to find a few consecutive days with no events that interest me. If I am feeling worn out when those times come along, I will take a few days off. Getting burnt out during the WSOP is the last thing you want. The players chasing bracelets create a schedule to avoid being in another tournament during an event with a small field. Do whatever is comfortable for you. Just make sure you don't get burnt out.

As in all tournaments made up mostly of satellite qualifiers, you should abuse the bubble mercilessly. I have watched numerous players blind off to their last chip trying to get in the money in a WSOP event. Figure out who is there to cash for the minimum and who is playing to win, as picking on the wrong person on the bubble can be detrimental. In the main event, I would go wild on the bubble, raising basically every pot, especially if I had a big stack. Very few players that get into a $10,000 tournament for only $100 want to bust on the bubble. People have even folded A-A pre-flop just to try to get in the money. Pushing any two cards is clearly profitable against someone who is folding A-A.

The WSOP is so profitable for the pros because so many amateurs show up, more than for any other tournament series. We have ESPN and the hole-card camera to thank for this. Every year, numerous hopefuls come out to Vegas with $5,000, looking to strike gold. Almost all of them go home empty-handed. While I suggest taking shots at WSOP events, especially the smallest buy-in no-limit holdem events and the Main Event, don't invest a significant portion of your bankroll to do it. If you had a $5,000 bankroll, you would be crazy to invest $1,000 to play one of the events, especially if it would take you a long time to win that $1,000 back. If you are grinding up a bankroll, you don't want to lose 20 percent of it. If you have $30,000 though, I see no problem with playing a few $1,000 tournaments. Just make sure you aren't another one of the amateurs in the field with a whopping -75 percent ROI.

I may sound a bit negative about the WSOP. I am actually just amazed that any tournament series could be held in such high regard over any other. Most major tournaments have a series of events that lead up to their main event, but if you win one of those, you get a handshake and maybe a small trophy if you are lucky. If you win a WSOP event, you're put on the poker map. I strongly believe the WSOP is good for professional poker players, mainly because it gets the money out of the hands of the amateurs and it also gets great ratings on television. As far as I can tell, the WSOP is here to stay. I'd better start learning how to play razz and Omaha 8 or better so I can start winning some bracelets.

World Poker Tour

Professionals consider the World Poker Tour to be the toughest group of tournaments in the world. The buy-ins are large, ranging from $3,500 to $25,000, and the fields are tough. If you plan to play a WPT event, do your homework and bring your "A" game.

WPT events stand apart from all other tournaments because of their slow structure. You must know how to play with very deep, deep, medium and short stacks to have any shot of winning these events. Very few amateurs have won WPT events. The slow structure enables the professionals to slowly grind down weaker players until they are broke.

WPT events usually last around five days. At Bellagio, where quite a few WPT events are held, you play five 90-minute levels each day, which makes for fairly short, enjoyable days. Despite this, I always take the day off before an event to ensure that I play perfect poker for five days straight.

Unlike the WSOP and other events made up of mostly satellite qualifiers, most WPT events are comprised primarily of players that buy in with cash. So, you can't abuse the bubble as much. You should still try, but make sure you are not trying to steal from the wrong guy.

If you are considering playing a WPT event, I suggest you find one with a softer field. These are the ones with a decent number of satellite qualifiers, including events at Commerce, Borgata and Foxwoods. These events usually have a decent mix of pros and amateurs, making them very winnable. Unless you value actually winning a WPT title, stay away from the tough ones.

Since I have two WPT titles and the record is three, there is huge value for me in tying that record and I play most every WPT event. Also, I have a pretty good grasp on how other professionals play, giving me a decent edge on most of the field. If you finally reach the competence in your poker game that few possess, you may be ready to take a shot at the WPT. Just be sure you have a $1 million bankroll and nerves of steel.

Traveling the Circuit

Most poker players dream of traveling the live tournament circuit. Traveling to exotic locations around the world to play poker is something most people would die for. While this may seem like the easy life, it has its share of problems. I have spent a few years and a lot of money learning the tricks of traveling the poker circuit. I hope I can you a lot of time and money.

One of the toughest things is booking flights and hotel rooms. When I lose an event, I usually want to get out of that town and either head to the next stop or back home. Because of this, I always book one-way flights. I used to book round-trip tickets but found the cost to change or cancel a flight is simply too high. I have never had a problem getting a flight out of a city because it was overbooked.

Make sure you do not have to pay for the entire stay at a hotel if you check out early. I once booked a three-week stay in LA only to find out I could only be there for a week. The hotel refused to cancel my remaining stay because I had booked it using a discount code. I was stuck paying $3,500 for a hotel I could only use for a week. Luckily, I had friends that agreed to stay in the room while I wasn't there. This is another example of thinking outside the box to avoid being stuck with a huge bill. I also never get a suite unless it is basically the same price as a regular room, which is rarely the case. If you are only going to be in a city for a week, you don't need a nice room. All you are going to do is sleep there. If you can save $2,000 every trip by staying in a regular room instead of a suite, you will end up with $30,000 or so by the end of the year. Saving this $30,000 alone could easily swing a break-even year into a small winner.

It really makes me unhappy to be forced to stay in a casino after I lose a tournament. This is the main reason for leaving as soon as I bust from the last event I plan to play. I value my happiness pretty highly. It is worth spending a little extra for one-way flights. Also, if you leave a hotel early, you save on your hotel bill, which will usually make up the difference between one-way and round-trip fares. If you don't mind staying at a casino with nothing to do except play cash games for a few days, feel free to book round-trip flights. Do whatever works for you.

Call the casino and ask for a poker rate when booking a hotel room. You can stay at most casinos for under $100 per night if you tell them you are there to play their poker tournament. Book early because these rooms tend to sell out quickly. Again, if you can save $100 per night by using the poker rate, you will save a huge amount of money over time.

I tend to book my flight and hotel room around a month before I am supposed to arrive. As you approach the date of an event, you run the risk of paying more for flights and hotel rooms. I know some players that always book their flights the day before. From time to time, they are stuck with a huge bill simply because they failed to plan ahead. I always arrive one day before I play. Some players arrive on the day of the event. I find that if I don't get a good night's sleep, my EV drastically decreases. Also, if your flight is delayed, you might miss the event. This happened to me when I was flying from Pensacola, Fla., to Monte Carlo. I was set to arrive a day ahead of time but a huge storm in Atlanta delayed me by 12 hours. I arrived with enough time to get a little sleep before the big tournament. Quite a few players that were set to arrive the day of the event were too late to register. They ended up flying around the world only to be told, "Sorry, you can't play." That would put me on tilt for years.

Always show up at the airport with time to spare. Missing a flight is always a huge hassle. It only took missing one flight for me to find this out. Be at the airport, ready to check in at least 90 minutes before your flight leaves. Take things to work on or study while waiting in lines and sitting on the airplane. Always make the most of your time.

Carrying money is always a tricky subject. Most casinos allow you to register online for tournaments now, which is awesome because you don't have to travel with large amounts of cash. Wiring money to most casinos is a pretty big hassle so I avoid that when possible. I have found it much easier to wire money to the main cage instead of the poker room. I think this is because they deal with wired funds all the time, whereas it doesn't happen as often in the poker room. When I went to the WSOP for the first time, I wired all the money I had to the Rio. The cage misplaced the money and my friends had to front money for me for the entire week while I was waiting for the Rio to find my cash. If I do wire money now, I always take enough cash to last a day or two.

This should be obvious, but you don't want to keep a large sum of money at your house. Keep it in the bank or in a lock box at your home casino. I keep my money in the bank and at Bellagio, as that is where I play when I am home in Vegas. Keeping a lot of money at your house is just asking for trouble.

Most casinos are filled with unhealthy food. While I am not obsessive about healthy eating all the time, I still try to order whatever looks healthiest on the menu. Most places have a sandwich shop where you can get something like a turkey sandwich. Most places also have a salad or fruit plate. Don't spend all your time eating prime rib at the buffet, as this will quickly put you out of commission.

I have been fortunate not be drawn to the partying that goes on the day before a major event. In fact, I rarely party and spend all night out because I don't function well when I am tired. When you are at a casino to play a poker tournament, you are there to work. You should never be out all night drinking the day before the main event. You probably flew across the world to play a poker tournament. If you wanted to party, you could have stayed home.

Keeping in touch with loved ones is tough while on the road. If you have a girlfriend or wife, set up a video chat program on your computer so you can talk to her. Be sure to call from time to time so she doesn't worry about you. Remember that even though you are on a poker vacation, people still care about you.

I am sure there are many small things I have not covered here. Whenever you encounter a situation and are unsure of the optimal play, think about what would be best for your poker career and your happiness.

Chapter 9

Hand Examples

I firmly believe that putting yourself in other players' shoes is one of the best ways to get great at the game with only a small commitment of time. When you are at the poker table, you should pay attention to every hand and constantly put everyone on a range of hands so you can better learn that most important skill. Below are discussions of 30 hands I've played throughout my career. I will cover numerous topics, although you will see that my decisions often depend on my opponents. The hands are in no particular order because I want you to be able to jump between vastly different topics in the blink of an eye at the poker table. If you are in the habit of only thinking about pre-flop decisions and are totally confused when a post-flop decision arises, whatever knowledge you have will be useless. I strongly urge you to write down what you would do in each situation before you look at my play, so you can see if we are thinking the same way, and if we differ, you can hopefully see why. Good luck!

Hand 1

This hand came up in the eight-handed $20,000 Epic Poker League event. We were down to 16 players, with 12 getting paid. We were getting close to the money but not quite close enough to play like a nit and guarantee a $40,000 payday. The stacks are:

UTG: 50 BBs

2nd: 50 BBs

3rd: 50 BBs

4th: 35 BBs. This player is known to be good and aggressive, although he is generally on the tighter side. I have seen him get out of line twice over the last few years.

Hijack: 80 BBs. This player is super-aggressive and constantly applies pressure when he thinks he can get away with it.

Button: 45 BBs. This is me. I have generally played tight and aggressive.

SB: 40 BBs

BB: 40 BBs

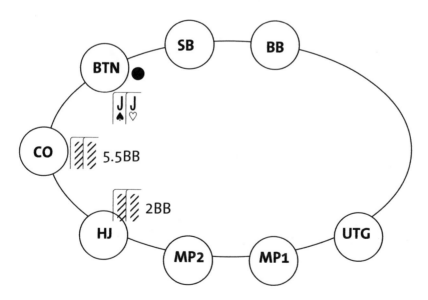

Action folds to the player in 4th position, who makes his standard raise to 2 BBs. Player 5 re-raises to around 5.5 BBs. He has been re-raising quite a lot in this event and has built his stack up from around 40 BBs at this table. I am on the button with J♠-J♣. This is a tricky spot because if I re-raise to around 12 BBs, I will be priced in to call player 4's all-in if he decides to go with his hand. I will be in rough shape against his range, which will be something like Q-Q+ and A-K. The hijack, while he did re-raise, probably doesn't have too strong of a range, as he is known to re-raise often.

I think my options here are to re-raise to around 20 BBs with the intention of calling either all-in, or to fold now. I don't think calling the 5.5-BB re-raise is ever an option. When someone cold-calls a re-raise, he often has a hand like J-J, 10-10 or A-K that he didn't want to fold or re-raise. Turning your hand face-up against good players is never a good option, especially considering that your stack will be fairly small compared to the pot. What matters most here is the initial raiser's opening range. If he is only raising something like 7-7+, A-Q+ and a few suited connectors, I should probably fold, as hands that beat me make up too much of that range. If he is raising very wide, I think re-raising is fine.

Given my reads, this is a fairly easy fold. Sadly, I re-raised, got all-in against the initial raiser's K-K and lost a large pot.

Hand 2

This hand came up in a $1,000 live tournament. We are a few hours into the day, so payout considerations are irrelevant. We are playing nine-handed. The stacks are:

4th: 60 BBs. This player is overly aggressive and loves to try to steal the blinds.

Button: I have 20 BBs. I have been playing fairly tight and aggressive because I have been short for a while.

The players in the blinds are both pretty tight, have around 50 BBs and don't get too far out of line.

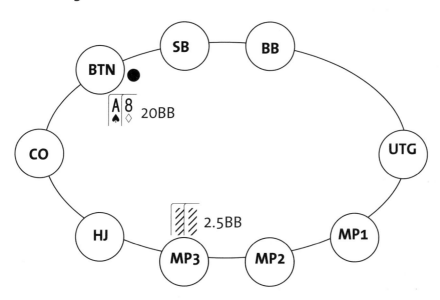

Player 4 raises to 2.5 BBs. The action is folded to me and I go all-in with A♠-8♦. In this spot, my opponent's range is very wide, as he has been getting away with stealing often. Having an ace in my hand greatly hurts my opponent's range because he has fewer combinations of hands that contain an ace. This turns into a simple math problem. I assume my opponent is raising 50 percent of hands and will call with 15 percent of those hands.

The equity from pushing is:

(proportion of folds)(size of pot) + (proportion of calls)(equity in pot - amount put in pot)

So, we have:

(0.85)(4.5) + (0.15)[42(0.3) - 20] = 3.825 - 1.11 = 2.715 BB profit

Clearly, this push is +EV. I would have a profitable all-in even if my opponent called more often. Also, I will rarely have less than 30-percent equity with any hand, so I can push in this spot often and expect to profit nicely. Obviously, if you start going all-in a lot, your opponent will call more often, but this play will remain profitable as long as you don't use it consistently against the same person. Feel free to tinker around with the formula to figure out when you should and shouldn't be pushing. Take into account that the SB and BB will each wake up with a monster around 3 percent of the time. This is why you should prefer to make these light re-raises from late position.

Hand 3

This hand is from a $10,000 WPT event. It is the middle of day 2, which means we are nowhere near the money.

Button: 50 BBs. This is me. I have been fairly aggressive, although not crazy.

SB: 100 BBs. This player has had more success at mixed games, although he is a WPT champion and certainly knows how to play no-limit.

BB: 50 BBs. This player has been fairly tight and aggressive.

Action folds to me and I raise to 2.5 BBs with A♠-4♣. The player in the small blind re-raises to 7 BBs. The big blind folds.

I only have two options here. I can either go all-in or fold. Given that the SB has been fairly aggressive, I think this is often a push. I can run an equity calculation, as in the previous hand, to figure out if pushing will be profitable. I need to know my opponent's re-raising range, which is tough, since players don't re-raise too often. I think he will re-raise my button raises fairly often.

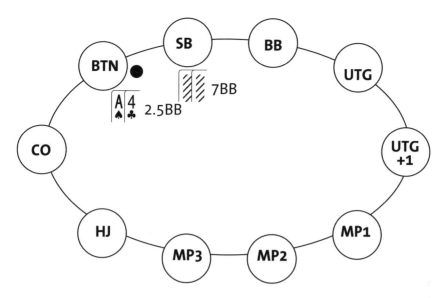

If he re-raises 28 percent of the time and will call with 28 percent of those hands, or a range of 5-5+, A-J+, I have:

$(0.72)(11) + (0.28)[102(.28) − 50] = 7.92 - 6 = 1.92$ BBs

This push isn't super profitable against the range I assigned the player, but it is still +EV. It will also let my opponent know he can't push me around. Notice again that this push becomes awful against a tighter range, and becomes significantly more profitable if he re-raises more than I assumed.

Defining ranges is very important because when you risk your stack, you want to be sure you have an edge. In this spot, I went all-in and my opponent quickly folded.

Hand 4

This hand is from a $20 online tournament. This is also a rebuy event, although it will not matter much in this hand. Everyone has around 80 BBs. We are playing 20/40.

I raise UTG to 120 with 4♦-4♠. Action folds around to the small blind, who calls. I have no reads on my opponent, as this is the first hand of the tournament.

The flop comes Q♥-Q♠-5♥.

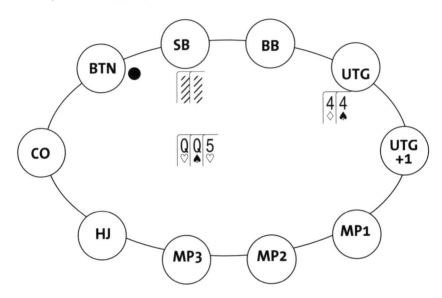

My opponent checks and I make a standard continuation bet of 160. Continuation-betting in this spot is mandatory. I want my opponent to fold all random overcards because they have decent equity. I also don't want to check back and let my opponent bet the turn when a card higher than a 5 comes, as I will probably have to fold. My opponent check-raises to 320, which is the minimum raise. I think his range is something like a queen, a 5, a flush draw, any pair and a few hands like A-J that he thinks may be good. While 4-4 may be ahead of this range at the moment, it is in terrible shape. I lose to most pairs, any 5 and any queen, and I am behind flush draws. I am only in good shape against hands like A-J, and even then I'm not in great shape. Weak players constantly call here and fold to turn bets. A much better play is to fold and move on to the next hand.

Hand 5

This hand is from a $10,000 WPT event I played at Foxwoods. We had just gotten in the money. Once this happens, I tend to not get too out of line while waiting for the short stacks to bust, but I still try to chip up. The relevant stacks are:

Hijack: I have 50 BBs. I have been fairly loose and aggressive so far.

Cutoff: 30 BBs. This player has been tight so far.

Button: 70 BBs. This player is a WPT champion who has no problem taking flops and getting out of line.

SB: 40 BBs. This player is known to be super tight.

BB: 20 BBs This is an amateur who tends to play straightforwardly.

I raise with A♠-10♣ to 2.2 BBs out of my 50-BB stack. The button calls and we see a flop of K♠-10♦-3♥.

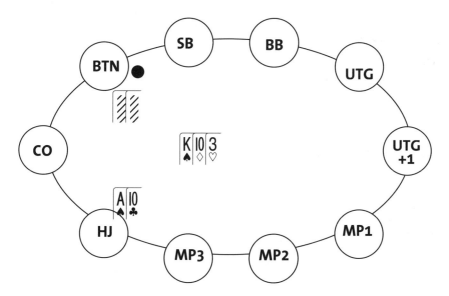

I make a 3-BB continuation bet and my opponent calls. He could have a fairly wide range at this point. I imagine he would raise with top pair, top kicker or better. This leaves us with a range of pairs 10 or higher, Q-J, A-Q, A-J, Q-9 and J-9. He is also capable of floating with air here from time to time, although I imagine most of his floats would be with gutshots.

The turn is the A♣. Before I get too excited, I need to see how this affects his range. If he has a gutshot with an ace, he will almost certainly bet the turn if I check. If he has something like K-9 or J-10, he will almost certainly fold to a bet, which is bad for me. If he has one of the missed gutshots, he will probably bet if I check. So, betting only gives me value from hands like K-Q and K-J that may check behind. If I check, I allow him to bluff his air, value-bet most of his value hands and save money when he has Q-J. So, I check. He bets 7 BBs into the 12-BB pot and I call.

The river is the 5♣. I want him to continue betting with air, so checking is the only option. If I lead into him here, he will call with any value hand worse than mine and raise if he has better. So, it's almost always bad to lead with medium-strength made hands. I check and he bets 16 BBs. I have a pretty easy call. Again, check-raising makes no sense because he will only call when I'm beat. I think he would value-bet all aces and all worse 2-pair hands. He may or may not continue with his gutshots, but that doesn't matter much. I call and lose to his Q-J.

Notice if I had bet the turn and he had raised, I would be in an awful spot and probably end up broke. Instead, I left myself with around 13 BBs, which I used to take eighth place in the event. If you pay attention, there are numerous spots in tournament poker where you can give up a little value and have a few chips left when you are beat. This trade is almost always worth making.

Hand 6

This hand is from a $500 online tournament. We are early in the event. Everyone has 200 BBs.

A player I don't know limps from second position. I have A♥-3♥ in fourth position. I make it 5 BBs. You can either raise or limp behind in this spot. I like to raise early in an event in order to find out how often and aggressively players are going to defend their limps. If they call and play well after the flop, I am probably better off calling behind and taking a flop. If they either fold pre-flop or call my pre-flop raise and check-fold post-flop when they miss, then I should be raising. Everyone folds to the limper and he calls.

The flop comes Q♠-8♠-3♠. My opponent checks.

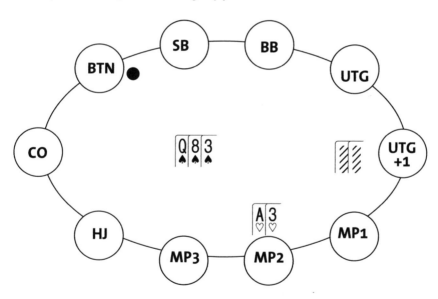

The equity difference between continuation-betting and checking is minimal in this spot. If I bet the flop, my opponent will probably continue with all decent flush draws and hands like middle pair or better, all of which I'm not too happy about being up against. If I check back the flop and he bets the turn, I should probably fold most of the time. If he checks the turn, I can then bet for value and protection; he may still call with a flush draw, but now I am in decent shape. I should bet against aggressive opponents that will bet the turn simply because I didn't continuation-bet the flop. I would tend to check against a passive, straightforward player, since he will probably not bluff the turn too often. In a $500 tournament, which is fairly large for online, I decide to bet 2/3 pot because players at this level tend to be aggressive. I take the pot down with the continuation bet.

Notice how much thought went into a simple continuation bet. Think about these situations away from the table, so you will have no problem making the optimal play when the situation arises.

Hand 7

This hand is from a $1,500 WSOP event. We are fairly early in the day. The relevant stacks are:

4th: 200 BBs. This is an older player that likes to limp.

Hijack: 200 BBs. This is a 40-year-old guy that won his way in through a satellite.

Button: 200 BBs. I have been fairly tight and aggressive so far.

Action is folded around to player 4, who limps. Player 5 raises to 3 BBs. When players make small raises over limps, you need to figure out if they are raising with their standard opening range or adjusting to take advantage of the limper. Since I know this $1,500 is a big deal for this player, I assume he has a decent hand that he would normally open-raise. I call with 10♠-10♣. I really like calling in spots like this because I am on the button and my hand will be greatly disguised. If I re-raise to around 10 BBs, I will usually take a flop in position against the initial raiser. I will be unsure about his range and will often see a tricky flop with overcards. Also, if I re-raise and my opponent re-raises, I will often have to fold the best hand. The limper calls as well.

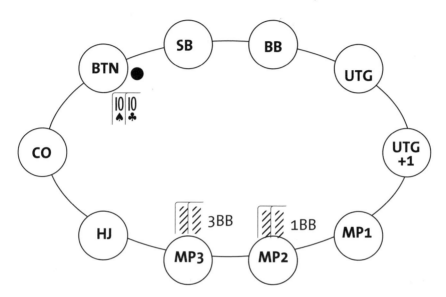

The flop comes A♣-5♠-2♦. Everyone checks to me and I check back. I plan to bet the turn if a card lower than a 10 comes and continue checking if the turn is an overcard to my pair. I could bet the flop here but I think I get more accurate information about the strength of my opponents' hands if they check through the turn as well.

The turn is the Q♠, which isn't good for me. Everyone checks again. At this point, I assume I am behind and plan to check-fold to any river bet. Even if I am ahead on the turn, I will often not be ahead when the river comes.

The river is the J♥. The raiser bets half-pot and wins. I could have considered stabbing on the flop but after that, I think I am forced to simply give up. Notice how I gave myself a great shot to win a pot with 10-10 without putting much money in the pot. In spots like this, you are giving up a small pre-flop win in exchange for the opportunity to stack your opponent if you flop a set when he has a strong holding.

Hand 8

This hand came up in the same $1,500 WSOP event as the hand above. We are a bit deeper in the day, although nowhere near the money. The stacks are:

UTG: 50 BBs. This is me. I have been playing fairly loose and aggressively, as I normally do in WSOP events.

2nd: 90 BBs. This is a young player I have never seen before. He has generally been loose and aggressive.

BB: 100 BBs. This player is around 50 years old and loves to see flops.

I limp with 8♠-8♦ from first position. I could certainly raise in this spot but against weaker competition, which is common in WSOP events, I really want to see a flop. I would tend to open-raise or fold in a larger buy-in WPT event. The young player to my left raises to 3 BBs. I imagine his range is fairly strong here, even though he has been rather aggressive so far. I don't think he is going to go out of his way to try to outplay me from such an early position. I call. The big blind calls as well, which doesn't mean much, as he likes to see flops.

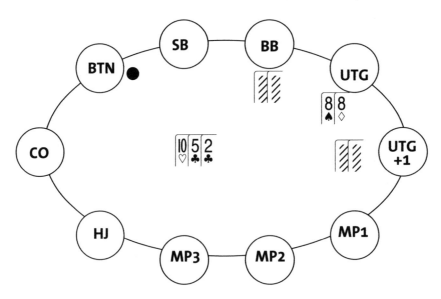

The flop is 10♥-5♣-2♣. Everyone checks.

The turn is the 6♠. The BB checks and I bet 2/3-pot. In this situation, the initial raiser probably has overcards, as he would have certainly bet an overpair on the flop. I also imagine he would bet any paired hand on the flop. Checking lets me know he is either slow-playing a monster, like 10-10 or 5-5, or he has nothing. Sets are a tiny part of his range, so I can assume he has nothing. The BB could have a piece of this board, although he probably doesn't have a 10, as he would have bet either the flop or turn. This leads me to believe I have the best hand by far. I don't like checking the turn because there are a lot of bad rivers that could easily cost me the pot. I would also not be too prone to check-folding basically any river because my range looks so weak that the aggressive raiser may bet the river with any-thing. I bet the turn and pick up the pot.

If the BB had called my turn bet, I would have checked behind or folded to his bet on most rivers. If the raiser had called my turn bet, I would have check-called most rivers. When you make a bet early in a hand, try to have a plan for later streets. Thinking only one street at a time is like thinking only one move at a time while playing chess. It is a recipe for disaster.

Hand 9

This hand is from a $10,000 online tournament, which is the largest buy-in event that runs online. The blinds are 25/50. Everyone has around 500 BBs.

Action folds to me on the button and I raise to 3 BBs, or 150, with A♠-9♣. A player in the big blind, who I think to be a solid winner online, calls. The flop is 9♠-6♥-5♦. The BB checks and I make a stan-dard continuation bet of 200 into the 325 pot. My opponent instantly raises to 550 out of his 25,000 stack. I know my opponent is loose, aggressive, and perfectly capable of making plays, so folding is out of the question. Re-raising is a poor option because it will force my opponent off all worse hands, so calling is the only real play. There are numerous bad turn cards for my hand. I must be willing to call down on most of them.

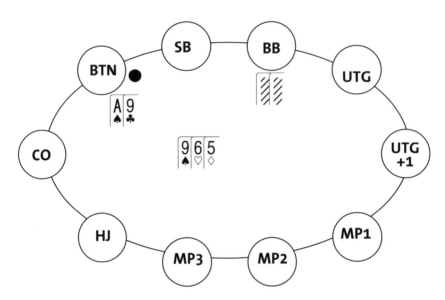

The turn is the 3♥. My opponent bets about 2/3-pot, 900 into 1,400. I fully expected him to continue betting on most turns. Even though this is a total blank, it would make sense for him to bluff here because he is trying to represent such a strong range by check-raising the flop that no turn should scare him. He would also bet on all overcards because those will generally make my range weaker. So, since I expect him to bet on every turn card and I am unsure which ones actually help him, if I think I was ahead on the flop, which I certainly do, I have an easy call on the turn. As on the flop, I don't plan on folding to too many river bets.

The river is the 10♠. My opponent checks. Now I think he either has a weak two pair, an overpair, top pair or nothing. I expected him to check-call with made hands, and to check-fold or fire a third barrel with air. Situations come up all the time where my opponent will only call my river value bet when I am beat, and this is one of those spots. It makes checking behind an easy decision. My opponent turns over K♣-8♣ and I win a nice pot.

Hand 10

This hand takes place in the same $10,000 event as the previous hand. We are playing 25/50. The stacks are:

2nd: 500 BBs, or 25,000 chips. This player is unknown to me, which makes me think he got in through a satellite.

4th: I have 550 BBs, or 27,500 chips.

Button: 450 BBs, or 22,500 chips. This is the player that tried to run a bluff on the previous hand.

Player 2 limps and I raise with A♣-A♠ to 5 BBs, or 250. No other play makes sense here. I would never limp behind with A-A and stacks this deep. You want to start building a pot, especially when you currently have the nuts. The player on the button calls. He could have a decently wide range made up of pairs, decent aces, suited aces, good Broadway hands and suited connectors. The initial limper also calls, probably with something like a small pair, suited connectors or a suited ace.

The flop comes 4♦-3♣-3♦. The initial limper leads out for 400 into the 825 pot. I view this as a bet to find out where he is at. If this is the case, a large raise will usually blow him off his hand, which is never good. I could call, but with a few draws out and very deep stacks, I am fine putting a little more money in the pot. I make it 1,050. The button folds and the limper calls. I think he has a weak overpair or maybe some sort of straight or flush draw.

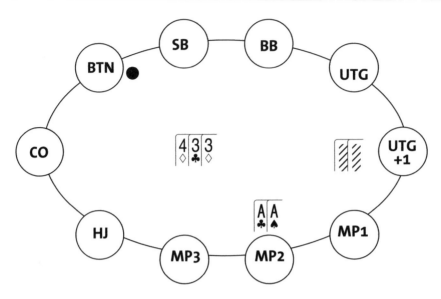

The turn is the A♥, which gives me a lock on the hand. My opponent checks, which doesn't really mean anything. The ace is generally bad for his range because if he had a pair, he now has to worry about the ace, and if he had a draw, he missed. My bet should be fairly small to try to induce a crying call. I bet 1,650 into the 2,925 pot. Looking back, I would have bet slightly smaller, maybe around 1,200. My opponent calls.

The river is the 2♦. This is a great card for me because if my opponent had a flush or straight draw, he probably just hit it. When a player draws to a hand like a straight or flush and gets there, he tends not to fold to any reasonable bet. If my opponent has a pair lower than aces, he will almost certainly fold to any bet. So, I need to make a fairly large bet to get value from the draws that just completed. My opponent checks and I bet 5,900 into the 6,225 pot. Another option would be to overbet the river to try to get maximum value from the flushes. I could bet something like 9,600, but I think some decent or scared players, like my opponent, might fold. My opponent tanks for a while before calling with 6-5, and I win a nice pot.

Hand 11

This hand occurred in the same $10,000 online event. We are now playing 50/100, making stacks half the size as in the previous hands, although we are still deep-stacked. The stacks are:

4th: 300 BBs, or 30,000 chips. This is me. I have been fairly aggressive so far, winning quite a few uncontested pots.

Hijack: 380 BBs, or 38,000 chips. This is an excellent player that adjusts well to every situation. He tends to be aggressive.

I raise with A♦-Q♦ to 3 BBs, or 300, from middle position. The player to my left re-raises to 1,050. His range could either be very tight or very wide, depending on what he thinks of my game. Given my previous aggression and our history together, I think he will be re-raising fairly wide. I could 4-bet him, but I will be out of position throughout the hand and will have no clue where I stand, so calling is the clear play.

The flop comes K♣-Q♥-5♣ and I check.

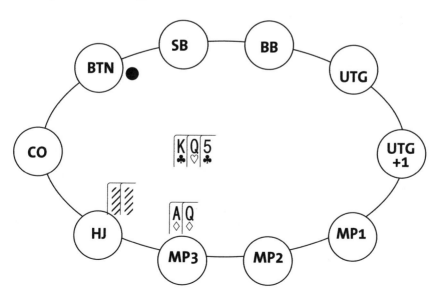

This is almost always my play when I'm first to act in a 3-bet pot from out of position and I'm not the aggressor. My opponent bets 1,600 into the 2,250 pot. I can't justify any play except a call. Folding would be far too weak. Even though I'm crushed by A-A, K-K, Q-Q, A-K and K-Q, I still beat a lot of hands in my opponent's re-raising range.

The turn is the 5♦. I check and my opponent checks behind. I now think I have the best hand a decent amount of the time, although it is tough to be certain. Good players will usually check back here with most weak kings and most queens. While my opponent may double-barrel with air from time to time, I don't think he will always do this.

The river is the 9♣. This is a pretty bad card for my hand because I now lose to Q-9 and J-10 in addition to the hands previously listed. If I bet here, I am unlikely to be called by a worse hand besides exactly Q-J and Q-10, so I check. I would probably call if my opponent bet here; my range probably looks fairly weak to him, since I checked the turn and river. I expect he would try to get me off my probable middle-strength hand if he has total air. My opponent thinks for a while before checking behind with A-9. If he didn't get a decent amount of showdown value on the river, I would have probably snapped off a little bluff.

Hand 12

Here is another hand from the $10,000 online event. We are playing 100/200. The stacks are:

Hijack: 150 BBs, or 30,000 chips. This is me. I have been fairly aggressive, although I still have not shown down many hands.

SB: 115 BBs, or 23,000 chips. This player just got moved to the table and is unknown to me.

BB: 100 BBs, or 20,000 chips. This is a solid, winning online player.

Action folds to me and I raise to 600 with J♦-6♦ from middle position. I could obviously fold this hand, but I like raising here from time to time to mix things up, especially if players aren't playing back at me too often. Both blinds call. When the small blind calls, you should assume this greatly widens the big blind's calling range because he is now in a decent relative position and is getting better odds. The small blind's calling range should be fairly tight, although most players defend much too loosely.

The flop comes A♠-K♦-Q♦, giving me a gutshot and flush draw.

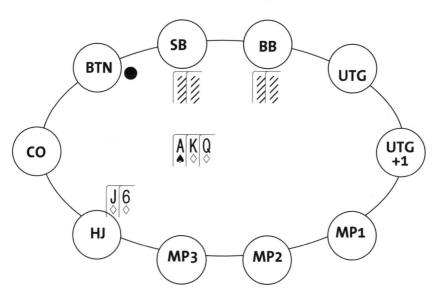

Both players check to me and I bet 1,200 into an 1,800 pot. Given how deep-stacked we are, I think betting here is mandatory. I am not concerned with getting blown off my hand, as I can easily call and raise. Any bet size between half- and ¾-pot is fine. The small blind calls and the big blind folds. Most people would raise with the nut-flush draw and top pair, so I believe the small blind has a hand like top pair, a pair plus gutshot or a weaker flush draw.

The turn is the 5♦, completing my flush. To my surprise, my opponent leads into me for 2,000 into the 4,200 pot. If my opponent is a weak player, which could be the case, he could show up with a weaker flush quite often. He could also have something like top pair and no longer want to give free cards. He will probably bet the river with a flush, and I can then go all-in, getting maximum value. He will probably fold to a turn raise if his hand is weaker than a flush. If I call, he will probably bet the river, either for value with hands like two pair or as a bluff. The only hands I may be able to get it in with that are behind right now are A-5 and maybe J-10. Raising the turn is therefore not a good option, so I call.

The river is the 4♥. My opponent bets 4,000 into the 8,200 pot, with 15,200 left in his stack. I am starting to believe he does have a de-cently strong hand like two pair, or maybe a slow-played straight. He will call any raise with a flush or straight. He may be able to get away from the two-pair hands if I push, but I don't think those make up much of his range. He will probably fold to any raise if he has decided to lead with some weird top-pair hand. So, most of his strong range will call a push and most of his weaker made-hand range will not call any raise. This makes going all-in the best option, so I push. My oppo-nent instantly folds and I win a nice pot. He probably had something like A♥-10♦ and thought leading the turn was the right play.

Hand 13

This hand is also from the $10,000 online tournament. My opponent is the player in the previous hand. We are now playing 200/400. The stacks are:

Cutoff: I have 160 BBs, or 64,000.

BB: 37 BBs, or 15,000. This player seems generally weak, although he may be able to make some moves.

Action folds to me and I raise to 1,200 from the cutoff with J♠-7♠. I would prefer a raise to 1,000 instead, as stacks are starting to get shorter, but 1,200 is fine. My opponent in the big blind re-raises to 2,600. When you see players in the blinds re-raise to a smaller than normal amount, unless it is their standard re-raise size, they almost always have a very strong hand. I love to call in these spots and take a flop as long as I am getting decent immediate and implied odds. I am looking to flop two pair or better, or a flush draw. I would much prefer a hand like J♠-10♠ to J♠-7♠ because J♠-10♠ can flop a lot of straight draws. I call 1,400 more.

The flop comes K♣-J♥-7♥.

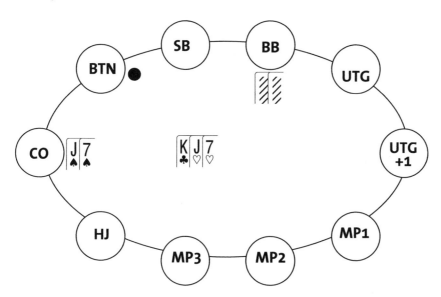

Luckily, my opponent goes all-in for 12,400 into the 5,400 pot. Amateurs love to make this play when they have a hand they don't want to see outdrawn. In this spot, I expect to see A-A, A-K and maybe a few crazy bluffs. With my opponent's entire range crushed, I have an easy call. Note that I would have an easy fold if the flop were K-J-6 instead, which is not what I was trying to flop. I make a trivial call and my opponent shows A-A. The river is an ace and I lose a nice pot.

Clearly, my opponent played his hand terribly because, unless I flopped a monster, I was going to fold. His all-in bet did nothing except force out hands with very little equity while keeping in hands that have A-A in bad shape. He would have been much better off betting small and keeping me in the pot with a hand like middle pair.

Hand 14

Here is one final hand from the $10,000 online event. The blinds are now 300/600. The stacks are:

3rd: 20 BBs, or 12,000 chips. This player had a backing deal with a major online site. He is an older player that is known to get wild from time to time.

Cutoff: 50 BBs, or 30,000 chips. I know very little about this player, as he is new to the table.

Button: I have 100 BBs, or 60,000 chips.

Action folds to seat 3, who limps. I don't know what to think about his limping range, although I imagine it is either very strong or very weak. When you don't know someone's range, imagine a few ranges he could have, assign a likelihood percentage to each and continue playing. The cutoff also limps, which I think he would do with a wide range. Once one player opens for a limp, players tend to limp behind with a much wider range, expecting to see a cheap flop. I raise to 3,600 with K♠-Q♣.

Action folds back to the initial limper, who raises all-in for 12,000 chips. The second limper folds. There is 17,100 in the pot and I have to call 8,400 more, meaning I have to win 33 percent of the time to break even. I will assign my opponent two ranges, one tight and one loose. For simplicity, I will assume he has each range half the time.

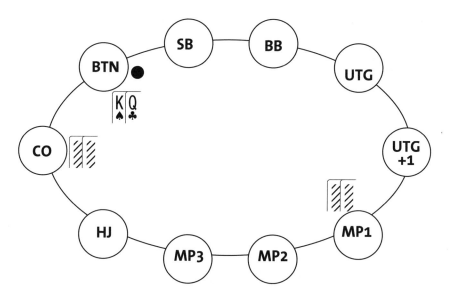

I have 28-percent equity against a range of A-A to 10-10 and A-K, and 62-percent equity against a range of middle pairs and a bunch of suited and unsuited connectors.

My average equity is 28(0.5) + 62(0.5) = 45 percent. This is more than enough to call, since I only need 33 percent to break even. Notice that you could assume he is pushing with the tight range more often, which would make a call closer. I make the call and my K♠-Q♣ beats his insane bluff with 6♣-4♠.

Hand 15

This hand occurred in a $500 live tournament. We are playing 50/100. We are fairly early in the day. The stacks are:

2nd: 32 BBs, or 3,200 chips. This player is older and has already lost 1,800 chips from his 5,000-chip starting stack.

4th: 62 BBs, or 6,200 chips. I have been playing tight and aggressively.

Hijack: 90 BBs, or 9,000 chips. This player is young and seems to be loose and aggressive.

Cutoff: 45 BBs, or 4,500 chips. This player seems to be aggressive but not far too out of line.

Player 2 limps, as do I with Q♣-J♣. I like playing cheap flops with good suited connectors in spots like this. Notice that if I raise, I may be re-raised by either the initial limper or someone behind me, which I don't really want. Folding is also an option I generally don't take. The player behind me limps and the cutoff raises to 500. Since he is aggressive, he could be doing this with a wide range of hands. The initial limper and I both call. The limper in the hijack folds, which is basically always a mistake. His limping range should com-prise hands he wants to see a flop with, and getting such great odds, he should call. If he has a hand that flops poorly, like A♠-6♣, he should either fold or raise pre-flop instead of limping.

The flop comes A♥-10♦-6♣.

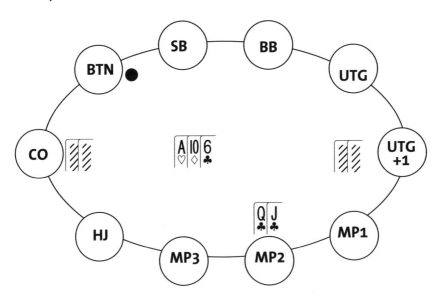

Everyone checks. This doesn't tell us much about the initial limper's range, but it does let us know that the cutoff probably missed this flop. He could certainly have a hand like K-K, but will almost certainly fold the hand to enough aggression later.

The turn is the Q♠. This gives me a pair plus gutshot, always a good thing. The initial limper now bets 300 into the 1,750 pot. While this is a very weak bet, I think calling is the right play, as he only has 2,400 left in his stack and I am getting excellent immediate odds. If I raise to 1,000 and he goes all-in, I will have to make a crying call. I call and the initial raiser calls as well. His range is probably similar to my hand, junky pairs plus a junky draw. I plan to check down if I don't hit on the river.

The river is the K♥, giving me the nuts. The initial limper bets 1,300 into the 2,650 pot, leaving very little behind. While it would be nice to figure out a way to stack the player behind me, I think it is going to be tough. I really want to raise the river; the river bettor will probably call off if he has something like two pair or a set. I think a min-raise on the river, which will put the bettor all in while giving the initial raiser on the cutoff something to think about, is probably the best play because he may think I am making an insane bluff and find a call with two pair. Instead, I go all-in. This isn't horrible, but it is suboptimal.

Even if you play well, you will make mistakes from time to time. Learn from your mistakes so you don't repeat them. If you mess up the same situation over and over, you are probably not doing something right. In this hand, everyone folded and I won a nice pot.

Hand 16

This hand took place in a $1,000 sitngo tournament at the WSOP. First place gets all the money in these events, so there is no point trying to blind off in order to go deeper in the event.

Everyone has around 10 BBs. We are currently eight-handed. A 30-year-old recreational player goes all-in from third position. He has been mildly aggressive, although he has only shown down good hands. I have A♠-J♣ in the cutoff seat. Most players would snap-call, as this is a pretty great hand for a 10-BB stack, but you should determine your calling range in these situations, so you can call more efficiently in the future.

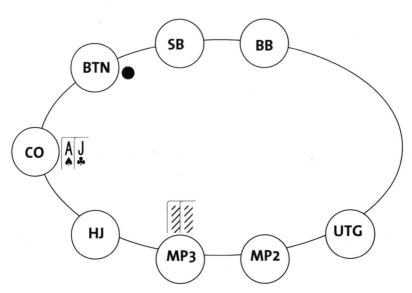

I first need to assign my opponent a range of hands. Since I think he is decent and aggressive, I believe he will be pushing any pair, any two Broadway cards, any ace and a few suited connectors. A-J has around 58-percent equity against that range, giving me an easy call, even with three players yet to act. Notice that I need to be more than 50 percent to win because of the players behind me. I also want to profit a bit from the call, so I estimate I need around 55-percent equity to call. If I think my opponent is pushing this range, I should be calling with something like A-10+ and 7-7+.

Next, I need to figure out if I can call if my opponent is pushing tightly. If I assume he will push 5-5+, A-5s+, A-10+, K-J+, any suited Broadway hand and a few suited connectors, then A-J only has 50-

percent equity, which isn't good enough to call. Against this tighter range, I should be calling with A-Q+ and 9-9+.

When you get short, don't think you need to get all-in as soon as you get a decent hand. You are often much better off waiting for a spot where you can be the first person to go all-in. Calling off your stack against an early-position raiser is only good if you have a monster.

I called and lost a flip to 7♥-7♣.

Hand 17

This hand came up in a $2,500 WSOP event. We are playing 250/500-50. The relevant stacks are:

UTG: 60 BBs, or 30,000 chips. This is me. I have been playing loose in position and tight out of position.

BB: 30 BBs, or 15,000 chips. This is a younger kid that has been mildly aggressive but certainly not out of line.

I raise J♣-J♦ from first position. The big blind calls. I imagine his range is fairly wide, although this is player-dependent, as some people defend their blinds often and some rarely defend. When someone raises small from first position and you are in the big blind with a hand that will flop well, like a small pair or suited connectors, you should basically always see a flop; your opponent's range will be fairly tight, meaning he will have a tough time getting away from his hand post-flop. Despite this, many players fold in the blinds because they think they are behind in the hand, which you should know by now is not a good enough reason to fold, especially with huge implied odds.

The flop comes 8♣-3♠-2♣.

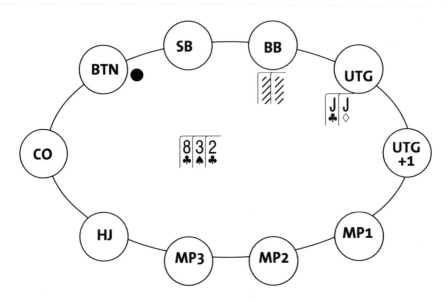

My opponent checks and I bet 1,800 into the 3,300 pot. My opponent has around 15,000 chips behind. I would prefer a slightly larger bet to induce a push from my opponent's weaker holdings. I don't think he can get away from most pairs or draws in this spot, so I should try to force him to push over my continuation bet. To my surprise, he just calls. This makes me think his range is fairly wide, most likely something like a pair or draw, although if I were in his shoes, I would probably push all of those hands, as well as my monsters to balance my range. I can discount all the overpairs that are better than my hand because he probably would re-raise with those pre-flop, making my hand very strong in this situation.

The turn is the 4♠. He checks and I bet 3,600. The 4♠ doesn't really change much unless my opponent had exactly A♣-5♣ or 6♣-5♣. I think my opponent will still have a tough time getting away from any pair in this spot, so I need to bet, especially with the numerous draws out. My opponent has around 13,000 behind, so I chose an amount that will basically force him to go all-in or fold, which is what I want because I almost certainly have the best hand. He goes all-in and I make the fairly easy call. He shows 8♠-6♠ for a pair plus flush draw and gutshot. I hold up and win a nice pot.

Hand 18

This hand was played in a $1,000 online tournament. We are deep in the money and down to 27 players. Most of the players have been loose and aggressive, although I expect some to tighten up a bit as the payout jumps start to become larger. We are playing 10,000/20,000-2,500. The stacks are:

Hijack: 70 BBs, or 1,400,000 chips. This is me. I have been playing very loose and aggressively, trying to steal the blinds whenever possible.

Cutoff: 33 BBs, or 660,000 chips. This player has been raising often when the action is folded to him, although he hasn't pushed over any of my raises yet.

Button: 70 BBs, or 1,400,000 chips. This player has been loose and aggressive, stealing often and re-raising fairly often.

SB: 15 BBs, or 300,000 chips. This player has been tight for the most part.

BB: 43 BBs, or 860,000 chips. This player is new to the table and I have very little information on him.

The action folds to me in the hijack and I raise to 45,000 with J♥-10♥. If the short-stacked players to my left had been re-raising all-in fairly often, I would be a little more cautious raising hands like J♥-10♥. A lot of players only raise hands they plan on calling with against a short stack's push, but this is generally a mistake. You always need some bluffs in your range, and since J♥-10♥ has some blockers and it flops well if I'm called, raising is usually fine. Everyone folds to the big blind, who calls. I imagine he will defend fairly often, as my raise is just over a min-raise. This is fine with me; my hand flops well and I will be in position throughout the hand.

The flop comes 7♥-3♥-2♥.

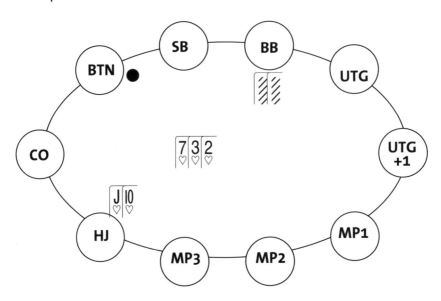

My opponent checks. Even though I've flopped a monster, I need to bet, as my opponent could have decent equity in this hand if he has a heart, and may be unable to fold a hand like 8♥-7♣. Even if I had flopped the nuts here with something like A♥-J♥, I would still continuation-bet; I am fairly deep-stacked and I would love to win all of my opponent's chips. I bet 72,000, a little more than half of the 120,000 pot, and my opponent calls, leaving 750,000 behind. He probably has a hand like a pair with a draw, or maybe as little as a weak pair with no draw. I don't think he has a flush or a set, so I am generally in good shape.

The turn is the 2♦. My opponent checks and I bet 160,000 into the 264,000 pot. I want to start threatening my opponent's stack. I don't want to let him draw to a bigger flush for free, and I want him to think I'm trying to force him off his likely marginal made hand. A small bet here would give him a great price to outdraw me, which is never good. While I may keep him in when he is drawing dead with something like 8♣-7♣, I think I am better off trying to get the maximum from his entire range. If he calls and the river is a heart, I will check behind. If the river is a non-heart, even if it pairs the board, I will probably go all-in. Sadly, my opponent folds and I pick up a small pot.

Hand 19

This hand is from a $500 live event. Most players have been fairly tight and aggressive, which is standard at some live events. The stacks are:

UTG: 50 BBs. This is me. I have been fairly aggressive but not out of line.

2nd: 80 BBs. This player is a tight, older gentleman that is a regular on the tournament circuit.

Button: 60 BBs. This is a young player that seems to respect my raises too much.

I raise 9♣-8♣ from first position to 2.75 BBs. There are antes in play, which is why my raise is a touch larger than I would usually make. I like raising hands like good suited connectors from under the gun in order to balance my range. I don't want to raise only monsters from first position because it will make me easy to play against after the flop. The player in second position and the big blind both call, giving us a three-way pot.

The flop comes A♦-9♦-9♥. The big blind checks. Even though I have basically flopped the nuts, I still need to make a standard continuation of around half-pot. In spots like this, you have to hope one of your opponents has an ace, which is fairly likely. If I check and try to get fancy, I could easily lose if a diamond comes, or turn my hand face-up by check-raising either the flop or turn.

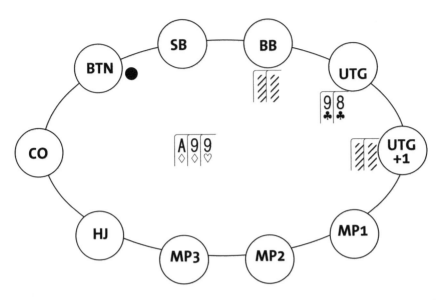

I will continuation-bet in this spot with my entire range, including the nuts. If you only continuation-bet here with hands like an ace or worse, your play will become fairly transparent. Against decent competition, you must mix some monsters into your range. Sadly, both opponents fold and I win a tiny pot. When you bet in these spots and everyone instantly folds, don't be sad because you lost your action. Simply muck your hand, collect the pot and move on to the next hand.

Hand 20

This hand is from the same $500 live event as above. We are around 10 places away from the money. The stacks are:

4th: 50 BBs. This player has been opening up his range as we approach the bubble. So far, no one has played back at him.

Hijack: 20 BBs. This is a young guy that plays well most of the time.

Button: 50 BBs. This is me. I have been generally loose and aggressive.

The player in fourth position raises to 2.2 BBs. He is probably doing this with a very wide range. The hijack goes all-in for his 20 BBs and I look down to see A♥-A♦.

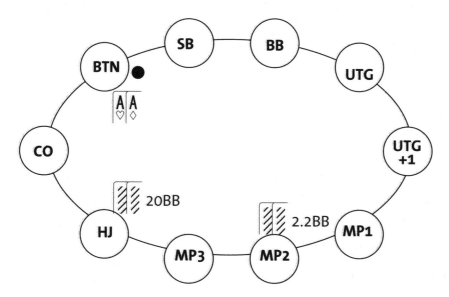

I have three options here. I can call, min-re-raise or go all-in. When a player pushes for around five times the initial raise or more, I tend to call with most of the hands I plan to play because I want to be able to get away from weaker hands like A-Q or 9-9 if the initial raiser goes all-in. So, I will tend to min-re-raise in this spot if the hijack has around 12 BBs or less, and call if he has more. I will often go all-in with a few hands I don't really want to play three-handed, like A-K, Q-Q and J-J. I will tend to call with A-A, K-K, 10-10, 9-9 and A-Q. I will be pushing with very few hands, but it doesn't matter much because I really can't fold those hands in this spot and I don't want to let my opponent see a flop with something like J♠-10♠. When you call in this spot with A-A, try to act as if you have a tough decision. Don't put on an obvious act, but at the same time, don't snap-call and celebrate.

I call. The initial raiser thinks for around 30 seconds and goes all-in. I snap-call. He turns over A♠-K♣, the initial pusher has 5-5 and I end up with a pile of chips. The player with A-K has a fairly easy fold in this situation. Given my range to call, the push is something like A-A, K-K, 10-10, 9-9 and A-Q. He needs to just find a fold and move on. When you are on the bubble and having your way with a table, which he was, there is no need to risk your stack when two players have both said they are willing to put all their money on the line. Give up the 2.2 BBs and continue stealing on the next hand.

Hand 21

This hand came up in a $200 online tournament and is similar to the previous situation. The stacks are:

3rd: 10 BBs. This player has been pushing rather often, probably because he has been short for a while.

Cutoff: 100 BBs. This is me. I have been playing my standard game.

Button: 80 BBs. This is an excellent, loose-aggressive player that has been around a while.

SB: 100 BBs. This is a solid online regular.

BB: 80 BBs. This player is new to the table and I know nothing about him.

The player in third position goes all-in for his 10 BBs and action is folded around to me, with 10-10. In spots like this, where you know you will see at least one hand from your opponent's range, you should try to determine the worst hand you can call with. I need around 54-percent equity to break even because players behind me are yet to act. If I give him a range of any pair, any Broadway, any suited ace and some suited connectors, I can call here with something like 8-8+ and A-J+.

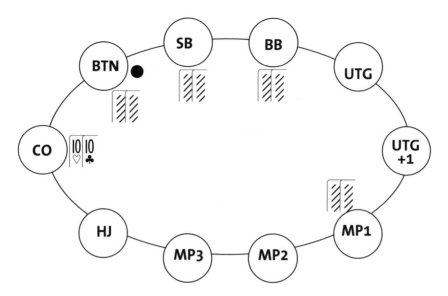

I tend to just call when a player has 6 BBs or more and min-re-raise when he has less than 6 BBs. This is because players seem to have no trouble calling a 5-BB all-in with a marginal hand after someone in front of them has called, but they play more straightforwardly when it becomes a little more expensive. In this spot, since my opponent has 10 BBs, I think a call is very standard. When I call with 10-10, I fully plan on folding to a re-raise from any of the large stacks behind me. In this hand, the big blind goes all-in. Since I know nothing about him, I assume he has a range like J-J+, A-Qs+ and A-K. Against this range, 10-10 only has 35-percent equity, giving me an easy fold. In spots like this, if the big blind turns over anything besides one of these hands, take a note and don't fold if the situation comes up again. I make an easy fold and the big blind beats the initial pusher's 8♦-7♦ with Q♠-Q♣. Notice that I would have lost an extra 9 BBs if I had re-raised the initial raise to 19 BBs. Saving 9 BBs, even when you've lost 10 BBs to the pot, is always a huge victory.

Hand 22

This hand took place in a $500 online tournament. The stacks are:

SB: 80 BBs. This is a good regular that isn't scared to make moves.

BB: 47 BBs. This is me. I have been playing a fairly tight and aggressive game, as the rest of the table is very tough.

The small blind raises to 3 BBs. I find J-J in the big blind. He could be raising with a fairly wide range, especially if he views me as a tighter player. If this is the case, calling is probably the best option, as he will likely fold to my re-raise. If he knows who I am and that I like to play pots from the big blind against the small blind, both by calling and re-raising, then I like re-raising.

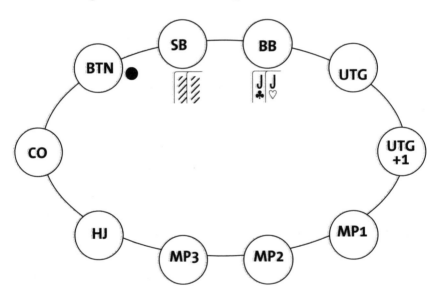

J-J is going to be in a tough spot post-flop quite often, so I am perfectly happy getting all-in pre-flop. I re-raise to 7.5 BBs. I don't re-raise to 9 BBs in this spot; this would make it tough to have bluffs in my range because I would be close to committing myself with strong, but not great hands. If I re-raise to 7.5 BBs, which is 2.5 times my opponent's raise, I have plenty of room to fold if I get pushed on.

My opponent instantly goes all-in and I snap-call. He turns over 8♠-6♠ and I win a nice pot. I firmly believe if I made it 9 BBs pre-flop instead of 7.5 BBs, he may have realized he had no fold equity and simply folded. Instead, I got him to give away 47 BBs with a weak holding.

Hand 23

This hand took place in a $300 live tournament. The stacks are fairly shallow, which is often the case in small buy-in live events. The players have generally been weak, limping often. The stacks are:

UTG: 15 BBs. This player has been limping from time to time and rarely raises pre-flop.

2nd: 30 BBs. This is an older player that likes to see cheap flops.

4th: 22 BBs. This is me.

Cutoff: 30 BBs. This is a weaker live player that frequents the tournament circuit.

The players under the gun and in second position limp. I expect their ranges to generally be fairly weak, although the player under the gun may be trying to trap with a monster. Action folds to me and I take a peek at K♦-K♥. I raise to 2.75 BBs. This is obviously much smaller than the raise size I suggest in *Volume 1*, but when you are playing against overly weak opposition, you can drastically vary your raise size to try to induce action. In a high-stakes tournament, in a similar situation against good players, who probably wouldn't have limped under the gun in the first place, I would have made it something like 4.5 BBs. The cutoff calls. I think he has something like A-J or 7-7 and doesn't know what to do with it. His best play with these hands is to either go all-in or fold.

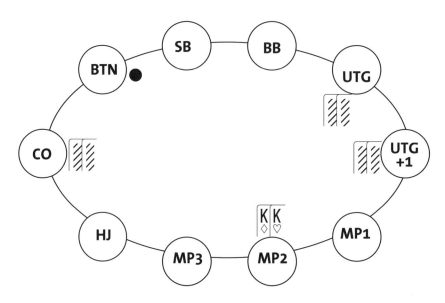

Action folds back to the initial under-the-gun limper, who goes all-in. Some players will only do this with a monster and some will do it with hands they think are monsters, like 6-6 and A-J. In this spot, I wouldn't fold K-K to anyone because it would be a huge error if someone were bluffing or overvaluing something like J-J. I would probably fold 10-10, which may seem super tight, but 10-10 is in bad shape even if a player is overplaying something like J-J or A-J. I call, the cold caller folds and my K-K loses to the limp-pusher's A-Q. I think the under-the-gun player is much better off raising or pushing A-Q than going for the limp and re-raise, as most players will only call off when they are either flipping or ahead of A-Q. If he simply raises or pushes, he may be able to get it in when he has his opponent dominated.

Hand 24

This hand is from a $100 online event. The blinds are 10/20. The stacks are:

4th: 150 BBs, or 3,000 chips. This is a well-respected online pro with decent live results.

Hijack: 150 BBs, or 3,000 chips. This is me.

BB: 100 BBs, or 2,000 chips. I know nothing about the big blind except that he has already fired out a two-barrel bluff and been caught.

Action folds to player 4, who raises to 3 BBs. I call with A♣-J♦. This hand flops decently well. I don't want to re-raise before the flop because if I'm re-raised or even called, I will have no clue where I stand in the hand, especially if an ace or jack flops. Some players will incorrectly assume I can't have a decent ace in my range when I call, so that adds a bit of deception to my range, which is always good. The big blind also calls, which I imagine he will do with a fairly wide range.

The flop comes 7♠-4♦-2♦.

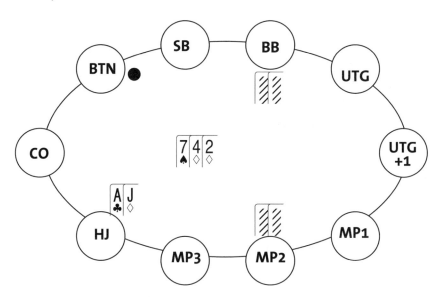

Both players check to me. I could bet or check here. Any time the initial raiser checks and you are in last position in a three-way pot, feel free to take a stab with a wide range because you can be confident that the pre-flop raiser missed the flop. This means you only have to worry about the player in the blind. This time I check, which I'm not a fan of, looking back. Even if I'm currently ahead in the hand, I will be forced to give up on most turns if someone bets, and I also have to worry about basically every turn card.

The turn is the 5♦, and they check to me again. The 5♦ is a wonderful card for me because now, in addition to my possible best hand, I have a weak diamond draw, which would give me a few more outs or induce one of my opponents to call with something like K♦-10♣. Any time you have a hand with showdown value plus a draw, it's likely that one or the other will come through for you. I bet 120 into the 190-chip pot and take it down.

Hand 25

This hand took place in a $1,500 live tournament. The field is generally soft and passive. We are playing 150/300. The stacks are:

3rd: 150 BBs, or 45,000. This is me. I have been the most aggressive player at the table by far.

Cutoff: 100 BBs, or 30,000. This player has been willing to see flops with junky hands but seems to play standard post-flop.

I raise A♠-Q♥ to 900 from middle position and the cutoff calls. He could have a fairly wide range, as he likes to see flops with all sorts of hands, ranging from pairs to suited gappers to Ax, and the occasional random hand like 9♠-5♣. Everyone else folds.

The flop comes 7♣-2♠-2♣. This is a spot where I would prefer to check my middle-strength hands, like A-Q or 6-6, but in order to balance my continuation-betting range, I need to throw out a bet. If I only checked my medium-strength hands, most opponents would quickly figure out what I was doing, fire a few barrels and force me off my hand. So, I make a standard continuation bet of 1,500 into the 2,250 pot. My opponent calls, which probably means he has something like a 7, a flush draw, a 2 or a random float with overcards.

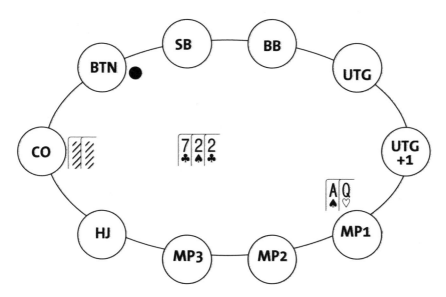

The turn is the J♥. I could certainly continue with a bluff here, but I elect to check. My opponent checks behind. If he had bet the turn, I would have had a fairly easy fold against most non-aggressive play-ers. If I knew him to be a habitual floater that bet the turn whenever checked to, I couldn't justify a check-fold. Against generally passive opponents, I think it is acceptable. When he checks behind, I expect him to show up with something he didn't want to get check-raise-bluffed off of, like a 7, a small to medium pair or a flush draw.

The river is the 6♦. I check again. Betting doesn't make sense because I will often be beat when called and will rarely be called by worse. My opponent now bets 2,700 into the 5,250 pot. I should call if my op-ponent will only bet the nuts or nothing, as I beat most missed draws. If he had something like 6♣-5♣, he would probably check back the river, so on average, I think this will be a call because by betting, he is representing a slow-played 2 or maybe some weird 7, which I think a lot of passive players would just check back on the river. If he is capable of betting hands like a 7, 6♣-5♣ or even something like 3-3, then I have an easy fold, because even though he is betting with fairly weak hands, I can't beat most of them. Always consider a check-raise bluff on the river if your opponent will bet a wide range but only call off with a monster. This time I called and lost to A♦-2♥.

Since my opponent showed up with basically the nuts, I didn't learn much about his river betting range. Losing is not a good enough reason to say my call was bad. For example, if my opponent would bet the river with only a missed flush draw or a 2, my call was almost certainly correct, even if I was wrong this time. Don't beat yourself up when you make a call that turns out to be wrong. You will make money in the long run if you are accurately thinking about your opponent's range.

Hand 26

This hand took place in a $200 online tournament. The blinds are 15/30. The stacks are:

Hijack: 100 BBs, or 3,000 chips. This is a solid online player with a decent amount of live experience.

Button: 100 BBs, or 3,000 chips. This is me.

The hijack raises to 90 and I call with 7♥-5♥. I can re-raise, call or fold with this hand. I think all three plays have fairly similar equity, although early in a tournament, I like seeing a few flops. Everyone else folds.

The flop comes A♠-Q♥-2♦. My opponent checks. I expect him to show up with a bad ace, a queen or a medium pair. Against that range, I don't mind a bet if I follow through with the bluff on the turn and river. Checking is also fine, but I shouldn't just check down if my opponent continues to show weakness.

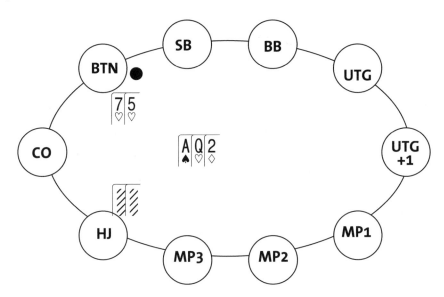

The turn is the 4♥, an awesome card for me. My opponent checks again. It would be criminal for me to do the same. If my opponent calls, I can be pretty confident he has a medium-strength hand like a queen or middle pair, and I will be able to barrel him off when the river isn't an ace or queen. On an ace or queen river, his likely marginal hand will gain some strength and be able to easily call down because I will be less likely to have an ace or queen. I would obviously bet for value if I hit my gutshot or flush on the river, which would nicely balance my river bluffs. I bet 150 into the 225 pot and he calls.

The river is an ugly A♦. My opponent checks and I check behind, losing to K♠-Q♦. While I am unsure if he would have folded that hand, I would still love a bet when the river was not an ace or queen. It is important to have a plan for each future street when you bet. If you have a plan, it is tough to get totally lost in a hand.

Hand 27

This hand is from a $200 online tournament. We are around five hands into the event and I have no reads on anyone. We are playing 10/20 and everyone has 3,000 chips.

The player in third position raises to 60 and I call on the hijack with 5♣-5♥. I see no other option in this situation. Always be willing to take a flop with a small pair when you are deep-stacked and have position. Re-raising has a little merit, but not much. The big blind also calls.

The flop is 8♦-5♠-4♦.

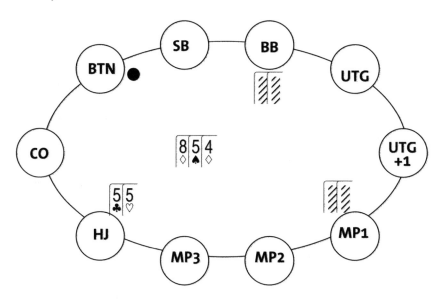

Both players check to me, which is never what I want to see when I have a set. With a board this draw-heavy, betting is mandatory. I make a standard bet of 140 into a 190 pot. The big blind calls; he probably has a draw or a marginal made hand like 8-7 or 6-5. The initial raiser folds.

The turn is the A♥, which is not good. While this card certainly doesn't hurt my hand, it hurts a lot of my opponent's hands, which will probably cost me action. He checks. I have to bet again to protect against draws. He will probably fold all weak made hands, which is not good, but I can't give him a free card because a good part of his range isn't drawing dead. Since I think he will fold most weak made hands to any bet, I think I should bet fairly large. I bet 420 into the 470 pot. Notice that if I bet something like 250, he will be getting 3-to-1, which probably isn't too far from the odds he needs to correctly call. You always want to make your opponent make a mistake. He calls.

The river is the J♣, another total brick. Now I think my opponent either has a busted draw, which he will fold to any bet, or a strong made hand, like A-8, A-5, A-4, 8-5 or 5-4. I think he will call any reasonable bet with these hands because my hand either looks like a strong made hand, which is tough to have, or a busted draw. I bet 1,020 into the 1,310 pot and my opponent snap-calls with K♦-5♦.

I have no clue what my opponent was thinking here, as he doesn't beat any made hand and only beats a few busted draws. Sometimes players make big calls in really bad spots. Since my opponent has two diamonds in his hand, it is much less likely that I had a flush draw. If I did have a flush draw, it would probably have an ace or jack, although I probably wouldn't bet a jack on the river. All in all, his call is pretty weak. Never berate someone who makes a bad call, whether he was right or wrong. The last thing you want is for your opponents to stop calling three barrels with middle pair.

Hand 28

This hand is from a $10,000 WPT event. We are fairly early in day one. The blinds are 100/200. The stacks are:

2nd: 150 BBs, or 30,000 chips. This is a mediocre live player that seems to play fairly straightforwardly.

Cutoff: 150 BBs, or 30,000 chips. This is me. I haven't been caught doing anything out of line at all so far.

The player in second position raises to 600 and I call with K♠-J♠ from the cutoff. Re-raising is never good here; folding, at least this deep-stacked, usually isn't a great option. Be careful not to lose a ton of money with hands like A-10s and K-Js if you flop top pair and your opponent fires multiple streets. Top pair with a decent kicker is not the nuts when a lot of money goes in the pot.

The flop comes Q♠-Q♦-9♦.

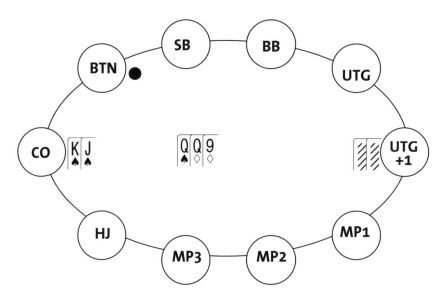

My opponent bets 800, which could mean anything, and I float. I have a gutshot, a backdoor flush draw, an overcard and position. I couldn't ask for much more. Unless my opponent has a 9 or better, or a draw, he will almost certainly check-fold the turn.

The turn is the 5♥. My opponent checks, which I fully expected, and I fire 1,800 into the 3,100 pot. He instantly raises to 5,000. This is one of those spots where my play was great but my opponent simply has a hand. If I had turned a 10 and my opponent check-raised, I would have reluctantly called down. I would fold to the check-raise on any other turn because, unless my opponent was crazy, which certainly wasn't the case here, he had at least a queen. I think for a while and fold. My opponent is nice enough to show 9-9.

If he had just called the turn, I would have considered firing the river. He basically turned his hand face up by check-raising the turn. If he had simply continued betting or check-called the turn, he would have gotten a lot of value from all my made hands. Instead he won just one small bet from me, which I am happy about. One thing I like to do in these spots is to mildly act as if I have a tough decision. When I fold, I generally say something like "nice bluff." This will often induce my opponent to show his hand, which is free information. Someone who check-raises the turn usually has a supreme hand.

Hand 29

This hand was played in a $3,500 WPT event.

It is early in day one and not much has happened so far. We are playing 100/200. The three players in this pot all have 150 BBs, or 30,000 chips. The hijack is an older player that I have seen around. I am in the small blind. The big blind is a young kid I have not seen before.

Everyone folds to the hijack, who makes it 600. He probably has a fairly standard raising range for an older player from late position, something like pairs, suited aces, Broadways and some suited connectors. I call with 5♠-5♥ from the small blind and the big blind calls as well.

The flop comes Q♣-3♣-2♠. I check, as does the big blind. The initial raiser bets 1,200 into the 1,800 pot. This is a fairly easy fold.

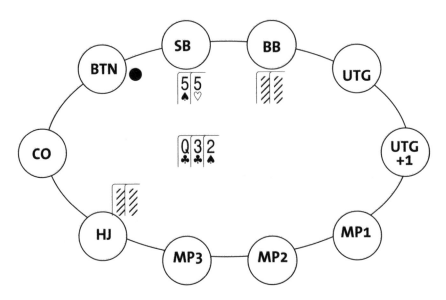

There are a few problems with calling. Either the big blind or the hijack could have me beat and I will be drawing thin, the hijack could be bluffing with something that has a lot of equity against my hand, like 9♣-8♠, or the big blind could be going for a check-raise with a draw, forcing me off my equity. I could check-raise the flop as a bluff, but I don't like bluffing off a pile of chips right at the start of a tournament in a marginal spot. So, if I check, it needs to be a check-fold.

But checking isn't my only option. I could lead for around 1,200, hoping my opponents fold all their air, which wouldn't be too terrible. I could also expect them to play fairly straightforwardly; the big blind has to worry about the initial raiser, and the initial raiser will probably miss this flop and play face-up. If you've read this entire book, you know I don't like donk bets because they are difficult to balance, and this is no exception. I would love to be able to check-raise my strong draws and sets and get action, which means I don't really want to lead with them. That means most of my donk-betting range, if I had one, would be marginal made hands and weak draws, all of which I would have to give up with on the turn. Considering all this, I think check-folding is the right play against decent competition.

Hand 30

This hand came up a little later in the same $3,500 WPT event. We are still playing 100/200. The stacks are:

Button: 100 BBs, or 20,000 chips. This player lost a fairly large pot earlier when he made middle pair and couldn't fold it.

SB: 150 BBs, or 30,000 chips. This is me. I haven't done too much so far.

BB: 150 BBs, or 30,000 chips. This player arrived late, so I have no reads on him except that he is older.

Everyone folds to the button, who limps. I have Q♠-9♦ in the small blind. I could raise or fold in this spot, but since the limper tends to trap himself post-flop, I think I should limp in and try to flop something like a pair before piling money into the pot. I limp and the big blind checks.

The flop comes Q♣-8♠-4♠.

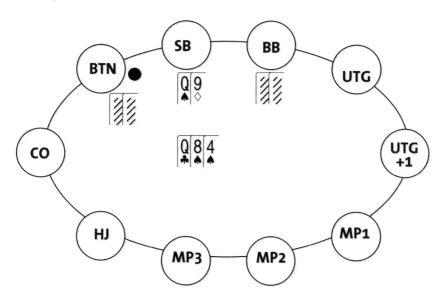

I could check or bet. I generally like betting in a limped pot. No one represented a strong hand pre-flop, so everyone will check through on the flop a decent amount of time, which isn't good for my weak top pair. I bet 400 into the 600 pot. The big blind folds and the button calls. I expect him to show up with an 8, 4, middle pair or draw. I think he would often raise the flop with a queen or better, so I think I have the best hand.

The turn is the 2♥, which is great for me. I bet 1,000 for pure value into the 1,400 pot and my opponent instantly calls. I don't really think the turn changed his range at all. He either has a worse made hand or a draw.

The river is the 2♦, which is also great for me. If I bet in this spot, I certainly think my opponent would call with all made hands and fold all busted draws. If I check, I am unsure if he would bet or check his made hands, but I know he would at least consider betting his busted draws. This is a close decision, and I decide to check. If I were to bet, it would be on the larger side because my opponent would call any reasonable bet with any pair.

My opponent quickly bets 3,000 into the 3,400 pot and my chips almost beat his into the pot. I have an easy call because I think all his made hands are worse than mine and all his draws were missed. In fact, I almost have the nuts. I don't think going for a check-raise on the river makes much sense because he would probably find a fold with all his junky made hands, which means he will only call if he has beat or I barely have him outkicked, which is tough to do with a 9 kicker. My opponent mucks his hand, which means he had a busted draw with no showdown value, and I win a nice pot.

Chapter 10

Questions and Answers

I have been teaching people to crush poker for years. I have made a point to copy quite a few of their frequently asked questions, as I thought they could be useful sometime in the future. Since you should have a broad knowledge of poker by this point, try to answer the questions before reading my answer. If you get any wrong, try to figure out why. If you have no clue, figure out why you have no clue and correct it. Poker is a game about finding the answers for yourself. The questions will cover various topics, both on and off the felt. Most of them will be fairly basic but should at least give you a glimpse into the mind of a beginning player. I hope you can learn a little something from these questions.

Q. I have seen this play a couple times when playing live tournaments. A big stack in early position grabs a handful of chips and splashes them into the pot. He does not take time to count out the chips. He simply grabs a pile and throws them in. What does this mean?

A. When a situation like this comes up, it is usually best to let someone else find out the answer for you. Pay attention to what happens when someone calls and go from there. Also, try to induce him to show his hand by saying something like "Nice bluff" or "Keep making that play; it will get you broke." Basically, you are trying to get free information so you can snap him off when he makes the play again. In general, I would assume this is a play with a marginal made hand like top pair, weak kicker and he is saying, "Call if you have me beat." Clearly, this is a terrible play, and players that use it probably aren't that great. Really though, it is very player-dependent.

Q. I was wondering what you think about the future of poker. Many people think the games will become tougher and unprofitable. Do you think this will happen? Is poker a good investment for my future?

A. If online poker becomes legal in America, poker will boom again. If it doesn't, it will likely stay where it is or slowly decline. Even if poker does get tougher, you can still make a pile of money as long as you work hard and stay ahead of the curve. But I find it hard to believe that the U.S. government will not legalize poker in some way in the near future. By regulating it, they stand to make a ton of money. I fully expect online poker to be totally legal over the next few years, making the games very good. Hopefully, the government won't significantly increase the rake.

Q. Do you think being coached by you will make me a winning player?

A. While I can't guarantee being coached by me will make you a poker superstar, if you listen to what I say and apply the changes I suggest to your game, I am confident I could make the vast majority of people profitable at poker. That doesn't mean you will be bringing in $10,000 per month, but if you play with players that are worse than you and are patient, there is no reason most people should be unprofitable at the lower-stakes games, easily bringing in a few thousand dollars per month.

Q. Do you think using a heads-up display (HUD) is necessary to beat online poker?

A. I used to never use a HUD. Over the last year or so, I have started paying more attention to stats and my results have slightly improved. I recently cashed for $317,000 in a $1,000 buy-in online tournament and it is tough to say if using a HUD helped me or not. I would venture to say it did. A HUD's value is tough to quantify. That being said, as long as you don't totally rely on it and use it mostly to slightly sway you one way or the other in tricky spots, I think HUDs are a great thing.

Q. What is the best way to switch from mainly playing sitngos to playing cash games?

A. When moving from one form of poker to another, I suggest you move down quite a few levels and put in a lot of hours learning the game before moving up. I also suggest you watch training videos pertaining to the game you are trying to learn. You should also find a book to read about the game, as well as a study group to discuss ideas with. Take it slow and put in a lot of hours at the table before playing for stakes that really matter to you.

Q. What type of win percentage can you expect at poker?

A. This depends entirely on your skill level, your opponents' skill level and the possible edge in the game you are playing. In general, winning at around 10-percent ROI in sitngos, 5 big blinds per 100 hands in cash games, 70-percent ROI in online multi-table tournaments or 150-percent ROI in live tournaments is considered very good.

Q. What games should a decent player grind on a daily basis?

A. It depends on your life and how much time you can devote to poker. Cash games are generally good for most players, as you can get in and out fairly quickly. The same goes for nine-handed sitngos. I only suggest multi-table tournaments if you are fairly free and don't have too many commitments, as they take a lot of time.

Q. You have stated that a big leak most players have is to bet small when they make a very strong hand. What is the best way to get value out of those? It seems like if you bet big, players will just fold. Should I check, giving them a free card? Should I check-call or check-raise?

A. Play your total bluffs and strong hands similarly. If you put your opponent on a weak range, you should generally bet smaller with your entire range unless you think a big bet will always get folds, assuming that is what you want. In general though, you want to bet a large amount when you have a strong hand because that is how you build a big pot. You will be pleasantly surprised that most players will pay you off with something like top pair or better. Simply bet around 5/6 pot and hope to get paid. If they fold to these bets often, start mixing in bluffs until they catch on, and then go back to betting the nuts that way.

Q. You mention in one of your videos that once you know you are a winning player, you don't need to worry quite so much about your bankroll. What is a good sample size to actually know if I am a winning player?

A. For cash games, I would say 200,000 hands is generally a large enough sample size to know if you are a winning player. For sitngos and multi-table tournaments, 3,000 games is enough. However, you should see your win rate increasing as you play more games, as you should be more skillful. If the opposite is true, figure out why. I say your bankroll matters a little less because I suggest you take shots at great games here and there. If you know you can drop back down and grind up more money if necessary, there is nothing wrong with taking shots occasionally. Make sure you stay disciplined.

Q. Would you play $1/2 no-limit in a casino the same as you would play $.05/.10 online?

A. I would play a little tighter in the live game, although the games are probably comparable. I also wouldn't re-raise with weaker hands pre-flop live, as I would online, as most of your value in low-stakes live games will come from making the nuts and getting paid off, whereas some of your value online will come from pushing your opponents off the best hand.

Q. Is it smarter to play 20 tables at once online to try to grind out money or fewer tables to try to learn to play better?

A. This depends on your financial situation. If you need money, play a lot of tables and grind out a profit. When you do this, you have to realize you will not learn to play better, which will make it tougher for you to move up in the long run. So, you are gaining a small amount of money now and forfeiting the chance to gain a lot more later. I suggest you learn to play well and move up that way.

Q. What is the best thing to do when you are losing over and over again and simply never get good cards?

A. When you are losing, assuming losing bothers you, which it shouldn't, spend some time away from the table and study the game. Watch poker videos, post hands in forums and read books. Get outside and enjoy life. Losing at poker should not dominate your emotions. Losing is part of the game. Get used to it.

Q. Do you have any advice on double-or-nothing sitngos, where half the field double their money and the other half get nothing?

A. Play tight and don't call pushes on the bubble unless you have a monster.

Q. I have a hard time making it to the top few places in large, multi-table tournaments. It seems like I always finish between 27th and 9th place. What am I doing wrong?

A. You are probably playing too tight. You have to be aggressive late in tournaments in order to withstand the constantly increasing blinds. If you play tight, waiting for premium hands, you will only win pots that belong to you. You have to steal a lot in order to make it. I hope the strategy I outlined in *Volume 1* helps with that.

Q. I like to watch a lot of poker shows on TV. I get the impression from your videos that a lot of the TV pros play poorly. Is this true?

A. Most of the pros on TV play far from optimally, as they are TV personalities, not poker players. Sure, they probably won at poker ten years ago, but that doesn't really mean anything if they haven't won anything since then. Watch the young, well-known, online players that get on TV. They usually play technically sound poker that will crush most opponents.

Q. When someone check-raises, do they usually have the nuts?

A. They generally have one of three ranges. They tend to have a well-balanced range of strong hands and bluffs, a range made up of top pair or better, or a range made up of strong hands, like two pair or better. Folding is probably the best option against all these ranges, unless you have a strong hand or a good draw. Don't let them know you constantly fold to check-raises though, or you will become exploitable.

Q. *I recently came into $2,000. I would like to get a nice two-monitor setup, which I can get for $1,000. I currently play on an old computer, but it still works. I would also like to pad my bankroll with a $500 reload bonus online and purchase some poker videos. How do you suggest I divide my money?*

A. I suggest you spend a little on poker videos and put the rest in your bankroll. If you can double your bankroll every few months, spending $1,000 will force you to work a few extra months. Say you have $1,000 and can turn it into $5,000 within the year. You could also start with $2,000 and turn it into $9,000 within the year but you have to play on an old computer. Is it worth $5,000 to play on a bad computer for a year? I think it is. You could then spend $1,000 out of your $9,000, which isn't nearly as significant as spending $1,000 out of $2,000. Basically, the bigger you can make your bankroll, the quicker you can move up.

Q. *Which sites online are best for building your bankroll?*

A. I suggest you play where there are very few regular players. This usually means selecting good tables on the main sites where there are very few regulars or at smaller sites where you are playing with a few random guys. The same goes for live poker. Play where the random guys play. You don't want to play with people that are competent and play every day. That will cost you money.

Q. *I have found by watching your videos that I re-raise way too often with small pairs. What is a good re-raising range?*

A. Your re-raising range should depend entirely on your opponent. Against a strong player, you should be re-raising a range made up of strong hands as well as hands that are too weak to call. If your opponent is a calling station, you should re-raise strong hands and decent hands, like A-J or K-Q. Figure out your opponent's range and playing style and go from there.

Q. Recently on the first hand at the final table of a $3, 18-person sit-ngo, I went all-in with K-K for 20 BBs and everyone folded. Should I have raised small instead?

A. It depends on everyone's stack size. If everyone has less than 10 BBs, which will be the case in a lot of sitngos, feel free to go all-in. If you and most other players have more than 15 BBs, you should tend to raise to around 2.2 BBs.

Q. What are typical weaknesses of players $1/2 no-limit players at local dog tracks? I notice a lot of players love to limp and see flops. What should I do about this? Also, how should I play the drawing hand, A-K?

A. Most of the players in $1/2 games at local dog tracks love to see flops and generally overvalue hands like top pair. You will also see some people sitting with 20 BBs and others with 500 BBs, causing you to play a significantly different strategy against each opponent. If you have a strong hand, you generally don't want the limpers to fold, assuming there are a lot of them. You would much rather they call with incorrect odds. Also, A-K isn't a drawing hand; 9♠-6♠ is a drawing hand. If you are in the small blind with A-K and eight people limp in front of you, make it $28 or so, assuming you have $200 in front of you. As you get shorter, you should raise a bit more so you can push any flop.

Q. I currently do not get rakeback. What am I missing out on?

A. Rakeback is a program by which the online sites give an affiliate some percentage of your rake in exchange for their signing you up to play on their site. Normally this is between 30 and 40 percent of the rake you pay. Since most smart poker players know this, the affiliates have come to an agreement with the players such that if the affiliate gets 40 percent, they give 35 percent back to the player, making both parties a decent amount of money. When I played sitngos online when I was 18 years old, I would regularly make $10,000 per month from rakeback and around $10,000 per month from actually playing. Rakeback doubled my income. Playing without rakeback is like shooting yourself in the foot and trying to ride a bicycle.

Q. How do you find your niche in poker?

A. Stick to one form of poker when learning. Once your bankroll is huge, you can venture into other areas of the game. I started playing sitngos and played them nonstop for around four years before switching to multi-table tournaments. Whatever form of the game you decide on, learn to be the best and grind it hard until you have a large bankroll.

Q. I am confused about equity. You say, "I am 33-percent to win so I need 2-to-1 pot odds to call," but my brain tells me this should be 3-to-1. How do you figure out equity when you are playing?

A. Odds of 3-to-1 mean you need to win one in four times, or 25 percent of the time. You simply add the two numbers together (1+3) then put them in the denominator and have a 1 as the numerator, so 3-to-1 is 1/4, or 25 percent. So, 33 percent of the time would be 2-to-1, or 1/3.

Q. I have witnessed things online to make me think the game is rigged. Am I correct?

A. No. You are much more likely to be cheated at live poker than online. That being said, I only think I have been cheated at live poker three times in my career, and I was at fault each time, as I was playing in random home games instead of at casinos. Online poker is simply not rigged.

Q. I want to start discussing hands so I can become better at poker. Where would you suggest?

A. I post and talk about hands constantly with people on the www.FloatTheTurn.com forums. Check it out.

Q. I have a leak where I raise a big pair like J-J, get called and see a flop with three undercards. There is a lot of betting and raising and it seems like I am always beat by either a set or a bigger pair. What am I doing wrong?

A. It sounds to me like you are getting a lot of money in with hands like weak overpairs, whereas these hands are basically bluff catchers once a lot of money goes in the pot. Consider checking back the flop or just calling continuation bets. Suppose someone raises and you decide to call with K-K for deception. The flop comes Q-6-2. Assuming you are both deep-stacked, if your opponent bets, you should be happy to just call down. Raising the flop basically turns your hand face up, saying you have something like K-Q or better, allowing your opponent to continue only with hands like A-Q or better, which puts K-K in pretty terrible shape.

Q. When everyone folds to me in the small blind and I have around 8 BBs, which hands should I be raising, calling and folding?

A. You should be going all-in with every hand with an 8-BB stack, assuming the big blind isn't going to call really wide, and most won't. If he is going to call you fairly wide, you can fold hands like 3-2, 7-2, 8-3, etc., but you should still be going all-in with around 90 percent of hands. You will bust out quite often doing this, but once you get short, you simply can't blind off, which leaves you with zero equity. When you gamble, you always have some equity. Don't turn something into nothing by being scared.

Conclusion

Throughout this book, I have strived to explain everything I know about being a professional tournament poker player. I am confident that if you put in many hours of study and constantly make smart decisions, you can make it in this competitive world. If you keep your head up when things go poorly and don't go crazy when things go great, you will succeed. Strive to play in games where you have an edge, constantly practice putting players on ranges, and seek to learn everything you can from players that are better than you. Most importantly, make sure you enjoy life. None of this is worth anything if you spend your life hunched over a poker table. Despite the many pitfalls in the poker world, a few people have figured out how to make everything work. Realize though, that you must never stop learning. If you become stagnant, you are almost guaranteed to fail. I hope someone has read this book and is well on the way to becoming the next poker superstar. Make sure you say "Hi" when you see me on the felt. I plan on being there as well. Good luck.